THE REGIONS OF FRANCE

THE BACKGROUND OF MODERN FRENCH LITERATURE

BY

C. H. C. WRIGHT

PROFESSOR OF THE FRENCH LANGUAGE AND LITERATURE
IN HARVARD UNIVERSITY

GINN AND COMPANY
BOSTON · NEW YORK · CHICAGO · LONDON
ATLANTA · DALLAS · COLUMBUS · SAN FRANCISCO

COPYRIGHT, 1926, BY C. H. C. WRIGHT
ALL RIGHTS RESERVED
PRINTED IN THE UNITED STATES OF AMERICA

326.2

The Athenæum Press
GINN AND COMPANY · PRO-
PRIETORS · BOSTON · U.S.A.

TO THE MEMORY OF
MY SISTER

PREFACE

THIS volume is not written to prove a theory. I have merely tried to provide a helpful guidebook for the better understanding of the writers of modern France and of the civilization to which they belong. Histories of French literature, to the number of which I have myself contributed, are not entirely sufficient for the foreigner, who is often at sea as to political, religious, and social conditions. I have therefore endeavored to sketch the background of French literature during the period from 1789 to 1914, and to show both how it explains that literature and how literary works throw light upon it.

I beg to call attention to the following points:

1. Much attention has been given to the Restoration and to the Monarchy of July because of the extraordinary intellectual richness of those times. Ch. Adam, in his history of modern French philosophy, says with truth of the years from 1828 to 1834 in particular that they saw the fermentation and the expression of most of the great ideas of the century.

2. I have felt myself occasionally authorized to use as contemporary evidence works written later than the period they describe. Flaubert's *Education sentimentale* for obvious reasons, owing to the author's careful documentation, may be cited as testimony to conditions during the times portrayed. Hugo's *Misérables* did not appear until the sixties, but the author had been an eyewitness of many of the historical events to which he refers.

3. We must keep our judgment clear and be on our guard against exaggerations. Writers of fiction and of poetry pitch their notes higher than do scientific historians. At the same time, as their works are more read they have a correspondingly better chance of being misleading. The age of Romanticism was

not monopolized by eccentric Jeunes-France. There were a thousand decorous *bourgeois* to one obstreperous innovator. Moralists like the younger Dumas give incomplete pictures. They castigate vice but neglect virtue, thereby distorting life. Nothing could be more one-sided than the literature of Naturalism.

4. Every successful writer, however sensational, has imitators who exaggerate still more. Thus are created a literary tradition and *poncif* often very remote from reality. Much of the poetry and prose of the Third Republic was affected by the abnormal and morbid writers Baudelaire and the Goncourt brothers. Their influence stamped itself deeply on literature, but the writers of their schools, however numerous and talented, are as lacking in proportion as the masters. In this sense it is true that today the fiction and the drama of Paris do not represent France. Romain Rolland says in the volume of *Jean-Christophe* called *Dans la maison*: "The theatres of Paris? Do you imagine that a hard working person even knows what is going on there? Pasteur did not go ten times in his life. Like all foreigners, you give disproportionate importance to our novels, to our boulevard performances, to the intrigues of our politicians . . . I will show you, when you so desire, women who never read novels, young Parisian girls who have never been to the theatre, men who have never busied themselves with politics,—and among Intellectuals, too." Precaution in this respect is therefore necessary when we use fiction or the drama as documentary evidence in the study of modern French manners and morals.

In writing this volume my sources of information have ranged over a very considerable field of political and religious history, philosophy, and sociology, as well as literature and art. I have tried to acknowledge my indebtedness to others by means of the Bibliography. In the cases, however, in which I may have used references without general or specific acknowledgment my intention has not been to deceive and I here record my apologies.

PREFACE

I have translated most of the prose quotations from French authors, but it seemed that more would be lost than gained in translating verse. French technical terms have been given very freely, usually with English equivalents. It is hoped that the book will be intelligible even to those whose knowledge of French is slight.

I thank my colleague Professor Louis Allard of Harvard for reading and criticizing certain chapters.

C. H. C. W.

CONTENTS

CHAPTER	PAGE
I. THE LAND OF FRANCE	1
II. THOUGHT AND POLICY UNDER THE REVOLUTION AND THE EMPIRE	20
III. REVOLUTION AND EMPIRE. MANNERS AND LITERATURE. THEMES AND POPULAR TYPES	37
IV. REVOLUTION, EMPIRE, AND RESTORATION. LITERARY FORMS. REVOLUTIONARY AND IMPERIAL ART	57
V. RESTORATION AND MONARCHY OF JULY. RELIGION AND POLITICS	71
VI. RESTORATION AND MONARCHY OF JULY. DEMOCRATIC MYSTICISM. POSITIVISM. THE NAPOLEONIC LEGEND	86
VII. RESTORATION AND MONARCHY OF JULY. SOCIETY. SOCIAL AND LITERARY TYPES	102
VIII. RESTORATION AND MONARCHY OF JULY. SOCIAL AND LITERARY TYPES (CONTINUED)	120
IX. RESTORATION AND MONARCHY OF JULY. ROMANTIC THEMES AND TYPES	137
X. RESTORATION AND MONARCHY OF JULY. ROMANTIC THEMES AND TYPES (CONTINUED). ROMANTIC ART	152
XI. SECOND REPUBLIC. SECOND EMPIRE. POLITICAL AND RELIGIOUS DISCUSSIONS. INTELLECTUAL INFLUENCES	174
XII. SECOND EMPIRE. SOCIAL AGITATION. THE AGE OF MATERIALISM	196
XIII. SECOND EMPIRE. SOCIETY. THE CLASSES. LITERARY TENDENCIES AND THEMES	212
XIV. THIRD REPUBLIC. INTELLECTUAL EPOCHS	233
XV. THIRD REPUBLIC. THE HISTORICAL AND POLITICAL SETTING	246
XVI. THIRD REPUBLIC. VARIOUS SOCIAL TYPES	267
XVII. THIRD REPUBLIC. LITERARY AND ARTISTIC TENDENCIES AND TYPES	281

BACKGROUND OF FRENCH LITERATURE

PAGE

APPENDIX
  A. *Genre Troubadour* 305
  B. Romanticism 306
  C. The *bourgeoisie* 308
  D. *La Bohème* 309

BIBLIOGRAPHY 311
INDEX 319

ILLUSTRATIONS

	PAGE
Map (The Regions of France)	Frontispiece
The Sabine Women, by David	23
Caricature of Costumes	33
Example of the *genre troubadour*	43
Men of Fashion under the Restoration	53
Frontispiece of the Works of Berquin	55
Frontispiece of an Edition of Ossian	61
Firemen, with Classical Helmets	67
Knights of the Extinguisher	72
Le ventre législatif, by Daumier	79
The *vieux sergent* of Béranger, by Charlet	97
Mayeux detects his Likeness to Napoleon, by Traviès	99
A *visage de keepsake*	104
Fashion under Louis-Philippe	107
A Masked Ball at the Opera in 1843	111
Descente de la Courtille	113
The *grisette*, by Gavarni	117
Uniforms of the National Guard	122
The Rag-picker, by Traviès	127
Les poires, by Philipon	129
Monsieur Prudhomme, by Henry Monnier	131
The *gamin*, by Charlet	133
The Raft of the Shipwrecked *Medusa*, by Géricault	157
Virgil and Dante, by Delacroix	159
The Death of Queen Elizabeth, by Delaroche	166
The Old Oak, by Dupré	171
Napoleon III and his Generals	179
Costumes of *cantinières*	181
Ratapoil	182
Liberty on the Barricades, by Delaroche	197
Blanqui	199
New Year's Day on the Boulevards in 1862	205

	PAGE
La Vie parisienne, by Chéret	209
The Empress Eugénie, by Winterhalter	215
At a First Performance under the Second Empire, by Marcelin .	217
Marchand de coco, by Bertall	219
Burial at Ornans, by Courbet	231
A Typical "Ramollot".	235
Diversions of the People . . . , ...	237
Second Condemnation of Dreyfus in 1899	253
Betting at the Races	269
Newspaper Hawker	271
Street Peddler	276
Military Drill, by Guillaume	277
Le Moulin de la Galette, by Renoir	283
L'Absinthe, by Degas	285
Proletarian Type	290
The Hay-Makers, by Bastien-Lepage	293
Le Bois sacré aux arts et aux muses, by Puvis de Chavannes . .	295
The Wedding, by the *douanier* Rousseau	299
From a Program of the *Chat-Noir* Theater	301

THE BACKGROUND OF MODERN FRENCH LITERATURE

CHAPTER I

THE LAND OF FRANCE

THE American, accustomed to spacious geographical measurements and magnificent distances, and possibly misled by such catch phrases as the "tight little isle" of England into thinking that all European nations are diminutive, is confirmed in such an opinion about France when he hears that it is considerably smaller than Texas. But within its area of a little more than two hundred thousand square miles France offers a topographical and climatic variety that few of our states, except perhaps a long-drawn-out California, stretching from North to South, can equal. Within the boundaries of continental France one finds both palm and pine; the term "sunny France", true enough of the Riviera, is a misnomer at Brest in Brittany, where it rains on one hundred and eighty days of three hundred and sixty-five; France contains bleak mountainous districts, like the southern Causses, where in the long winters the ground is covered with snow, while the *Côte d'Azur* basks in the sun and Picardy flounders in mud. Rarely does so compact an area on the American continent offer such geographical variety.

In this interesting country dwell races as different as the landscapes. Just as the European classes New Englander, Hoosier, and Oregonian together as Yankees, so one who has not traveled in France fails to distinguish between the calculating Norman and the effervescent Gascon, and does not realize that the centralization of French administration, the spread of primary education, the development of railways, the mixing pot of universal military service have still left ethnological differences in the inhabitants. The peasants and dwellers in small towns have until recently clung to their own homes in a way utterly at variance with our overland migrations and journeyings westward; so that even today, though the limits of the old provinces have theoretically vanished, each district has its racial individuality. The Norman is hard-headed and practical; the neighboring Celtic Breton, Renan and Loti both tell us, is more dreamy and emotional; the talkative Southerner monopolizes the debates of the Chamber of Deputies and thinks aloud ("Quand je ne parle pas, je ne pense pas", Daudet makes his Numa Roumestan say); the uncouth rustic of Auvergne, angular and slow of speech, has often been the object of gibes by frisky and sophisticated Parisian jesters.[1] Moreover, scattered through France are groups of people who seem quite alien to their neighbors: the Bigoudens of Pont-l'Abbé on the southern coast of Brittany, addicted to bright colors, are supposed to come from some untraced Oriental migration; the inhabitants of the *Bocage vendéen* in southwestern France are said by some to descend from the remnants of old Hunnish invasions, and the critics of Clemenceau, the "tiger" of modern France, point to his high cheek bones and Mongol cast of countenance; the women of Arles are praised for the Greek configuration of their faces; there are many districts, as in Brittany or in the valley of the Tarn, where French is acquired as a foreign language and spoken slowly and with effort by the peasants, and the language of the Basques is one of the puzzles of philology.

Though geography and ethnology thus seem to have made a chaos of France, nevertheless the physical configuration of the land renders its description by river basins and by the old provinces fairly easy. The leveling process of the Revolution, with

---

[1] See, for instance, old farces like Labiche's *le Misanthrope et l'Auvergnat*. The Auvergnat in mid-nineteenth-century literature was the water-carrier, the porter, or the coal-man.

its administrative "reforms", tried to obliterate the provinces by the formation of departments, and yet only partly succeeded. On the other hand, geology could not be thwarted, and the mountain ranges and heights of land simplify the study of French physical geography. Moreover, at the political confines of the nation, except in the plains of Flanders and the northern frontier in general, the country is trimly bounded by mountains, streams, or seas. The Pyrenees separate France from Spain, the Alps divide it from Italy, and the World War has driven back the northeastern frontier from the Vosges mountains to its old outposts on the Rhine.

Under the pre-Revolutionary régime France was divided into thirty-two administrative divisions, corresponding closely but not absolutely to the old provinces, or fiefs, whose gradual annexation to the domain of the king formed the realm of France. Normandy, Brittany, Burgundy were such provinces. These provinces were themselves made up of a quantity of small, homogeneous districts called *pays*, whose limits were often determined by agricultural or climatic as well as by geographical conditions. These names are as persistent in the usage of today as are those of the old provinces, and one meets allusions to Périgord, Beauce, or Médoc as readily as to Poitou or Languedoc. In 1790 the Constituent Assembly broke up the old provinces into eighty-three departments, with names generally borrowed from mountains, rivers, or other geographical features. These departments were intentionally made to overlap the boundaries of the old provinces, so as to destroy the past in the interest of a new uniformity. They were created of a size that would make it roughly possible, before the days of railroads, for the center to be reached from all the parts in the course of a day. By 1870 the number of departments had grown to eighty-nine. The loss of Alsace-Lorraine reduced the number to eighty-six, but the World War has brought back the old area.

The starting-point for the study of French physiography is the great *Massif central*, the kernel of which is found in the mountains of Auvergne, culminating in the Puy de Sancy, the highest mountain of central France (6188 feet), in the region of the Mont Dore. Here one is in the midst of volcanic territory. Not far away to the north is the Puy de Dôme, on the summit of which, crowned by its ruined pre-Roman temple, Pascal's brother-in-law, in 1648, conducted experiments on atmospheric pressure. From here the eye ranges over a wide panorama of extinct volcanoes, with the rounded tops where once sank the depressions of burning craters. At the foot of this mountain is Clermont-Ferrand in its region of petrifying springs and carbonic-vapor grottoes, where the somber cathedral of gloomy Volvic lava stone overlooks the birthplace of the austere Jansenist Pascal. Here is the central home of the Auvergnat population, sturdy and persistent, but prone to wander afield and to seek in cities like Paris the money not to be found on the rough hillsides.

To the north and to the west the mountains of Auvergne flatten out in smaller hills, plateaus, and river valleys to the plain. But eastward and southward they connect with the great range of the Cévennes, which help to form the height of land cutting France in two from the Vosges to the Pyrenees. Like an enormous screen the Cévennes divide the sunny and parched basin of the lower Rhône from the misty north. Here are some of the most interesting natural curiosities of France and some of its most fascinating historical memories. During the days of Louis XIV the hardy Cévenol mountaineers, in their mountain fastnesses, clung firmly to their faith in spite of the cruelties of the royal dragoons (the *dragonnades*); and the Camisards of the Gévaudan, after the revocation of the Edict of Nantes, fought with frenzied fury their Catholic foes.[1] To the north, on the borders of Auvergne, in the district of Velay, is the old town of Le Puy, once described as "the most picturesque place in the world". Here are cathedrals and chapels perched aloft on steep rocks rising almost perpendicularly from the plain; here

---

[1] Ferdinand Fabre is the great French novelist of the Cévennes, particularly of the southern parts near his native Bédarieux.

are memories of La Fayette, born a few miles away at the old manor of Chavaniac; close at hand is the ruined castle of Polignac, cradle of one of the most famous families of the old French aristocracy; near by are scenes commemorated by George Sand in the *Marquis de Villemer* and *Jean de la Roche*. A few miles away Robert Louis Stevenson started on his wanderings through the mountains with his donkey Modestine. On the outskirts of the Cévennes, in the Gévaudan, stretch the poverty-stricken, lofty regions of the Causses, without trees or water, chill and bleak, their stony surface swept bare by the winds and all the vegetation cropped to the roots by grazing sheep.[1] But on the edge of this country, deep in hollow cañons, flows the Tarn, with its hamlets clinging under projecting cliffs, sometimes inaccessible by road, and near by the dolomitic wilderness of *Montpellier-le-Vieux* seems a huge city carved out of stone.

Southward the Cévennes connect by subsidiary ranges with the Pyrenees; northward is the district of le Forez, one of the interesting hilly regions; here flows the Lignon, which, though scarcely more than a rippling brook, is one of the most famous streams of French literature, for on its banks Céladon (the hero of d'Urfé's famous pastoral romance, *Astrée*) wooed his fair shepherdess. Still farther north are the highlands of le Morvan, with groves of beech, oak, and chestnut, a last projection of the *Massif central* into the basin of the Seine. This region is occupied by a sturdy race whose women are famous as nurses. Here are Autun, of which Talleyrand was once bishop, the home of Philip Gilbert Hamerton, the artist-critic who did so much to interpret the French to the English; and the old abbey town of Vézelay, where crusades were preached in the Middle Ages and where was born Théodore de Bèze, the great reformer and suc-

---

[1] The Gévaudan was the scene of the activities of the "*grande bête du Gévaudan*", perhaps an escaped animal, whose depredations in 1764 and 1765 were magnified by popular tradition and superstition into those of a mysterious and furious monster. Stevenson, in his *Travels with a Donkey*, calls him the "Napoléon Buonaparte of wolves".

cessor of Calvin at Geneva. Westward lie the sunny slopes of the Côte d'Or in Burgundy, covered with famous vineyards, where Vercingetorix resisted Cæsar to the end at Alesia (Alise-Sainte-Reine). Northward still the height of land becomes the plateau of Langres and the district of Chaumont, headquarters of the American army, until it finally circles round to the Vosges or merges northward to the Argonne and the Ardennes.

The Pyrenees raise their lofty peaks between France and Spain. Less visited by foreign tourists than the familiar Alps, the region contains such well-known places as Pau, the birthplace of Henry IV; Lourdes, the greatest pilgrimage resort of France; the semi-independent republic of Andorra, one of the oldest communities in Europe; and the queer little Spanish enclave of Llivia, surrounded by French territory and connected with Spain, ever since the treaty of the Pyrenees in the seventeenth century, only by an international road. The Alps, dividing France from Italy, extend through a land at least part of which came to France in the nineteenth century under Napoleon III. Savoy, though its language is French, long belonged to the kingdom of Sardinia; it was the ancestral home of the present royal house of Italy, whose cry is still "Avanti Savoia". The Jura mountains help to separate France from Switzerland. Crossing the hollow Trouée de Belfort, saved to France by Thiers as a protective outpost against Germany after the Franco-Prussian War, we come finally to the wooded Vosges, which divide the lands of purely French language from Alsace.

The mountain ranges of France, together with projecting spurs or plateaus only a few hundred feet high, divide the land into five well-defined river basins: the Seine, the Loire, the Garonne, the Rhône, and the Rhine. A few subsidiary coastal basins of some secondary streams are joined to the larger ones.[1]

---

[1] The newest geography emphasizes the connecting links rather than the dividing line between districts, the *seuil*, or "threshold," instead of the *ligne de partage des eaux*; but the adult Frenchman of today was taught in school the physical configuration of his country by river basins.

THE LAND OF FRANCE

The Seine rises in the plateau of Langres and, flowing leisurely in a winding course, which tends, on the whole, in a northwesterly direction, finally throws itself into the English Channel. Uninteresting in its upper parts, its banks become more varied and picturesque as it approaches and passes Paris. It traverses the old province of the Ile-de-France and, indeed, helps to form, together with the Marne, the Oise, the Aisne, and the Ourcq, that inland "Island of France" which was the nucleus of the domains of the old French monarchy. At Rouen, birthplace of Corneille and of Flaubert, the Seine reaches the capital of Normandy.

Normandy is one of the provinces whose aspect is most familiar to the foreigner, because it is the one usually seen first by the Englishman or the American reaching the continent, and the peasants of artists like Millet, himself a Norman, have often been of the Norman type. Normandy was the great literary province of the seventeenth century, as Anjou and Touraine had been of the sixteenth. Below Rouen the Seine, after repeated S-shaped curves, pours its sluggish waters into a wide, muddy estuary. On the north are the cliffs overlooking the great modern seaport of Le Havre, dating only from the days of Francis I, and birthplace of Bernardin de Saint-Pierre (the author of *Paul and Virginia*) and of Casimir Delavigne; on the south lie the lush pastures and rich thickets of the Vallée d'Auge, where the quaint old town of Honfleur, with a name of Celtic origin, watches enviously from its silted harbor its successful upstart rival across the bay. Honfleur recalls the days when its hardy navigators, fishermen, explorers, and privateersmen ranged over the western seas, and still remembers that from its port Paulmier de Gonneville once sailed forth to explore Brazil, Jean Denis to discover Labrador, and Samuel de Champlain to found Quebec. Here, in more recent times, the place gave birth to the historian Albert Sorel, the poet Henri de Régnier, and the Mark Twain of modern France, Alphonse Allais. Here, too, lived Baudelaire and the describer of Norman scenes, Jean Revel, and here the American Homer

Martin pottered away in poverty, before posthumous fame made him one of the great artists of America.

North of the Seine the chalky cliffs of upper Normandy face, across the gradually narrowing Channel, the chalky cliffs of England, with which they were connected before some convulsion of nature made the Straits of Dover. Along this coast, with its inland district of the Pays de Caux of which Maupassant wrote, one comes to the seaports or watering places of Fécamp, Etretat, and Dieppe before reaching the mouth of the Somme, a river flowing generally northwestward through the territory in Picardy devastated during the World War and occupied largely by the British armies,—Saint-Quentin, Péronne, and Amiens. At Amiens lived for many years Jules Verne, prophet of aërial and submarine navigation, once beloved by hundreds of thousands of youths for his wonderful tales of extraordinary adventure. Picardy was famous as one of the centers of Gothic architecture. It was the birthplace of Calvin.

Into the Seine from the north flow such rivers as the Aube, which passes near Brienne, where Napoleon went to the military academy, and where, in 1814, he defeated the allies in one of the important contests on the battle fields of Champagne; the Marne, which goes by Langres (birthplace of Diderot), Châlons, Epernay, Château-Thierry (now known to every American but chiefly famous before the war as the birthplace of La Fontaine), and Meaux (the bishopric of Bossuet); the Oise, which enters the Seine a little below Paris and receives on its way the Aisne.[1] North of the Marne, in Valois, Brie, and Champagne, is land many times fought over, with names famous in history, scene of the first and second battles of the Marne and the fierce contests on the Aisne,—the valleys of the Ourcq, Belleau Wood, Reims, the Chemin des Dames. Already, in 1814, in the district near the Chemin des Dames, Napoleon had been defeated in battles which led to the downfall of the First Empire and the exile to Elba.

---

[1] Pontoise, on the Oise, is the home of the French counterparts of the "Wise Men of Gotham". *Revenir de Pontoise* = "avoir l'air niais".

On the south the Seine receives the Yonne, which floats down to Paris the barges laden with wood from the Morvan and the Nivernais[1]; the Loing, whose reedy waters flow under the old bridge at Grez, so often portrayed by artists, on the edge of the forest of Fontainebleau, where Stevenson fell in love with his American wife and hobnobbed with Sir Walter Simpson, his Bohemian companion on the inland voyage among the waters of northern France; the Eure, which passes through Chartres with its great cathedral, one of the marvels of French Gothic architecture and the inspiration alike of poet, of intellectualist, and of decadent, of James Russell Lowell, of Henry Adams, and of Huysmans.[2]

Going westward along the shore from the mouth of the Seine, the traveler passes through the region of Lower Normandy, land of William the Conqueror; of the seventeenth-century Malherbe, apostle of common sense in poetry; of Saint-Evremond, in the same century, soldier, man of letters, and a connecting link between the literatures of France and England; and, in our own times, of Barbey d'Aurevilly, the "diabolical" *conteur* and critic; of Octave Feuillet, the society novelist of the Second Empire, and of Remy de Gourmont, the critic and æsthete.

Southwest of Normandy there projects into the western sea the granite peninsula of Brittany, divided by its central hills into a northern and a southern watershed. On the boundary of the two provinces is the Mont Saint-Michel, and between their projecting arms lie the Channel Islands, belonging to England and last remnant of the old Duchy of Normandy, where the king is only duke. In these islands the traveler from New England is surprised to come upon doughnuts (*merveilles*) and baked beans. Lonely Brittany, with its Celtic speech, its strange customs and superstitions, and the seafarers of Loti's *Pêcheur d'Islande*, is in some respects a different country from the rest

---

[1] See Daudet's *Belle-Nivernaise*.
[2] Lowell's *Cathedral*; Henry Adams's *Mont Saint-Michel and Chartres*; Huysmans's *la Cathédrale*.

of France, from which it was independent until the end of the fifteenth century. It is a conservative land of the past, naïvely religious, except among the radical and socialistic laborers of the arsenals at Brest, but, like Normandy, devastated by alcoholism. Some of its districts are thickly strewn with prehistoric menhirs and dolmens, like the famous regions of Carnac and Locmariaquer on the south coast; others are scattered with elaborate stone crucifixes and religious monuments, halting places for the great processions, or *pardons*, which the peasants carry out with eager piety sometimes reminiscent of paganism. At Sainte-Anne-d'Auray is one of the most important pilgrimages of France, and near the village the large kneeling statue of "Henry V" in regal robes, erected in memory of the legitimist pretender the comte de Chambord, testifies to the conservatism of the populace. To Brittany belong Chateaubriand, the æsthete of Catholicism, buried on a lonely islet in the harbor of his native Saint-Malo; Lamennais, the pariah of Catholicism, born also at Saint-Malo; Renan, the apostate of Catholicism, who came from Tréguier, near the northern coast. On a sandy and desolate peninsula inclosing the Gulf of Morbihan on the southern shore, Le Sage, creator of Gil Blas, saw the light of day at Sarzeau. Brizeux was one of the great poets of nineteenth-century Brittany, and in contemporary times Anatole Le Braz and Charles Le Goffic have sought to make it their own in verse, fiction, and criticism.[1]

The basin of the Loire includes territories of very different nature. The river is the longest one in France, but because of the shallowness of its lower reaches, interrupted by sudden and destructive inundations, it is one of the most untrustworthy. This is a result of deforestation. The lower course is protected by embankments, or levees, which unfortunately are not always strong enough. The Loire rises in the lofty *Massif central* and flows due north for some distance, after which it gradually sweeps round to the west. First it crosses the mountain district of le

---

[1] Landerneau, the Little Pedlington of modern French literature ("Il y aura du bruit dans Landerneau") is in Northern Brittany.

Velay and the upland region of le Forez; then, roughly dividing Bourbonnais (ancestral home of the Bourbon dynasty) and Nivernais, it waters the marshy plains of Sologne near Orléans and goes through Touraine and Anjou before reaching the sea near Saint-Nazaire. Emile Guillaumin describes rural life in Bourbonnais, and René Boylesve provincial life in Touraine. The Loire, with its tributaries, waters one of the most interesting parts of the country historically, and goes through the heart of the land. At Orléans are memories of Jeanne Darc, and along the river below the city the shattered French troops resisted the invaders in the Franco-Prussian War. From Blois to below Tours we are in the country of the famous Renaissance châteaux,[1] and the center of the rich life of poetry and song connected with the names of the Pléiade in the sixteenth century and familiar to readers of Dumas's romances. Tours, in the "jardin de la France", is the scene of parts of *Quentin Durward* and the birthplace of Balzac, and we are near the places of some of his stories. Here is the burial place of Ronsard, and not far away were the homes of Descartes and Rabelais. Rabelais's seemingly fantastic geography in his land of the giants Grandgousier and Gargantua is in reality merely a description of the hamlets, willow groves, and river fords near his native town of Chinon. Here we are near one of those quaint regions of France inhabited by troglodytes, or cave dwellers, where one may see chimneys emerging from a field or lace curtains at windows in the face of a cliff.[2] Saumur was the home of Balzac's heroine Eugénie Grandet; Angers on the Maine, a tributary of the Loire, is the chief city of Anjou, land of Du Bellay, the poet of the Pléiade who, far away in Rome, wrote of his love for the gently curling smoke rising from the chimneys of the native hamlet, and of his homesickness for the *douceur angevine*.

[1] Blois, Chambord, Chenonceaux, Chaumont, Amboise, Azay-le-Rideau, and many others.

[2] See also the village of Bourre, in Loir-et-Cher, between Tours and Bourges; also Troo in the valley of the Loir (Ronsard country).

In its upper course the Loire clings closely to its watershed, but as it reaches the open land the districts to the north give more space for human habitation. To the north of Orléans stretches the plain of Beauce, once so poor that its gentlemen "went to bed to have their breeches patched",[1] and, as Rabelais said, "breakfast on yawns", but whose flat, treeless spaces are now the granary of France. In the region of Vendômois, near the Loir,[2] was born the great sixteenth-century poet Ronsard, who sang of familiar haunts like the Fontaine Bellerie and the forest of Gastine.

The southern tributaries of the Loire are more numerous than the northern ones. The Allier, flowing almost due north, skirts homes of the romanesque ecclesiastical architecture of Auvergne, as Brioude and Issoire, crosses the fertile Limagne, and passes by Vichy, famous for its springs. In the mountains near Brioude, perched among the pines, is the old fortress abbey-monastery of La Chaise-Dieu, once the richest in France, where a pope, Clement VI, was buried, where the Cardinal de Rohan was banished in disgrace after the Affair of the Diamond Necklace, that great scandal which involved Marie-Antoinette just before the outbreak of the Revolution.

The Cher comes from the mountains of Lower Auvergne and describes a wide circle almost parallel with the Loire, which it enters just below Tours, passing not far from Bourges, the old capital of Berry, and flowing under the Renaissance château of Chenonceaux.

The Indre is a placid stream which goes by Loches, birthplace of Alfred de Vigny, with its memories of Charles VII and Agnes Sorel; here may be seen the dungeons into which Louis XI cast his prisoners. On its upper course in Berry it passes near Nohant and waters the district which George Sand described in her pastoral romances like *la Petite Fadette, la Mare au*

---

[1] An old proverb said:
  C'est un gentilhomme de Beauce,
  Qui est au lit quand on refait ses chausses.

[2] Le Loir, a small and indirect tributary of la Loire.

diable and *le Meunier d'Angibault*. The neighboring valley of the Creuse, which pours into the Vienne, particularly Gargilesse, is also in places commemorated by George Sand, and her *Histoire de ma vie* and *Promenades autour d'un village* once made the region famous and the resort of artists. Berry was the home of George Sand's godson, the poet of *névroses*, Maurice Rollinat.

The Vienne rises in the bleak plateau of Millevaches on the western slope of the *Massif central*. It flows through le Limousin and its chief town Limoges, once famous for its enamel ware, and whence so much china is exported to America,—birthplace in modern times of President Carnot and of Emile Montégut, —and after passing through Chinon and the Rabelais country it reaches the Loire above Saumur. It receives the Creuse on the right, and on the left the Clain, a sinuous stream in pretty vales, which twists about the hill where stands Poitiers.

Two other short tributaries of the Loire deserve mention: the Thouet, which flows by Parthenay, one of the most picturesque towns of Poitou, and the Sèvre Nantaise that takes one by Tiffauges, castle of Gilles de Raiz, the original of "Bluebeard", and Clisson, again one of the quaintest towns of France.

Among the rivers flowing into the ocean between the mouth of the Loire and that of the Garonne the most important are the Sèvre Niortaise and the Charente. The former comes from the hills of Poitou, passes by Niort, where Madame de Maintenon was born, and before reaching the sea crosses the marshy plains of the Marais vendéen that René Bazin has described in his sad *la Terre qui meurt*. To the north is the Bocage vendéen, where the inhabitants so long resisted the troops of the Revolution. On the Vendée, a short tributary of the Sèvre, is Fontenay-le-Comte, now a half-dead town but in the sixteenth century the intellectual capital of Lower Poitou. A few miles away, on a hillock once an island among the now drained marshes, the ruined cathedral of Maillezais recalls Rabelais, who lived here and at Fontenay-le-Comte, and his patron the bishop Geoffroy d'Estissac. The Charente, coming from le Limousin, goes past Angoulême, set high on a hill overlooking the plain, birthplace of Margaret of Navarre and of the important seventeenth-century rhetorician Balzac, a very different man from the great novelist; past Cognac, the home of brandy and the birthplace of Francis I, and Saintes. Not far from Angoulême is the magnificent Renaissance château of La Rochefoucauld, once the estate of the famous author of the *Maxims*, and on the coast between the Sèvre Niortaise and the Charente is La Rochelle, heroic citadel of the Huguenots, which resisted so valiantly the siege of Richelieu that only a small fraction of its inhabitants was left to surrender.

The basin of the Garonne is, historically and architecturally as well as by its scenery, of the greatest interest. The Garonne rises in the Pyrenees and pours into the Bay of Biscay by a long and wide estuary called the Gironde. It passes by Toulouse with its brick churches and public buildings, one of the intellectual centers of old France, a home of conservatism and reaction during the religious persecutions of the past; Agen, home of Julius Cæsar Scaliger, the pedantic Aristotelian critic of the sixteenth century, who helped to saddle French tragedy with the unities; Bordeaux, brilliant and spacious, recalling Montaigne and Montesquieu, a busy modern seaport with a glorious past as well, whose prosperity is built not only on seaborne trade but on the rich red and white wines of famous vintages, lighter than the heavy Burgundy. Into the Garonne there flow many streams from the right. The mountain Ariège comes from the Pyrenees. The Tarn, pouring through desolate cañons, passes by Albi and its fortress-cathedral, the headquarters of the medieval Albigensian heretics. It receives the Aveyron, which also rises among the bleak *causses* and flows through Rouergue, with the town of Rodez perched high aloft like a mountain town of Italy. The Lot comes from above lonely Mende and goes through the district of Quercy with its chief town, Cahors, birthplace of the poets Clément Marot and Olivier de Magny in the sixteenth century and of Léon Gambetta in the nineteenth. Léon Cladel and Emile Pouvillon are modern novelists of Quercy. Before reaching Cahors the river traverses a wonderful valley of rugged cliffs with rocks of varied shapes and hues. To the north of Cahors the *causses* of Quercy, similar in geological formation to those of the Tarn but somewhat less bleak, let the rain percolate through their porous surface until, far below the ground, the water forms huge grottoes and flowing streams. Among these caverns is the great abyss of Padirac, from the bottom of which one travels on a subterranean watercourse deeper and deeper into the ground. At the adjacent pilgrimage of Rocamadour the chapels and shrines cling to the steep cliff, so that, beginning with the roofs, one can climb down instead of up until one reaches the village at the bottom of the valley. The last important tributary of the Garonne is the Dordogne, a varied river with varied affluents, ranging from the Cère, dashing through mountain gorges, to the quiet Isle, which itself receives the semi-stagnant Dronne, creeping past old Brantôme (of which the sixteenth-century gossip of that name was lay abbot), with its thousand-year-old abbey and its painted grottoes. This is the district of Périgord and the town of Périgueux, with its extraordinary semi-Byzantine cathedral. Périgord is the land of prehistoric remains, where have been found old skeletons and early drawings going back to the fourth, third, and second ages of humanity. It is the land where Michel de Montaigne was born and lived to read and meditate in his rural château overlooking wide-ranging vineyards and sunny slopes.

Thus the basin of the Garonne incloses districts famous in the past, such as Gascony, Armagnac, Périgord, Quercy, and Rouergue. It is a part of France where many of the inhabitants speak with an accent and intonation different from that of the North. From Gascony, too, came all those wandering and adventurous "Cadets of Gascony", younger sons of landed families, proud and haughty, but impecunious soldiers of fortune, resourceful, witty, and cheerful, given to wild exaggerations and always falling on their feet. Henry IV is reported to have said to a gardener unable to make anything grow on a barren patch of land: "Plant Gascons, for they will thrive anywhere."

The Mediterranean coast of France belongs to the basin of the Rhône, but on the western coast of the Golfe du Lion, mistranslated in English "Gulf of Lyons", the territory is watered by individual streams flowing directly into the sea. Part of this land, definitively French only since the seventeenth century, has retained a Spanish appearance, and Perpignan might be Catalan almost as well as French. At Carcassonne the fortifications, elaborately restored, show what a walled city of the Middle Ages was like, and he who yearns for the horizon recalls Gustave Nadaud's poem, with its refrain, "Je ne verrai jamais Carcassonne." Some towns flourish yet: Montpellier has its spacious neoclassic promenades, as well as memories of the times when its medical school was one of the leading resorts of Europe. Narbonne, on the other hand, has dropped from some hundred thousand in olden times to a mere score of thousands; and a place like Mauguelone, near Montpellier, once a thriving town and bishopric, is today only a half-abandoned church by the lonely sea. Back in the narrow gorges of the Hérault the tiny hamlet of Saint-Guilhem-le-Désert, lost in the wilderness, alone remains to recall one of the great medieval pilgrimage routes connected with the early history of the *chansons de geste*.[1]

The Rhône, flowing from its glacier in Switzerland, near the Saint-Gothard, is French only after it has left the Lake of Geneva. It twists round the Jura mountains and goes south to the Mediterranean, becoming more and more individual as it flows. The southernmost regions are Languedoc and Provence, —glorious names in medieval life and letters. Today they are to a great degree treeless, and in winter are windswept by the cruel *mistral* that blows from the snow-capped Alps. In summer they are torrid and parched, and end by the sea in marshy

---

[1] M. Joseph Bédier's theory of the origin of the medieval heroic poems, which tends to connect them with the conscious literary work of people at the great stations on the pilgrimage routes of France, is gradually replacing the theory of the folklorists. These considered the *chanson de geste* to be the outgrowth of primitive anonymous popular ballads.

swamps, where mosquito-bitten towns like Aigues-Mortes live on their past glory, or in barren wastes like the pebbly Crau, or marshy Camargue, at the delta of the Rhône.[1] Perched on the crags, in a landscape recalling the Inferno of Dante, is the deserted city of Les Baux, whose lords once claimed the titles of Kings of Arles and of Emperors of Constantinople. It still displays whole streets of half-ruined Renaissance houses, some partly hewn from the rock, while the castle rises in state above the whole. Arles brags of its Greek origin and the beauty of its women; Nîmes is Roman but keeps up a pseudo-metropolitan air today; Tarascon sulks over Daudet's *Tartarin*; and Avignon recalls the sojourn of the popes many centuries ago. But the atmosphere is clear and bright, and the native, exuberant and voluble, thinks no place its equal. The Provençal poet Mistral, author of *Mireille*, with Roumanille and Aubanel, sought to revive the glories of the old language and to restore it to its rank in literature.[2]

Beyond the delta of the Rhône and Marseilles, the chief seaport of France, the coast gradually becomes Italian, as near the Pyrenees it is Spanish. The cloudless skies and the olive trees are those of another country, until one remembers that much of the land was Italian until the reign of Napoleon III, and that Nice was the birthplace of the Italian Garibaldi. Across the waters to the south is the Corsica of Napoleon I and of Mérimée's *Colomba*.

Mountainous Savoy was the country of the two brothers, Joseph and Xavier de Maistre. In the early nineteenth century its wandering urchins were the chimney-sweeps' boys of Paris, or with their trained marmots they begged in the streets, and Guiraud's famous sentimental ballad, *le Petit Savoyard*, was once in every school reader. Today Henry Bordeaux is fond of its scenery as a background for his stories. Grenoble, in Dauphiné, was the birthplace of Stendhal.

---

[1] Jean Aicard is the modern novelist who has written of the Camargue.
[2] Paul Arène and Paul Mariéton have written of modern Provence. Zola was born there.

At Lyons, "second eye of France" and once a close rival of
Paris in commerce and letters, the Rhône receives its chief
tributary, the Saône, where Philip Gilbert Hamerton made his
summer voyage. To the north of Lyons, in Burgundy, are
Mâcon, birthplace of Lamartine, and Dijon where Bossuet was
born. Paray-le-Monial is the chief place of pilgrimage in
France after Lourdes, where in the seventeenth century the
cult of the Sacred Heart arose from the ecstatic visions of the
nun Marie Alacoque. The old district of Franche-Comté, once
Spanish territory, has as chief city Besançon, the birthplace of
Victor Hugo, "vieille ville espagnole", as he terms it.[1]

The World War has restored to France a large territory in the
valley of the Rhine, where for so many years only portions of
some of its tributaries belonged to that nation. Strasbourg,
where Rouget de Lisle composed the *Marseillaise*, has returned
to its old allegiance, and the French name Saverne replaces the
German Zabern, where the episode of the lame shoemaker perhaps had no little to do with inducing the German War Lords
to goad France to war. This is the land of Erckmann-Chatrian's
stories and of René Bazin's *les Oberlé*, as Lorraine and Metz are
the land of Maurice Barrès and of *Colette Baudoche*, and the
scene of the writings of André Theuriet and Emile Moselly.

In that part of Lorraine which remained French, Nancy, on
the Meurthe, the old capital of the duchy of Lorraine, found
itself, as a result of the Franco-Prussian War, really a frontier
town; Epinal, on the Moselle, was long the home of the rough
images d'Epinal known to every French child, cheaply printed
and crudely colored pages of pictures in broadside form, with
brief accompanying letterpress containing fables, legends, or
fairy tales; at Domremy, near the Meuse, is the home of the
greatest heroine of French history, Jeanne Darc. Near the
Meuse is land the names of which are famous in American history as the scene of the greatest battle ever fought by our

---

[1] Burgundy prides itself on wit and salt, on good eating and good drinking,
on being the home of the songs called *noëls bourguignons* and of *Bourguignons salés*. The epigrammatist Piron was a Burgundian.

army, in the Argonne. Saint-Mihiel, Verdun, Varennes, where Louis XVI was arrested in 1791, Clermont-en-Argonne, and Sedan, where Napoleon III surrendered in 1870 and where the World War came to an end in 1918, are found here.

Northeastward to the sea the Escaut, or Scheldt, and its small, sluggish tributaries water French Flanders and Artois before flowing through Belgium into Holland. Arras was the home of Robespierre, Carlyle's "sea-green incorruptible". All this land, recently devastated, was always of great historical importance, but is now architecturally less interesting than the south. It was one of the most thoroughly industrialized parts of the country, packed with a manufacturing and mining population, and the innumerable battles fought upon its soil through the ages had destroyed many of its antiquities.

CHAPTER II

THOUGHT AND POLICY UNDER THE REVOLUTION AND THE EMPIRE

THE history of modern France begins with the Revolution. The bloody cataclysm which then occurred changed, if only outwardly, the governmental and social organism, and it is customary nowadays in France to consider the Revolution as the birth of freedom, regardless of incidental despotism and terror, and regardless of the fact that, as Arthur Young pointed out, France had a milder government than any large country in Europe except England.

The Revolution, however startling its manifestations, was not the sudden phenomenon that it appears to be when we read about it in historical manuals, although the extreme consequences of its outbreak were unlooked for. Nor were its causes the strict consequence, as Taine would have us understand, of certain characteristics of the French temperament, the *esprit classique*, a sort of abstract-reasoning process. Instead of being rigidly logical the Revolution was, at least during the days of the Girondists and the Jacobins, under the lead of political mystics, swayed by words and phrases; though men acted, as they thought, in the name of pure reason. The Jacobins especially tried to materialize their theories and ideals by bloodthirsty tyranny and the murder of their more conservative antagonists.[1]

---

[1] A few words concerning the legislative bodies and parties of the Revolution may be helpful. The States-General met at Versailles in May, 1789, for the first time since the early seventeenth century. It contained three distinct bodies: the nobility, the clergy, and the commoners, or Third Estate. In June the Third Estate declared itself a National Assembly. In time, when the other parties had drifted back, it became known as the Constituent Assembly, because its purpose was to formulate a constitution. In 1791 it was replaced

THE REVOLUTION AND THE EMPIRE

The ultimate causes of the Revolution were economic, but the remedies were often sought in the untried theories of Rousseau and the dogmas of ideologists. The *immediate* effect of the eighteenth-century "philosophers" was small, and the Revolution took its course in a somewhat haphazard way, often through the action of a minority, who had, however, the strategic advantage of having wrested power from a divided opposition. So many forces came into play, ranging from religious animosities to personal spite, that no period in French history is more difficult to unravel, and there is none in which it is so difficult justly to apportion praise or blame. Moreover, since the Revolution was such a complicated phenomenon, almost every historian has approached the period from the point of view of his sympathies or his scholarly bias, and every interpretation has seemed, at least to some readers, one-sided or incomplete. Though we dismiss the rhetoric of Carlyle as worthless, and confine ourselves to historical writers, we encounter divergent opinions even among defenders of the Revolution. Thiers and Mignet wrote before the Revolution had received sufficient perspective, and were influenced by the political atmosphere of their times. Michelet glorified the democratic Revolution, just as Taine, writing many years later, after the horrors of the Commune of 1871, was utterly to condemn it as the work of ghouls and

by its own creation, the Legislative Assembly. The chief parties in Paris were the Feuillants, partisans of the constitutional monarchy, as distinguished from out-and-out royalists; the Montagnards of the "Mountain", fierce opponents of the constitution (thus named because they sat on the upper benches), destined to be the nucleus of the Jacobins and of the ultra Cordeliers; the Girondists, anticonstitutionalists also, but less rabid in their policies. The term *Jacobinism* today is used to designate vindictive, unconciliatory radicalism. The drift was inevitably toward advanced policies, partly under the influence of the self-formed committee at Paris, the Commune, which usurped the powers of the regular municipality. The king was suspended and a National Convention was summoned to determine a new form of government. The Convention destroyed the monarchy and the king. The dominant Jacobin party persecuted the milder Girondists and terrorized France (Reign of Terror) until, in Thermidor, 1794, the reaction came and Robespierre was put to death. Then followed the Directoire and the reign of the profiteers, then the Consulate of Napoleon, and the Empire.

hyenas; Lamartine deified the Girondists, and Louis Blanc saw the advent of socialism. Among the more recent writers, M. Aulard, in his political history, confines himself of necessity to a single phase. After reading his stout volume one might imagine the Revolution to have been the work of jurisconsults and legists. Albert Sorel thinks principally in terms of international relations. The socialist Jaurès, on the other hand, is engrossed in the rise of the working classes. Then, again, an avowed partisan like the anarchist Prince Kropotkin deifies the very men on whom Taine pours gall and wormwood, and sees the soul of the Revolution in the Commune; or another writer, Mrs. Nesta Webster, a high Tory, relying almost entirely on contemporary partisan writings, calls the whole Revolution the result of underhanded intrigues of the Duke of Orléans and his paid hirelings, led by Choderlos de Laclos, author of the *Liaisons dangereuses*, to supplant Louis XVI on the throne.

The ultimate cause of the Revolution, it has been said, was economic, but such an explanation inadequately accounts for all the complex motives. The eighteenth century had scattered plentiful seeds of discontent and had prepared for the change. Intellectually, indeed, the greatness of the Revolution was in its antecedents, and its own men were for the most part but average people who borrowed from the crisis as much as they gave to it.

The eighteenth century was an age of venturesome theorizing. The self-confident spirit of rationalism, for which Descartes had been in part responsible, led people to find abundant defects in the political and social organism, and to offer remedies. The Revolution was largely a revolt against privilege and inequality as a result of the philosophical movement in favor of liberty and the Rights of Man. The theories were made timely by economic injustice and hardship. The wealthy privileged classes were envied by the rest of the tax-burdened population. Economic discontent received a "philosophic" justification and explanation in the new theories.

Years before the Revolution Pierre Bayle had preached re-

THE SABINE WOMEN, BY DAVID (LOUVRE MUSEUM)

ligious tolerance and had furthered freedom from dogma. The abbé de Saint-Pierre had advocated universal peace and fraternity. But it is to a greater degree in men like Voltaire, Rousseau, Montesquieu, and the *philosophes* that we find the ideas destined to ferment into destructive or constructive forces. Voltaire continued more vividly the tendencies of Bayle toward religious freedom, and his spectacular efforts to rehabilitate the victims of legal injustice aroused other critics. The positivism of the Encyclopedists and of the *philosophes* in general had emboldened people to favor innumerable schemes, however immature, for the amelioration of society. It became natural to preach the corruption of priests and the treachery of kings, as foes of rational progress and universal brotherhood. In a minor degree Montesquieu's analysis of institutions afforded a foundation for theories of reconstruction, but the extraordinarily fertile brain of Rousseau was, above all, the chief inspirer of new ideas, which the Revolution tried to carry into effect, of democracy and popular sovereignty, natural rights and the social contract. The thought and language of Rousseau underlie the words and deeds of the leaders of the time and the chief ordinances of the great tribunals, the Constituent and Legislative Assemblies and the Convention.[1]

Meanwhile the French government was rolling up increasing

[1] Some writers make much of the influence of secret societies. The Freemasons, then as now in France, were addicted to political intrigue; the duc d'Orléans was Grand Master of the French Masons, and most of the prominent Revolutionaries were members. There were also the traditions of the Illuminati, a former movement of republican free thought, founded by the German ex-Jesuit Adam Weishaupt, to free nations from tyranny and the people from serfdom. It has even been suggested that traditions of the Illuminati, as much as the direct influence of Plutarch and Rousseau and of Barthélemy's archæological and didactic novel, *le Voyage du jeune Anacharsis*, were responsible for the symbolism and nomenclature of the Revolution, and that the formula "Liberty, Equality, Fraternity" was derived from the rituals of the Illuminati and the Masons. The whole question is very obscure. Of much more obvious influence was the power of political clubs, meeting in old monasteries,—the Feuillants, the Jacobins, the Cordeliers,—who gave their names to Revolutionary parties. This religious terminology is constantly encountered in the early history of the Revolution.

deficits.[1] An extravagant court and reckless expenditures for the support of idle and useless officials were enough to arouse discontent, but in addition repeated wars had made it impossible to carry on the government without crushing taxes.

The growth of industrialism, too, crude as it was compared with the conditions of today, had contributed to the rise of a well-to-do *bourgeoisie* without political power and jealous of the oligarchical nobility. Some of the latter actually furnished weapons to the malcontents by the enlightened way in which they acknowledged existing defects, but the majority of the nobility were not so open-minded. So the middle classes looked jealously at the rich estates lying idle in the hands of the clergy and nobility. Even the peasants were seized with the spirit of rebellion against feudal privilege and began to burn and plunder.

New ideas reflected the changed feeling. The school of economists called the Physiocrats had based their theories on agriculture and argued that national wealth comes from the soil. But both in agriculture and in industry the *bourgeoisie* advocated freedom of labor, with no restrictions for capital and no

[1] In 1787 Arthur Young wrote the following strikingly prophetic lines: "One opinion pervaded the whole company, that they are on the eve of some great revolution in the government: that everything points to it: the confusion in the finances great; with a *deficit* impossible to provide for without the states-general of the kingdom, yet no ideas formed of what would be the consequence of their meeting: no minister existing, or to be looked to in or out of power, with such decisive talents as to promise any other remedy than palliative ones: a prince on the throne, with excellent dispositions, but without the resources of a mind that could govern in such a moment without ministers: a court buried in pleasure and dissipation; and adding to the distress instead of endeavoring to be placed in a more independent situation: a great ferment amongst all ranks of men, who are eager for some change, without knowing what to look to or to hope for: and a strong leaven of liberty, increasing every hour since the American revolution — altogether form a combination of circumstances that promise e'er long to ferment into motion if some master hand of very superior talents and inflexible courage is not found at the helm to guide events, instead of being driven by them. It is very remarkable that such conversation never occurs but a bankruptcy is a topic: the curious question on which is, *would a bankruptcy occasion a civil war and a total overthrow of the government?*" The work of Arthur Young is one of the most interesting pictures of France at the outbreak of the Revolution.

combinations for workers, the policy of *laisser faire* destined in time to bring upon the middle classes the same hatred by the populace that both felt for the nobility. For these theories of individual property entrenched the *bourgeoisie* still more among the "haves" as opposed to the "have-nots".

At the outbreak of the Revolution, therefore, the effective force confronting the royalty and the privileged classes was the ambitious, well-to-do *bourgeoisie*, and in the background was the populace, city mob or peasantry, with even more intense wrongs in the shape of personal and economic servitude. It too begrudged the clergy and the nobility their long usurpation of the land. Historians have blamed the king for not understanding the aspirations of the nation and for not allying himself with the new forces against a doomed reaction. Radicals, like Jaurès or Kropotkin, complain that the *bourgeoisie* was selfish and blind to the problems of the proletariat, so that it was justly submerged by mob violence. A prince of the royal family set an example of demagogy. The duc d'Orléans, chief of the younger branch, was anxious to lead the opposition to the king and to head a new constitutional monarchy; but he was unscrupulous in his methods. His readiness to stir the mob against authority reacted against him, and he became in time one of the victims of the Revolution.

The third estate therefore desired to replace autocracy by a constitutional monarchy, under a king who should be servant instead of irresponsible master of the nation, with the chief authority vested in a national assembly of representatives. The great contemporary examples of constitutionalism were England and the new American republic. Montesquieu had been an admirer of the English system of government, and his writings had in turn influenced that of the United States. Consequently there were historical precedents for a parliamentary government with two chambers and for a separation of the executive and the legislative functions. Moreover, America was extremely fashionable in educated liberal circles, and the theories and governmental vocabulary of the new republic were familiar to all.¹ On the other hand, there were the usual doctrinaires, who wished to organize France on the untried theories of Rousseau rather than on the historical experience of Montesquieu. The final result, the Constitution of 1791, was a hybrid and short-lived makeshift, by which there was only one parliamentary chamber, with the relations between king and legislature so vague as to invite disagreement and almost inevitable violence. The constitution was accompanied by a stirring Declaration of the Rights of Man, inspired by Rousseau and the Declaration of Independence, but it was in practice violated by a division of citizens into active and passive, whereby the proletariat was excluded from sharing power.

Thus the early Revolution had no serious thought of a republic, and the king seemed the best rallying-point for the reorganized nation. The unfortunate monarch, through dissensions over religion and through the intrigues of the queen's party with foreign powers, was himself partly responsible for bringing a republic nearer. In the midst of mental tension and suspicion of the king the Girondists, through petty politics, led into war a country which had recently proclaimed universal brotherhood, and let loose the struggles which devastated Europe and brought on the rule of Napoleon and the conflicts of the nineteenth and twentieth centuries. Nobody today can at heart blame Louis XVI for acting as he did, yet the flight to Varennes and the arrest of the fugitives gave a blow to royal prestige from which it could not recover. The nation considered its king derelict to duty and a truant. Events moved fast, and before many months the king was insulted in his palace, dragged before the Assembly, and given over as prisoner to the proletariat of the Paris Commune and to the levelers who wanted equality of fortune now that privileges had been done away with. So

¹ Aulard, *Hist. pol. de la Rév. fr.*, p. 20, n. 4, quotes Chateaubriand's *Mémoires d'outretombe* (ed. Biré, Vol. I, p. 232) as saying that just before the Revolution it was supreme good taste to affect America at Paris, England at court, Prussia in the army. The vocabulary of the French Revolution (Declaration of Rights, National Convention, etc.) borrowed much from America.

the Convention and the Republic came, and the king disappeared. The Convention held both legislative and executive control and had as autocratic a power as a king of the old régime; but a body of eight hundred men could not govern efficiently, and it was swayed either by the oratory of demagogues or by the committees, who usurped such authority that they, especially the *Comité de salut public*, became irresponsible and tyrannical governing powers. The rule of the Convention was presumably "provisional" until the end of the Revolution, and the democratic constitution of 1793, never put in force, was in time replaced, after Thermidor and the failure of the Convention, by the constitution of 1795, with its restricted electorate and the government of the Directoire.

The early Revolution, in spite of riots and paid instigators, had been guided, on the whole, by level-headed moderates. The government of the Legislative Assembly was a deterioration from the Constituent Assembly, but with the Convention all types of men had their fling. There were reckless, chronically oppositional intellectualists; there were irresponsible, immoral plungers and semicrazy revelers in filthy vituperation, like Hébert and Marat.[1] As harmful as any were mystical fanatics like Robespierre. Many people were hypnotized by the term "Revolution." Its ideals were sanctified into a semireligious dogma. Its achievement justified every method. Intolerance and murder in the name of liberty were perpetrated by the abstract visionary Robespierre. The "general will" of Rousseau, in which all acquiesce, grew to be, under the Terror, a tyrant over the people. Not only the aims but the implements of the Revolution were the object of worship, and the "Mountain" was *sainte*. The murdered Marat became the holy emblem of a country stabbed through the heart, just as the whole Revolution, as a mass, or *bloc*, is still an object of worship among modern radical fanatics.

It was in religion that some of the most striking experiments

---

[1] Marat was a skillful physician of scientific repute and the author of useful treatises.

were tried. Among the *bourgeoisie*, the Jansenists, for instance, numerically few but intellectually strong, wanted merely to free the Catholic Church from their own old persecutor, Rome. They had for many years worked for a semi-independent, or Gallican, church. On the other hand, the emotional revolutionists substituted for the old spirit of religion a mystical cult of mankind. The destructive satire of the Voltairian tradition, combined with the lay traditions of *philosophes* and economists, vulgarized by the atheism of Paris politicians, made them attempt to replace Christianity by the cult of "Reason". Others, especially Robespierre, under the spell of Rousseau's deism, in time preached the worship of the "Divine Being", dissociated from the God of revealed religion.

It is only by taking into account these tendencies, and by recalling the mystical fanaticism of the Revolutionaries, that we can understand the various manifestations. First came the attempt, abetted by Jansenists and Protestants, to reject the domination of Rome by organizing a national, or constitutional, clergy, owing allegiance to the Revolution and not to Rome, which was partly blamed for the corruption of the old régime and the conspiracies to retain the monarchy. Naturally a good proportion of the clergy and of the faithful refused to take the oath to accept the semi-heretical church. A schism ensued in which the innovators had political support and the nonjurors were supported by tradition. The rivalry of the two churches resulted in hostility and persecution. The constitutional clergy got between two fires: the Catholics and nonjurors on the one hand, and the atheists on the other.

Again, the disciples of the irreligious *philosophes* wished to do entirely away with Christianity. They persecuted constitutional and nonjuring clergy alike, and substituted a new calendar for the old one, wiping away Sunday.[1] But under the influence of age-long custom even they could hardly conceive of the cult of a philosophical principle, such as Reason, without

---

[1] American Catholicism after the French Revolution was much influenced by the persecuted and exiled French clergy, especially the Sulpicians.

a ceremonial. In the laicized cathedral of Notre-Dame an actress, dressed in red, white, and blue as the Goddess of Reason, was enthroned and honored with formal rites. Soon after, all buildings dedicated to religion were closed.

The trend toward atheism was unwelcome to the deist Robespierre, who, on June 18, 1794, staged the theatrical Festival of the Supreme Being, at which he officiated as a lay high-priest, proclaiming, in accordance with a decree which he had recently carried through the Convention, the existence of the Supreme Being and the immortality of the soul. This serious burlesque was of short duration, and in the last days of the Convention and during the Directoire one sees a gradual return of the Catholic religion, though with friction between the constitutional and the nonjuring clergies and with spasmodic persecution on the part of the authorities. Meanwhile a group of Rousseauistic deists tried to organize a new religion of humanity, called Theophilanthropy, and devised ceremonials for worship, marriages, and funerals, as well as holidays in honor of men like Socrates, St. Vincent de Paul, Rousseau, and Washington. Theophilanthropy lasted only a short time, but such was the religious confusion that when the tenth, or holy, day of the republican calendar (*décadi*) coincided with the old Sunday, it was not unexampled to find a church building used successively on the same day for rites of Catholicism, of the republican calendar, and of theophilanthropy.

Thus the religious history of the Revolution, to the time of Bonaparte, shows, first, a schism in the Church and a division into constitutional and papal Catholicisms; second, endeavors, on the one hand to sweep away religion entirely in favor of a worship of Reason, and on the other hand to replace it by a deism called the Cult of the Supreme Being. Even later, under the Directoire, the anticlericalism of those who could not in spirit disconnect the Church from the old régime, and a desire to give purpose to the tenth day of the republican calendar, caused them to emphasize holidays for the worship of country and the glorification of patriotic and moral virtues. Religion was merged into patriotism and the *culte décadaire*, or worship of country. Theophilanthropy was permitted, if not encouraged, as a religion for those who had none, or a moral support for those who already had an object of worship. But theophilanthropy appealed to a limited number and was above the level of the masses.

The Revolution had naturally begun by a political upheaval. The first schemes for economic regeneration had been chiefly moral utopias, so vague as to put any practical application out of the question. Philosophical economists were largely engrossed in abstract Rousseauistic theories concerning the Law of Nature, the Social Contract, or Natural Rights.

Soon the abolition of privilege and the shifting of wealth by legislation drew attention to questions of ownership and aroused a desire for property among the have-nots. The cleavage showed itself between rich and poor, and the latter were charged with assaults on property and with "agrarianism".

The division of classes was accentuated by the interference of the Paris proletariat, and every attempt toward reform was made nugatory by the influence of the mob. The history of the Revolution became largely that of the popular movements of Paris. Into proletarian dissatisfaction with the existing social order were injected Rousseau's fallacies of the goodness of man uncorrupted by the complications of civilization, and of the superior justice of primitive communism. Hence the glorification of the proletariat, which has persisted to the days of modern socialism and communism. The first endeavors were directed, especially under "physiocratic" tradition, toward equality interpreted as liberty of opportunity to acquire property. The peasants wanted land of their own, but the efforts were individualistic. A cottage, a field, a plow for everyone was the aim of Robespierre. He wanted a sovereign democracy, economically static, made up of peasant proprietors and city artisans. This individualistic agrarian "socialism" (to anticipate a term not then in use) was fed by the usual classical reminiscences and allusions to Solon and the Gracchi. It was instilled into the rabble, ignorant of ancient history, by pamphleteers or by the sensational fiction of the pornographic writer Restif de la Bretonne, especially in *le Paysan perverti* and in its sequel, *la Paysanne pervertie*.[1]

The next stage came with further terrorization by the city mob, the interpretation of liberty as a leveling process, and demands for the support of the poor by the rich. The demagogues as usual justified these demands by Rousseau and declaimed on the purity of human nature and the sovereignty of the people. The omnipotent state, as the expression of the majority (in this case the organized minority controlling the Paris Commune, and the Jacobin Club and "Mountain") became more tyrannical. The Girondists, who wanted authority federalized, were charged with being in league with the rich. The state, deified as an object of patriotism, grew more grasping and resorted unhesitatingly to confiscation and expropriation, in the direction of nationalization, the servitude of the citizen to the state, and the destruction of private enterprise. By the force of circumstances the Revolutionary policy tended more and more to power held in common, and even Robespierre seemed a moderate to the *enragés* of the populace.

Fortunately for the country this chaos was not actually reached. The legislative body never ventured to pass an agrarian law, though it could confiscate food and excess profits. After Thermidor and the downfall of Robespierre the reaction came. When communistic theories took definite form through the machinations of Babeuf, it was too late, and he was put to death under the Directoire, a government of the *nouveaux riches*.

---

[1] "We shall prevent all orders without exception from receiving neophytes, we shall make landowners of all those who work for them, and thereby we shall bring about the happiness of peoples. . . . We shall endeavor to diminish all huge fortunes and to increase those of the peasants by making them gradually proprietors. For that purpose we shall give vogue to a love-making verging on dissoluteness and we shall try, as far as possible, to ruin the nobles in order to force them to sell; we shall dismember the great fiefs, and we shall bring it about that the auction sales be by sections."—Quoted by Jaurès, *Histoire socialiste*, Vol. II, p. 1096

CARICATURE OF COSTUMES

François-Noël Babeuf, the founder of Babouvism, who took the name of Gracchus Babeuf, crystallized the radical consequences of the popular Revolutionary ideas. By political journalism and conspiracy a secret egalitarian club was organized, with passwords and ritual, for propaganda among the soldiery and elsewhere. It advocated class war under the pretext of equality, the confiscation of property, compulsory labor, the classification of industries, public warehouses, equal distribution of profits, abolition of private enterprise, even state ownership of children during education. Such a social upheaval never got beyond theory, and the Directoire promptly put Babeuf out of the way. Yet his conspiracy deserves careful attention because his chief lieutenant Buonarroti, of the family of Michelangelo, survived to bring his ideas to light at a more opportune time, and because they contain the germ of nearly all socialistic and communistic theories down to Bolshevism.

The humanitarian idealism of the early Revolution lapsed into the bloodshed of the Terror, and its fraternalism was obscured by economic poverty and the extravagance of profiteers of the Directoire. Napoleon's strong hand replaced chaos by order, though the order was that of tyranny. But Napoleon needed to justify his usurpation, or at any rate to make it acceptable, before venturing on ruthless Cæsarism. Before 1807, the time of the treaties of Tilsit and the zenith of his career, Napoleon posed as a liberator and a champion of democracy. The Revolution had proclaimed the sovereignty of the people, and Napoleon affected to be the true voice of the nation. He favored *la carrière ouverte aux talents* and bestowed honors on the low-born equally with the aristocrat. Before the Revolution it had been assumed that only nobles were fitted to command and be officers. He sought popularity as the *petit caporal*. The gray coat (*redingote grise*) as an emblem took the place of the white plume of Henry of Navarre. As the creator of a new Europe Napoleon was the reincarnation of Charlemagne and not merely a successor of Louis XIV. Meanwhile he gradually introduced as complete an autocracy as France had known.

When he felt he could do so, he showed himself a full-fledged tyrant. His drastic reorganization accepted such revolutionary innovations as served his new schemes of centralization. He encouraged the glorification of military imperialism and rewarded artists who painted his triumphs. He surrounded himself with generals with showy titles and uniforms. The imperial reign was an epic age, and *Veillons au salut de l'Empire* took the place of the *Marseillaise*.[1]

Napoleon began to exert his grip with the *coup d'état* of Brumaire. He rejected the schemes of the inventor of constitutions, Sieyès, by which the chief of the state was to be an irresponsible Grand Elector, what he considered a mere "fatted hog" (*pourceau à l'engrais*). He made himself First Consul, and took to himself substantially all the despotic power of the Committee of Public Safety. He then reorganized France without regard for schematism and theorizing, and with severe attention to fact. Idealism had proved a failure; Napoleon was a realist, and the very term *idéologue*, whether applicable to the past or to the present, was to him anathema.

The rule of Napoleon conferred some great administrative reforms on the country, and the codification of the laws was a blessing. But despotic centralization crushed many praiseworthy impulses. The nation was ruthlessly unified, like a regiment, and freedom of thought was suppressed. Newspapers were rigidly censored, and their number limited. Books like Mme de Staël's work on Germany could be confiscated and destroyed if the censorship, even after allowing publication, changed its mind. By the *Concordat*, which lasted for a century, Napoleon turned the ministers of religion into salaried dependents of the state and got control of their actions and of their speech. Especially he laid an iron grip on education. He established a system, called the University, controlling all stages of education. Strict military discipline with uniforms prevailed in the colleges and *lycées*. The foundation of all education was fidelity to the Emperor and to his dynasty.

[1] The word *Empire* had originally meant "state" and not "empire."

Thus Napoleon crushed intellectual opposition. He eliminated from the Institute of France the division of Moral Sciences, because its members were inevitably theorists and therefore hated ideologists. Sieyès was once asked what he thought. "I do not think", he replied. The activity of intellectual men was directed to ornate flattery and rhetorical eulogy. The average of taste is illustrated by the great vogue of "Lyceums" and "Athenæums", where popular lecturers gave courses in neatly rounded periods to audiences largely composed of women. The name of La Harpe is almost the only significant one remembered among a host of garrulous talkers.[1]

[1] For pictures of the Revolutionary period in fiction, see Balzac's *les Chouans*, Hugo's *Quatre-vingt-treize*, Dickens's *Tale of Two Cities*, Félix Gras's *les Rouges du midi*, and Anatole France's *les Dieux ont soif*. Balzac's *Une ténébreuse affaire* is a sort of detective novel dealing with life under Napoleon. For an ambitious but not oversuccessful endeavor to delineate life under the Empire, the Restoration, and the Monarchy of July see Paul Adam's series of novels: *la Force*, *l'Enfant d'Austerlitz*, *la Ruse*, and *Au soleil de juillet*.

CHAPTER III

REVOLUTION AND EMPIRE. MANNERS AND LITERATURE. THEMES AND POPULAR TYPES

THE turmoil of the Revolution found expression in habitual French methods of venting opinion, ranging from *salons*, clubs, and *cafés* to theaters, newspapers, and pamphlets. With the advance toward what we should now call radicalism the social strata became confused and the different sets were more mixed.

At first it was especially in the *salons* of clever and attractive women that public opinion was molded before it seeped through to the multitude, and that the bright flippancies of eighteenth-century literary wit and philosophic cleverness took on a political and economic tinge. In the neighborhood of 1789, in spite of new theories, they kept some of the conservatism of the old régime. There were royalist *salons*, moderate ones like that of Mme Necker, literary ones like that of Mme de Genlis, philosophical ones like that of Mme Helvétius, and artistic ones like that of Mme Talma. Mme Roland became in time the Egeria of the Girondists. Yet everywhere attention gravitated to politics.

The clubs were fertile breeding-places of revolution; and, descending the scale, the intrigues of adventuresses, or the gossip of *café* and street corner, kept the caldron seething. Individual *cafés* became party strongholds; the gardens of the Palais-Royal resounded with frothy oratory. Plays reëchoed prevailing ideas, and the company of the Théâtre-Français was rent with dissension. The newspapers, ranging from the conservative *Actes des Apôtres* to Hébert's periodical pamphlets, the *Père Duchesne*, outdid one another in scurrilous abuse.

The Revolution drove everybody into the street. People were too excited to stay at home or in the workshop. The desire for a clean sweep brought about far-reaching changes. The calendar was rewritten; cities were rechristened; there were no more masters and lackeys, but Citizens and "attendant brothers" or *frères servants*, who called each other *tu* and *toi*; costumes and headdresses received a political nomenclature; the neat knee breeches of the aristocratic régime gave way to the Revolutionary uniform of the *sans-culottes*, the long trousers of modern democracy. The shibboleths were those of social regeneration based on an amalgam of Plutarch and ancient stoicism, together with the emotionalism and sentimentality fashionable since the days of Rousseau and Diderot. Nothing exercised more influence on the oratory of the Revolution than the classical harangues of the rhetorician Thomas, with his academic eulogies of great men in history and letters.

As the Terror grew somber the enthusiasm for humanity became embittered by persecution and hardships resulting from the cost of living. Sentiment still gushed in literature, and a theater gave *Paul and Virginia* on the bloody day of Thermidor, when Robespierre's jaw was smashed;[1] but in theaters, between the acts, one of the company would sometimes read the names of those executed during the day, to an audience which had begun the evening by singing the *Marseillaise*, kneeling through the first stanza. Every man suspected his neighbor, and the Revolution, which had destroyed the Bastille to free a few prisoners, ended by cramming the jails and murdering their inmates.

The depreciation of the currency and the enormous rise in prices fell heavily on the ordinary citizen, but many were made happy by opportunities for speculation. Money seemed more abundant and came or went easily. Under the Directoire everything was a reaction against the Terror. There was hoarding and

---

[1] Two of the favorite works of the period, Carlyle reminds us, were the pruriently modest *Paul et Virginie* and the sewerlike *Chevalier de Faublas* of Louvet.

gambling in values, and those who possessed fabulous amounts of paper money rioted in debauchery. The Directoire was the period of the *nouveaux riches*, speculators, and contractors (*les riz-pain-sel*). Easy divorce made marriage a temporary contract; the loosening of social restrictions and of political surveillance turned life into a ceaseless quest for pleasure; dancing raged and public resorts were often but places of assignation. Already in 1787 Arthur Young had written: "Coffeehouses on the boulevards, music, noise, and *filles* without end; everything but scavengers and lamps." People had lost the art of conversation, so they danced and ate.

The fashions reflected the new order. Money easily made encouraged expenditure for clothes. As a reaction against the Revolutionary affectation of patriotic simplicity and the *sans-culotte* uniform of 1792, with its Phrygian cap and long, loose striped trousers, the men of the Directoire indulged in extravagancies of style. Some wore ill-fitting knee breeches, carelessly buttoned at the knee, with shapeless humped coats and heavy gnarled walking-sticks; others made their breeches as close as tights, with low slippers, variegated coats with trailing tails, and they carried long canes and gigantic monocles or glasses on wands. They had blond wigs above black (anti-Revolutionary) high stocks and chokers, with hair banged over the ears (*oreilles de chien*). They skipped and strutted through the streets, talking in a mincing speech which discarded consonants like *r* and *d*. These were the *muscadins*, perfumed with musk, the *élégants*, the *merveilleux*, or the *incroyables*, so-called because of their reiterated ejaculation, "C'est incoyable." This pronunciation has been called *garatisme*, and perhaps originated partly in imitation of the finical and conceited enunciation of the famous singer of sentimental ballads, or *romances*, named Garat, one of the worst *incroyables* and an insufferable fop.

On their part the women, or *merveilleuses*, of the Directoire discarded the republican *négligés* and toilets *à la constitution*. In 1788, says the actress Louise Fusil in her memoirs, literature and fashions still recalled Louis XV and Du Barry; in 1791 everything was Spartan and Roman, with the pictures of David and the plays on Brutus, Cæsar, Manlius, and Gracchus; under the Directoire the model was the Athens of Aspasia and Alcibiades, with tunics, sandals, and cameos. Though women might still read of virtuous Arcadian shepherdesses, yet with conscious effrontery they made their clothing transparent and scant. The *sans-culottes* were laughingly said to have been followed by the *sans-chemises*. Bare-armed, with dresses cut below the shoulders and slit up the side above the knee, they pretended to be imitating the modes of Greece. Mme Tallien, fascinating and powerful in political intrigue ("Notre-Dame de Thermidor") but outrageous in costume and manners, typifies the spirit of pleasure of the Directoire among women, as the Director Barras embodies its political dishonesty and personal immorality among men. But of course the immorality of the Directoire must not be exaggerated; France did not let virtue perish in spite of the Paris smart set.

With the advent of Napoleon manners became, at least outwardly, more restrained. Napoleon was bent on building up a new aristocracy, though the plebeian origin of some of his generals and of their wives, such as the former washerwoman, the Duchess of Danzig ("Madame Sans-Gêne"),[1] made the task no easy one. He was very severe about etiquette, and instituted elaborate court ceremonies and high functionaries, annexing many aristocrats of the old régime to give tone to his new world of fashion. Court costumes and uniforms became more and more elaborate, and the Empire styles for women took on a heavy stateliness which the diaphanous flimsiness of the Directoire had not been able to attain. But beneath their stiff brocades the hearts of the Junos of the Empire still beat with reverie and romance.

The Revolution, which created such a sudden upheaval in politics, made more gradual changes in literature. There the conservatives could not be done away with by the guillotine. The Voltairian traditionalists of pseudo-classicism held sway in

[1] See Sardou's play, *Madame Sans-Gêne*.

all the "higher" forms, from tragedy to descriptive poetry. To the Voltairian classicists the merit of poetry lay in overcoming an obstacle, the *difficulté vaincue*. They were partisans of political and social progress, but were literary conservatives. The teachings of La Harpe and the lectures of his *Lycée*, which he gave from 1786 for a dozen years, weighed heavily on the whole Empire period. The critics and theater-goers, *connaisseurs* of inherited taste, who would not look beyond the bounds of the old *répertoire*, kept drama in a rut down to the time of the romantic revolt of 1830. It was they who were chiefly responsible for the vogue of mechanical tragedies of Greece or Rome, and of lifeless comedies full of traditional stock characters, *soubrettes*, valets, *marquis*, countesses, and *procureurs*, inherited from eighteenth-century writers, but who no longer corresponded to life. Yet, as a matter of fact, theatrical audiences, in the aggregate, were less guided by absolute tradition than conventional historians of literature have implied. Professor Allard points out that the success of plays was determined quite as much by the vogue of individual actors and the personal preferences of these as by other reasons.

Another form of false classicism which had flourished in the eighteenth century and still remained popular, especially in love poetry, was a "boudoir classicism" of Ovidian and Anacreontic tradition. Greece was the home of voluptuous refinement. The amours of the gods and goddesses of mythology, Venus and Cupid, were the patterns and themes of this flowery art. It reached its highest form of genius in the poetry of André Chénier, beheaded under the Terror, its nearest approach to scholarly accuracy in the *Voyage du jeune Anacharsis* (1788) of the abbé Barthélemy, a semi-erudite romance of travel in ancient days, which helped to bring an idea of Greece, however false, to the Latin traditions of Voltairian pseudo-classicism. But its most pervasive manifestation came through the "idyllic, bucolic, elegiac and sensual" *Voyage d'Anténor* of Lantier which had a great vogue between 1798 and 1823, with its Alexandrianism and imitation of Ionian voluptuousness.

But the school of Voltaire had a rival in that of Rousseau; the school of rationalism, in that of emotionalism. The deification of primitivism and the "state of nature", of impulse and feeling, had provoked new currents in literature, in which the "pathetic fallacy" was constantly developed by correspondence between the outer world and inner feeling. The nature descriptions of Rousseau had led to the exoticism of Bernardin de Saint-Pierre, with the contrast between simple happiness and civilized suffering. Primitivism was also reënforced by the cult of early ages of history, true or spurious,—medievalism and the *genre troubadour*, or, with Chateaubriand, the æsthetic charm of early Christianity and the beauty of the Gothic church, and Ossianism and the mystery of Celtic legend and of Northern literatures. The influence of meditative English writers strengthened the tendency toward reflective melancholy and the idea of death, but as yet without the tempestuous revolt of later romanticism.

Meanwhile, to cater to the everyday moods which clung to life, there was evolved an abundant literature of moral eulogy of the simple existence, contrasted with the seductions and vices of the town, a prose and poetry for family consumption and the edification of ingenuous youth, with stress on virtue derived from goodness, for, as Mme de Staël said: "All true virtues come from goodness." In the breaking-down of the old pseudo-classical *genres* we shall indeed find all the tendencies enumerated above almost inextricably confused, and merged to form a literature of Sensibility. Literary taste became lachrymose sentiment and tenderness, which was often soft-heartedness or *sensiblerie* rather than true *sensibilité*. But sensibility, as a form of sympathetic feeling, was synonymous with virtue: "My friend, our children will learn from us to suffer and to love. Misfortunes give feeling, and is not feeling the source of virtues?"[1]

In the grand style of poetry the chief *genres* in vogue down

---

[1] Quoted by Welschinger, *le Théâtre de la Révolution*, p. 254, from a play on La Fayette, *le Prisonnier d'Olmutz, ou le dévouement conjugal* (1796).

SCENE TO ILLUSTRATE THE BEGINNINGS OF THE *GENRE TROUBADOUR*
From the works of the comte de Tressan (edition of 1822–1823)

through the Empire were, in addition to tragedy, the *discours,* the *épître,* the ode, and the set didactic poem in general. These transmitted the conventional precepts of neoclassic formalism without poetic inspiration. They were supported both by the vogue of antiquity in art and manners and by the imperialism of the new Cæsar. Even Revolutionary prose oratory thought it was reproducing the patriotism of ancient liberators and lawgivers. It abounded in allusions to Solon, Lycurgus, Leonidas, Aristides, Socrates, the Gracchi, Brutus, and Cæsar. It inveighed against tyrants and exuded moral and civic maxims on virtue and the rights of man. At first there was love of humanity, then "Tremblez, tyrans, et vous perfides" became the keynote of oratory and of the literature which reflected its tone.

So far as drama is concerned, the opening pages of Welschinger's *Théâtre de la Révolution* summarize its characteristics. Scores of plays, tragedies, and especially historical *drames* in prose and verse were written, and many acted, during the ten years, but we remember only a few, such as Marie-Joseph Chénier's plays, or Laya's "comedy", *l'Ami des Lois.* Authors dealt with topics of passing interest. "They sang in every rhythm the triumphs of the Revolution, of the Republic, of Democracy, of the Third Estate, of Liberty, of Reason, and of Friendship; the Genius of the Nation, Virtue, Sensibility, Tolerance, Love, Conscience, Beneficence, Valor, Hospitality, Duty, and Nature; they celebrated the Family, generous couples, reunited couples, republican couples, the happiness of fatherhood, civic marriage; they satirized the mania for clubs, the follies of the times, women addicted to politics, Jacobins, and Terrorists; they wept over the victims of convents and the severities of cloisters; they applauded the unfrocked, the marriage of priests, while they declaimed against the ancient inquisitors and the new Tartuffes; they embodied ridicules in types which became famous,—Madame Angot, Arlequin, Figaro, and Nicodème; they celebrated with equal enthusiasm the fourteenth of July, the tenth of August, the ninth of Thermidor, the eighteenth of Fructidor, the eighteenth of Brumaire, the Constituent Assembly, the Legislative Assembly, the Convention, and the Directoire; they exalted the victories of the Republican armies and the exploits of Bonaparte." Plays were dedicated to "virtuous wives", "noble magistrates", and "souls of virtue and feeling". Even love passages grew bombastic. Marivaux no longer reigned supreme, but the style often became one of stereotyped phrases about "torches of Hymen", the "girdle of Venus", "murmuring brooks", and "fateful oaths".

Plays like Marie-Joseph Chénier's *Charles IX, ou l'Ecole des rois* (1789) and *Caïus Gracchus* (1792) illustrate, the first the Revolutionary "national" tragedy, with sixteenth-century costumes instead of togas, and portraying the monarch as a traitor to country and honor, and the second the coupling of pseudo-stoic classicism of plot with contemporary politics and sensibility, aimed against Robespierre. Of *Charles IX* Danton is reported to have said: "If *Figaro* killed the aristocracy, *Charles IX* will kill royalty." Laya's *Ami des Lois*, presented in 1793, just before the trial of the king, was an anti-Jacobin attack under disguised names (Nomophage and Duricrâne) upon men like Robespierre and Marat. The *Victimes cloîtrées* of Boutet de Monvel (1791) popularized the idea of the sensual, hypocritical, and ferocious monk, who carries ruin to families and destroys society to satisfy his ambition and lust.

For the dramatic *social* types, real or conventional, as opposed to the political characters, one turns more naturally to comedies, comic operas, and plays interspersed with the songs called *vaudevilles*. The public liked to be bathed in tears by *drame* or serious comedy, or to be tickled by the satire of the vulgar newly rich, such as the fishwife become wealthy. The tearful drama of the eighteenth century and the pastorals of Favart had, before the Revolution, an offshoot in the tearful comic opera, such as Marsollier's *Nina, ou la folle par amour*, with music by Dalayrac, which was the starting-point for a literature of maidens driven to insanity or somnambulism through love, and women wore *chapeaux à la Nina*:[1]

[1] *Ermite de la Chaussée d'Antin*, January 1, 1813.

> Quand le bien aimé reviendra
> Près de sa languissante amie,
> Le printemps alors renaîtra,
> L'herbe sera toujours fleurie ;
> Mais je regarde . . . hélas! . . . hélas!
> Le bien aimé ne revient pas.[1]

Among genuine *drames* the *Abbé de l'Epée* (1800), by Bouilly (the *poète lacrymal*), and *Misanthropie et repentir* (1799), an adaptation of Kotzebue's *Menschenhass und Reue*, portraying the final reconciliation of injured husband and repentant wife, are good examples of the type. Women used to faint in such numbers at this play that a contemporary skit made a character say:

> Ne vous alarmez pas :
> Madame est la vingtième
> Aujourd'hui dans ce cas.
> Mais comme cela gagne, à la fin, moi, je tremble
> Qu'un jour acteurs et spectateurs,
> Auteurs, moucheurs, ouvreurs, souffleurs,
> Ne se pâment ensemble.[2]

Under Napoleon, and especially with the Empire, dramatic taste became more in accordance with tradition. The *drame* especially was derided by many as "chambermaid tragedy" (*la tragédie des femmes de chambre*). The tyrant exercised a close supervision of the theater, of which he wished to restore the old prestige as a glory of his throne. Official decrees differentiated between the plays suitable to various theaters: *vaudeville*

---

[1] There was published a collection of tales, *les Folies sentimentales, ou les Egarements de l'esprit* (1786). Mme de Staël wrote *la Folle de la forêt de Sénart* (cf. Grimm's *Correspondance*, ed. Tourneux, Vol. XIV, pp. 382 and 401). "Chevalier, j'ai fait une folle", she is reported to have said to the chevalier de Chastellux. "Madame," he replied, "I had thought it was your mother."—*Souvenirs du Baron de Frénilly*, p. 16, quoted in d'Alméras, *Paris sous la Révolution*

[2] *Comment faire* (1799). Cf. Jullien, *Hist. de la poésie fr. à l'époque impériale*, Vol. II, p. 323. The vogue of different adaptations of *Menschenhass und Reue* lasted on the Paris stage until the Second Empire. Cf. Rabany, *Kotzebue*, p. 184.

plays, plays in a style *grivois* (smutty), *poissard* (Billingsgate), *villageois* (rustic), melodrama, pantomime, and farce. The Théâtre-Français received Napoleon's patronage as a national institution; the actor Talma, interpreter of Corneille, was his favorite tragedian; and when, in 1808, a part of the Comédie française went to Erfurt to act before the *parterre de rois*, the *répertoire* was almost entirely taken from Corneille, Racine, and Voltaire. With the passing of Revolutionary disorder public taste also became more sedate. The dramatic standard was set by the educated *bourgeoisie*, the connoisseurs, professional men, and merchants,—prosperous baldheads (like bare knees,—*les genoux*, as the Romanticists were to call them), who enjoyed tragedy with an *ennui noble*. It is, then, not to be wondered at that juggling the rules became again the mark of the great dramatic poet, and inspiration was lost in frigid form. We need not be surprised at the wrath of the Romanticists a few years later, and can realize why they confused Racine with his degenerate successors. As early as 1797 Népomucène Lemercier's *Agamemnon* was acclaimed the culmination of classical tragedy. In 1813 the writing of a tragedy was such a simple task of carpentering that when Brifaut had half finished a play situated in Spain, but was obliged for political reasons to alter it, he merely shifted the scene from "Barcelone" to "Babylone", and called his work *Ninus II*. Even a tragedy like Raynouard's *Templiers* (1805), which aimed at being historical and national, lacks inspiration and smells of the lamp, though it won him his election to the Academy. That the partisans of regularity were firm in their convictions is shown by the fact that in 1809, when Népomucène Lemercier, by this time regarded as a traitor to classicism, brought out his so-called "Shakespearean" play *Christophe Colomb*, a man was killed and several were wounded in the riot at the theater.[1]

The purely comic spirit found a characteristic expression in

---

[1] On such occasions men were hired to hiss or to applaud, just as, nearly a hundred years later, during the Dreyfus agitation, hoodlums were paid to *conspuer Zola* outside the Palais-de-Justice.

the type of Madame Angot. *Madame Angot, ou la poissarde parvenue* (1796),[1] an *opéra-comique* by Maillot, and its sequel, *Madame Angot au sérail de Constantinople* (1800), by Aude, a "drama-tragedy-farce-pantomime", parodied the vulgar woman enriched and aping her betters. The memory of her name has lasted to the present, and *la Fille de Madame Angot* (1873), still constantly played in France, is one of the most melodious operettas of modern times.

The period of the Revolution, with its saturnalia of play and song, created or gave renewed vitality to several types of fool or lout. Some of them, with their stupidity intensified, have remained as bywords. The old stereotyped comedy character Arlequin, or Harlequin, remained in various plays an embodiment, half-comic, half-pathetic, of ignorance and shrewdness. Nicodème, who has since degenerated in common parlance to a simpleton, was given vogue in 1790 by Beffroy de Reigny ("le Cousin Jacques") in his *Nicodème dans la lune, ou la Révolution pacifique*.[2] By his good-natured combination of candor and untutored sense he is made to show up the follies of the time. Jocrisse appears in a standard example of the vaudeville-farce, *le Désespoir de Jocrisse*, by Dorvigny (1792). There he was a slow-witted and thick-headed valet, making constant blunders in his muddled bewilderment, a good specimen of the Wise Man of Gotham.[3] The same Dorvigny had given vogue, in his *les Battus payent l'amende* (1779) to Janot or Jeannot, the simpleton, always getting into scrapes, whose burlesque inversion of clauses brought together incongruous parts of the sen-

---

[1] The *genre poissard* in song (humorous imitation of fishwife language) had enjoyed vogue since the writings of Vadé. The fishwife under the old régime had many privileges and was a mistress of vituperation.

[2] Nicodème is found in the seventeenth century as the name of a character in Furetière.

[3] Jocrisse belongs to the type which reappears in the simpleton of the melodrama, the maladroit serving man. To Martine, in Molière's *Femmes savantes*, a *jocrisse* had been a weak, henpecked man. When Veuillot called Victor Hugo "Jocrisse à Patmos" he was comparing Hugo's grandiloquent platitudes to nonsense expressed in the style of the Apocalypse.

tence.¹ We are told in Grimm's correspondence² that, at the hundred and twelfth performance of *les Battus payent l'amende*, the house was packed, whereas, at the same time, not two boxes were occupied for the revival of Voltaire's *Rome sauvée*.³ One of the well-remembered types is Cadet Roussel. Aude made this pretentious ninny the hero of various farcical plays, including *Cadet Roussel, misanthrope*, a parody of *Misanthropie et repentir*, but the French mother today, in her nursery songs, is more apt to recall the hero from an anonymous ditty of the same period, where he is described as the owner of innumerable possessions, all in groups of three. On the other hand, Cadet Buteux, about whom the *chansonnier* Désaugiers wrote numerous songs, especially *pots-pourris*, personified the *gouailleur* wit of the populace, rough, satirical, but good-humored and sensible, in his accounts of successful plays. A French Baron Munchausen and precursor of Tartarin is M. de Crac, popularized by Collin d'Harleville in his *Monsieur de Crac dans son petit castel, ou les Gascons* (1791), the lying Gascon, gifted with the creative imagination and exaggerated falsehoods which American humor connects with the yarns of the old-fashioned Yankee. A "tall story" in French is a *craque*, though even Littré finds it hard to decide whether M. de Crac got his name from *craque*, or whether *craque* came from *M. de Crac*.⁴

Among real persons in Paris who acquired glory by dramatization was an eighteenth-century street singer and player on the rustic *vielle* (roughly designated as a hurdy-gurdy), named Fanchon, from Savoy. She was idealized and sentimentalized by Bouilly and Pain, in 1803, in *Fanchon la vielleuse*, as a kind and beneficent spirit. The song of Fanchon by Doche was one

---

¹ Jeannot was a good old rustic name. Jeannot lapin is one of La Fontaine's animals. Janotus de Bragmardo was an educated dolt of Rabelais.
² Ed. Tourneux, Vol. XII, p. 253.
³ This example shows that audiences were not so docile in their intellectual classicism as has been argued.
⁴ On the other hand, the *Dictionnaire général* gives an earlier example, from Destouches, of *craquer* as a familiar term to describe taking a person in by a lie.

of the famous melodies of the age and in theatrical terminology *fanchonner* was equivalent to a long dramatic success.[1]

With the coming of Napoleonic despotism regular comedy had to be conventional, but it did not lack smartness and polish. The *esprit* of Andrieux and Etienne, the pictures of manners by Picard, as the provincial life of *la Petite Ville*[2] (1801), are accomplishments of which an age need not be ashamed.

During the whole Revolution and Empire the comic operas, the *vaudevilles*, and the comedies were better than the tragedies. Some of the Empire comedies of manners give us, within the limits permitted by the censorship, an occasional fleeting picture of life.

The aspiring poetry of the Revolution and Empire was self-satisfied but mediocre. There was a vogue of translations from Virgil, Horace, Pope, Milton, and Tasso, as well as of still-born original epics. With Napoleon poetry became official, rhapsodical, and pseudo-classical in its rigid forms. André Chénier's poetry was almost unknown in his time, except to Millevoye, who had access to his unpublished works, so that we can disregard him; but such productions as Marie-Joseph Chénier's *Chant du départ*, or the better-known *Marseillaise*, are in language examples of the dithyrambic rhetoric then universal. Under Napoleon the "enthusiasm" of official poetry was as artificial in language, besides being forced in feeling. The same description applies to the much-esteemed didactic and descriptive poetry.[3]

[1] Compare the article in Jal's dictionary and Bouilly's *Mes récapitulations* for an illustration of literary metamorphosis.

[2] The *petite ville* of which one of the inhabitants, Riflard, praises the moral tone, "because all our women are virtuous and faithful to their husbands or to their lovers". Riflard, with his huge umbrella, left his name as a slang designation, still occasionally used in France, for an umbrella.

[3] The fate of much of this poetry is expressed in the cynical mock epitaph for Baour-Lormian, who had translated Tasso:

> Ci-dessous gît Baour, le Tasse de Toulouse,
> Qui mourut in-quarto, qui remourut in-douze,
> Et qui, ressuscité par un effort nouveau,
> Pour la troisième fois remourut in-octavo.

Ecouchard-Lebrun, called "Lebrun-Pindare", is the type of the soaring lyrical poet, as Delille is of the didactic writer. These authors represented the decay of a great tradition and its degradation to mere formalism and the imitation of imitation. The Empire Pindarism was as unreal as that of Boileau's ode on the capture of Namur. Poems on gardening or agriculture were stylistic rehashes of works like Virgil's *Georgics*, or of eighteenth-century town poets of nature, of the school of Thomson and his *Seasons*, such as Saint-Lambert and Roucher. Delille, universally admired in his life and honored at his death by a national funeral, was the embodiment in the *genre descriptif* of what Rivarol called the *style citadin*, and the high priest of that cult of words which distinguished between "noble" and "plebeian" (*roturier*) terms, against which the Romanticists were to react. Poetry became verbose rhymed periphrasis. There were even semihumorous didactic poems like Berchoux's *Gastronomie* :[1]

> Delille, dans ces vers nobles, harmonieux,
> A fait de la campagne un tableau précieux;
> Il peint l'homme entouré de ruisseaux, de prairies,
> Promenant dans les bois ses douces rêveries;
> Le loto, le trictrac l'attendent au retour.
> J'admire ces plaisirs d'un champêtre séjour;
> Mais je ne vois jamais l'homme des champs à table.
> Réparons, s'il se peut, cet oubli condamnable.
> Puissent tous mes lecteurs, approuvant mon projet,
> Pardonner à mes vers, en faveur du sujet!

[1] Jouy's *Franc-Parleur* says in 1814: "*Gastronomy*, to use a fashionable term, is an art which now has its rules, its poetics, and its professors. Societies are devoted to its cult; almanacs have spread the doctrines of the *gastronomists*; proselytes have multiplied; but amid this host of enthusiasts, all are not able to become artists. A poet had taught, with as much gayety as wit, 'The Art of dining at home'; another, with the same talent, reduced to precepts 'The Art of dining out'. The science of the 'gullet', as Master François [Rabelais] terms it, made an eminently creditable progress for the human mind." The gastronomical cult of the period reaches a climax in Brillat-Savarin's celebrated prose *Physiologie du goût* of 1825. The *Physiologie du goût* provoked Balzac's *Physiologie du mariage*, and thus various more or less scabrous "physiologies" down to the present.

But all poetry was not solemn or ponderously humorous. The reaction against the Terror encouraged frivolous and reckless verse and song. All the Trissotins of the seventeenth century seemed to have come to life again in the composers of epigrams, charades, madrigals, *bouts-rimés*, *logogriphes*, and *bouquets*. The pages of the *Mercure français* are full of enigmas in verse and prose, which people exercised their ingenuity in solving. Collections abounded called *almanachs* and *étrennes*. Jouy's *Ermite de la Chaussée d'Antin* speaks, in 1811, of the "numerous almanacs of our day, filled with anacreontic, erotic, satirical and gastronomical songs." The same writer complains that every man suspected of being able to read and write was teased to compose verses for women's albums: "Will you not compose something for my album, you who have written such pretty things in the albums of all the other ladies?" Popular songs ranged from suggestive licentiousness and boudoir Anacreontism, through pseudo-naïve sentimentality to the smut of the old *esprit gaulois*. Those were the days of the vogue of the *polissonneries* and the erotic elegies of the "half-Tibullus", Parny,[1] of Fabre d'Eglantine's *Il pleut, bergère*, as well as the *gaillardises* of Désaugiers. Désaugiers, indeed, personifies, better than anybody else, the song and *grivois* vaudeville of his day, full of epicurean optimism and good-natured satire. Presiding spirit of the *Dîners du Vaudeville*, and of the *Caveau moderne*, which latter was largely responsible for bringing out Béranger, as well as director for several years of the Vaudeville theater, Désaugiers immortalized himself by such exuberant songs as *Paris à cinq heures du matin*, and *Paris à cinq heures du soir*.[2] His *Monsieur et Madame Denis* portrays the Darby and Joan of French literature. By some of his rollicking vaudevilles he also contributed to the gallery of modern comic types: M. Vautour,[3] the grasping landlord, whose rapacity overreaches itself, and

---

[1] Parny's reputation was already made before the Revolution, but he was at the height of vogue under the Empire.

[2] Compare Boileau's satire *les Embarras de Paris*.

[3] *Monsieur Vautour, ou le propriétaire sous le scellé* (1805).

MEN OF FASHION UNDER THE RESTORATION: *GANDINS* AND *MIRLIFLORES*

From Dayot, *la Restauration*

who finds himself, much like an anti-hero of Scarron, on the point of being thrown in a chest from a window; M. Dumollet,[1] the tradesman of Saint-Malo, who repeats the adventure of Molière's M. de Pourceaugnac in search of a wife, with as annoying consequences; M. Pinson,[2] the shopkeeper's assistant out for a lark; Prince Mirliflor,[3] the handsome lover of fairy literature.

The racy *esprit gaulois*, smacking of the soil, thus found expression in the *chanson* and *vaudeville*; and the finished craftsmanship of a decorous and scholarly, more epigrammatic La Fontaine appeared in the fables of writers such as Arnault.[4] But cosmopolitan influences were to be seen in serious poetry and in the novel. The tearful Sensibility of Rousseau's school was often expressed in terms of English Melancholy and German Sentimentalism.

The reading public, now much increased, found enjoyment in the portrayal of *bourgeois* virtues and domestic sentiment. The tone of Rousseau's exhortation to mothers on bringing up children, the pictures of innocent youth in *Paul et Virginie*, the moral tales of Marmontel, the virtuous fables of Florian, the rustic scenes of Greuze, and the pictures of *genre* by Chardin had been reënforced in spirit for the French by the vogue of the Swiss Gessner, whose reputation had reached a climax under Louis XVI. His placid sentimentalism was in strange contrast with the violence of the Revolution, which it long outlasted. Gessner greatly encouraged in France the literature in prose and verse of which Berquin, with his *berquinades*, is a noteworthy representative. The Zurich writer had taken the pastoral idyl, and its conventionalized and bastard eighteenth-century descendants of Theocritus and Virgil, and had transformed them into virtuous Helvetians. The shepherd Corydon no

---

[1] *Les trois étages, ou l'intrigue sur l'escalier* (1808); also several sequels.
[2] *Je fais mes farces* (1815), a *folie-parade*.
[3] *La petite Cendrillon, ou la chatte merveilleuse* (1810). *Un mirliflore* had been since before the Revolution a name for a fop.
[4] For instance, *la Feuille morte*.

FRONTISPIECE OF AN EDITION OF THE WORKS OF BERQUIN (1802)

longer burned with passion for the handsome Alexis, but loved virtuously his chaste spouse. So French literature celebrates conjugal, parental, and filial affection, the idyllic happiness of youth and innocence, of life free from the vices of town, and writers instill pedagogical maxims of virtue and righteousness. The goody-goody sentimentality, as it now seems, of the prose and verse of Berquin, the *ami des enfants* and French translator of *Sandford and Merton*, helped to set the standard of literature written in many countries for over half a century for the delectation of youth. The moral poems of Berquin correspond to the "Mary-had-a-little-lamb" school of ethics in English, upon which school they undoubtedly exerted an influence.

CHAPTER IV

THE REVOLUTION, THE EMPIRE, AND THE RESTORATION. LITERARY FORMS. REVOLUTIONARY AND IMPERIAL ART

THE eighteenth century had witnessed the growth of reverie, the *genre triste* or *genre sombre*, which was to a considerable degree influenced by the English Graveyard School of meditative pessimists, Gray's *Elegy*, Hervey's *Meditations among the Tombs*, Blair's *Grave*, and Young's *Night Thoughts*, in time reënforced by such works as Goethe's *Werther*. Writers recorded a melancholy, often justified amid the disasters of the Revolution, but which long remained as a pleasurable literary mood, and was in time merged with general romantic pessimism.[1] Thus, Chateaubriand tells, somewhere in his many records of *ennui*, how he once *tried* to be unhappy but could not. Funereal verse was in vogue as a form of elegy, and the sweet haunts of Melancholy were staged amid settings of autumn and the dying year, pale moonlight, distant sounds of tolling bells, burial urns and cypresses or weeping willows, heaths and gloomy waterfalls, ruined castles and deserted cottages, moss-covered bridges spanning somber streams, lonely monasteries, decaying abbeys, and solitary hermitages. Mme de Staël had precursors for Corinne and Oswald amid the ruins of the Campagna, as had Chateaubriand for Father Aubry and the burial of Atala, and the spirit of the ruined past in the *Génie du Christianisme*.[2]

[1] So Gabriel Legouvé (W. Thomas, *le Poète Edward Young*, p. 451):
> Voilà donc tes bienfaits, tendre Mélancolie!
> Par toi de l'univers la scène est embellie;
> Tu sais donner un prix aux larmes, aux soupirs;
> Et nos afflictions sont presque des plaisirs.

[2] Compare, in art, the works of Hubert Robert and the engravings of the Italian Piranesi etc.

The *genre sombre* found a kindred spirit in the *genre troubadour*, which had a great vogue under the Consulate, the Empire, and the Restoration, with abundant manifestations in literature and art, and which survived for many years in the stiff bronze groups decorating the once fashionable French mantelpiece clocks under glass domes.[1] The expression *dessus-de-pendule* applied in French to literature has a distinct and readily understood application. In the *genre troubadour* the diffusive melancholy was combined with nostalgia for an unreal but vividly imagined Middle Age[2] conceived not as rude and barbarous but as the *bon vieux temps* of page and troubadour, of *preux chevalier* and fair *châtelaine*; or, with more mystery, of old nurses' tales, of fays, sylphs, and ghosts, of pilgrims and hermits haunting Gothic towers and ruined donjon keeps. Much of this abundant literature took the form of pseudo-ballad or *romance*, set to music. A striking example is the once universally popular *Ermite de Sainte-Avelle*, by Edmond Géraud, which Hugo tells us, in *les Misérables*,[3] every maiden in the early nineteenth century had upon her lips.[4]

An influence which shared popularity with the *genre trouba-*

---

[1] The groups were not all necessarily romantic. A favorite *dessus-de-pendule* was "Marius amid the Ruins of Carthage", perhaps popularized by the lines of Delille's *Jardins*, Bk. IV:

> Telle jadis Carthage
> Vit sur ses murs détruits Marius malheureux,
> Et ces deux grands débris se consolaient entre eux.

[2] There is an important letter in the *Ermite de la Chaussée d'Antin* (January 1, 1813) on the vogue of medievalism in manners. This considerably antedates the Romanticism of Hugo and his school.

[3] In the section called *En 1817*.

[4] For the text see the Appendix to this volume. The *romances* were not all medieval. They fall in with the general sentiment of the period and the current elegiac lyricism in a minor key, of which the pages of the *Mercure de France* give so many examples. A very popular *romance* was the *Fleuve du Tage*. One of the writers most in vogue was the vicomte de Ségur. Balzac, in *la Fille aux yeux d'or*, says that the name of La Fayette implied America; that of Talleyrand, diplomacy; that of Désaugiers, the *chanson*; and that of M. de Ségur, the *romance*. These mediocre songs often owed their success to the melody.

dour was that of "Ossian". Sometimes the currents merged, at other times they followed their individual courses. For years the Ossianic harp was as important as the classic lyre had been, or as the romantic lute was to be. The extreme limits of Ossianism are placed at 1780 and 1830. By the close of the latter period the names of Oscar and Malvina had, says Taine,[1] sunk to the class of *coiffeurs* and *grisettes*. It was especially under Napoleon that, partly because of his enthusiasm, the vogue of the false Celtic bard reached a climax, just as the literary forgeries published under the name of Clotilde de Surville exerted great influence on the *genre troubadour*. The *genre ossianique*, like the *genre troubadour*, was a form of pre-Romanticism, with more heightened gloom than the former and without the full-fledged tempestuousness of the latter. It remained abortive in that no great poet came forth entirely under its spell, but for a while it showed itself everywhere in literature and in art. Napoleon read Ossian on the ship returning from Egypt, and on the ship sailing to St. Helena. His foes Chateaubriand and Mme de Staël fell under the influence, as Lamartine and others did later. In the poet conceived no longer merely as a sentimental minstrel brooding over the past, but as the inspired prophet, or *vates*, of Hugo, we find perhaps in part a prolongation and transmutation of Ossianism. Mme de Staël made Ossian the key of her theory, in *De la littérature*, of the "Northern Homer", and of the contrast between Ossian and Homer, representatives of the literatures of North and South, of melancholy and cheerfulness. It is therefore not to be wondered at that Ossianism took such hold, as a relief from eighteenth-century analysis. The vague forms of Celtic lore were used as literary trappings, as the *merveilleux païen* had been by the seventeenth-century classicists, and as Christianity was to be by the Biblical poets of the Restoration. The Ossianic phantoms dethroned dryads and nereids, to be replaced in turn

---

[1] *History of English Literature*, quoted by Van Tieghem, *Ossian en France*, Vol. II, p. 28. Mme Cottin wrote a *Malvina*. Readers of *The Children of the Abbey* will recall the Oscar and Malvina of that estimable tale.

by the sylphs, gnomes, and witches of the *bas romantisme*. So prose and poetry reëcho with description of gray hillsides bathed in mist, tempestuous heaths, dashing torrents, shaggy oaks and storm-tossed pines, rough crags overlooking the lonely sea, lowering skies and the cloud-veiled moon,[1] meditations on fallen grandeur, the neglected heroism of warriors, the forgotten glory of bard and minstrel. M. van Tieghem[2] quotes a significant passage from Alfred de Vigny's *la Veillée de Vincennes*, illustrating the Ossianic elements transmuted in the brain of a real poet:

> What they sang was one of those Scottish choral songs, one of those old melodies of the Bards, resounding in the sonorous echo of the Orkneys. To me this melancholy chorus rose slowly and vanished all of a sudden, like the mists of the mountains of Ossian; those mists which form on the foaming froth of the torrents of Arven, gradually thicken and seem to be swollen and distended, as they ascend, by a countless throng of phantoms tormented and twisted by the winds. There are warriors, who are ever dreaming, with their helmets resting on their hands, and whose tears and blood fall drop by drop in the dark waters of the rocks; there are pale beauties, whose hair streams backwards like the rays of a far-off comet, and merges in the moist bosom of the moon; they pass quickly, and their feet vanish into the silken folds of their robes; they have no wings, yet they fly. They fly holding harps, they fly with downcast eyes and lips parted in innocence; they utter a cry as they pass, and disappear as they rise into the gentle light which summons them. There are aërial ships which seem to dash against somber shores and plunge into the thick billows; the mountains are bowed in sorrow, and the black hounds raise their misshapen heads, howling slowly as they gaze at the disk quivering in the sky; while the sea shakes the white columns of the Orkneys which stand like the pipes of a vast organ and pour over the Ocean a melancholy harmony a thousand times prolonged in the caverns where the waves are imprisoned.

The poet embodying the conventional lyric tendencies, the *poncif*, as the French call it, of this transitional age is the now

---

[1] The tempestuous moon belongs to the *genre ossianique*, as the translucent lovers' moon to the *genre troubadour*. Cf. Musset's mockery of *la lune comme un point sur un i* in his *Ballade à la lune*.

[2] Op. cit. Vol. II, p. 333.

FRONTISPIECE OF AN EDITION OF OSSIAN (1777)

neglected Millevoye. He expresses very well the general average of sentiment in his time. He is a disciple of the classicists or pseudo-classicists from Boileau to Parny, but he has also undergone the influence of the precursors of Romanticism, from Rousseau to Chateaubriand. The once famous *Chute des feuilles* and *le Poète mourant* illustrate Millevoye's art. He gave popularity to one of the favorite themes of Romanticism, the youthful poet dying in his prime. Millevoye is an important precursor in poetry of the Consumptive School (*genre poitrinaire*). A characteristic example of the lyric and elegiac sentimentalism, of which Guiraud's *Petit Savoyard* is still remembered, was Soumet's *Pauvre fille*, of 1814, which had great vogue under the Restoration:

> Mes yeux se sont mouillés de pleurs.
> Oh! pourquoi n'ai-je pas de mère?
> Pourquoi ne suis-je pas semblable au jeune oiseau,
> Dont le nid se balance aux branches de l'ormeau?
> Rien ne m'appartient sur la terre,
> Je n'ai même pas de berceau,
> Et je suis un enfant trouvé sur une pierre
> Devant l'église du hameau.

The novels of the Revolution and of the Empire were abundant, although only those of Mme de Staël and of Chateaubriand are read today. A number of these were by women, who developed what may be described as the *rhapsodical*, or, to characterize it to another generation, the *narcotic*, novel.[1] Fiction was considered for a while more suited to the female pen. Men were occupied with higher, especially martial, things. As a direct nervous reaction, perhaps, from the heart-rending events of history these novels were generally banal and lifeless,

---

[1] "You have not yet said anything about the comet; yet if I am to believe some of my neighbors it exercises a great influence on things here below. It is the comet which dries up springs and brings about a drought. When old women are ill, it is the comet which has caused their fever. When one yawns over the last works of Mme de Genlis, the comet is again the cause."—*Ermite de la Chaussée d'Antin*, September, 1811

except where there was a conscious imitation of the English School of Terror of Mrs. Radcliffe,—"horrible works of a frenzied 'Miss'."[1] In this case it was customary to pile on horrors in just as unreal a way.[2]

The emotionalism of the "lady novelist" proceeded in part from the exaltation of *Julie*, of *Werther*, and of Ossian. With an incomplete knowledge of the heart she wrote tales of passion and thwarted love. They are subjective romances, in which the hero or heroine alone is really important, and afford an outlet for the authoress's pent-up emotion, in reaction against the cold-blooded corruption of much of the eighteenth-century literature. They foreshadow in their inconclusiveness the inhibition of the will portrayed in the approaching *mal du siècle*. The heroes are chivalrous and distinguished, the heroines virtuous, and express their refined sentiments in noble language. "Lovers breathe forth their melancholy to the silent night on the banks of a raging torrent, sob beneath cypress trees and die of pure grief." Mme Cottin, who gave vogue to the name "Matilda", was one of the most popular novelists of the period. Mme de Duras's *Ourika* (1823) gave its name to shawls, hats, and a color. Tender-hearted readers of the experiences of this child of nature and "Atala of the *salons*", the unhappy girl from Senegal who loved her white foster-brother, wept over her sad lot and envied the sweetness of negresses of Guinea and Gaboon.

Very different were the naughty novels, the *genre polisson* of Pigault-Lebrun, which carry over the polished *grivoiseries* of the eighteenth century in a cruder popular form to Paul de Kock. Another kind was the "terrifying" novel, already referred to, especially represented by a writer now forgotten, but an important precursor in modern literature. This was Ducray-Duminil, a disciple of the English School of Terror, the *manière*

[1] Baour-Lormian, *Mon second mot* : "D'une Miss en furie effroyables travaux."

[2] A reaction against the English School of Terror is seen in *la Dot de Suzette* (1798), written by a man, Fiévée. The naïve simplicity of this little tale of virtue and sensibility makes it still interesting. It was one of the most popular stories of its day.

anglaise, whose *Victor, ou l'enfant de la forêt, Cœlina, ou l'enfant du mystère*, and others furnished situations and characters that Pixerécourt worked up into the melodrama. More than a million copies of *Cœlina* were sold.¹ From Pixerécourt the themes spread to the romantic drama. Pigault-Lebrun and Ducray-Duminil are also precursors of the *feuilleton* novelists. It was this literature which reproduced Lewis's wicked monk and ghostly "Bleeding Nun", both many times repeated in varying forms.² Lewis's Ambrosio, the monk tempted by the devil and becoming his victim, as well as Mrs. Radcliffe's friar Schedoni, in *The Italian, or the Confessional of the Black Penitents*, reënforced Boutet de Monvel's *Victimes cloîtrées* and the hostility to religion aroused during the Revolution, and helped to spread the figure of the wicked churchman, anticipating many traits of the Byronic hero.³

But it is especially with Mme de Staël and Chateaubriand that we come to those personal novels which had tremendous influence on literature and feeling: *Delphine, Corinne, Atala,* and *René*.

Mme de Staël was a genius instead of a woman of mediocre talent like her contemporaries. She projected her own emotional personality into her heroines. Delphine was usually interpreted as the expression of Mme de Staël's youthful feelings, and Corinne again as herself idealized, as she would have wished to be. Both women, especially Delphine, are *âmes sensibles*, and Corinne is the superior woman, the emancipated genius,

¹ "Delightful reading! I have read all those which have appeared during the last four years: the Castles, the Dangers, the Children of Mystery, of Love, of Happiness, Cécilia, Camilla, Rosa, Cœlina, Agatha, Rosalba."—*La petite ville*, Act II, Sc. i. "Another novel ending in A", Napoleon exclaimed impatiently when Chateaubriand's *Atala* came out.

² As late as 1854 Gounod composed an unsuccessful *Nonne sanglante*, with a libretto by Scribe and Germain Delavigne. Berlioz had previously begun a score, but, after a disagreement, Scribe took the libretto away from him.

³ Says a character in Balzac's *Muse du département*: "If you do not see at these words, 'dress rustled in the silence', all the poetry of the rôle of Schedoni, invented by Mrs. Radcliffe in *The Confessional of the Black Penitents*, you are not worthy to read novels."

transgressing or rising above social conventions in her luckless quest. They anticipate the high-strung women of romantic fiction, the heroines of George Sand at war with their environment and claiming the right to happiness.

It was for Chateaubriand, however, to stamp a deeper impress on the French mind than anyone since Rousseau. Through him we find the spirit of Melancholy projected more than ever upon literature, no longer as the result of society but inherent in man. One of the greatest egoists of modern times, Chateaubriand threw his brooding temperament upon his readers. He popularized the idea of moral solitude even in a crowd, the pseudo-philosophic contrast between life in exotic landscapes and in civilization, the yearning for an unattainable infinite, the lassitude by which the return to primitive life leaves us no happier than before. The *mal de René* was one of the greatest single factors in nineteenth-century romantic pessimism. Moreover, in all his works, whether the *Génie du Christianisme*, the *Martyrs*, or any other, he had the great gift of prose lyricism; he kindled the spirit of æsthetic Christianity and of poetic religiosity. He was one of the causes of the anti-Voltairian rebellion, one of the renewers of medievalism, and the great leader of the literature of poetic imagery. Yet, in a certain sense, Chateaubriand merely illustrates the Empire style of which he is the culmination. He was a conservative and balked at being called the father of the Romanticists. In *les Martyrs* he aimed merely at continuing in prose the epic tradition of the past from Le Bossu to his own day.

The art of the Revolution and of the Empire abundantly reflects contemporary tendencies. The coquettish improprieties of Boucher and Fragonard underwent an eclipse. Strangely enough in those emotional days, even the "sensibility" of Greuze was out of fashion and that artist was reduced to poverty. Instead, for a time, a pictorial neoclassicism held sway, under the guidance of Louis David. There had been a considerable revival of interest in artistic doctrines and the philosophy of art, illustrated in archæological research by the comte de Caylus and the German Winckelmann. In painting Vien had led the reaction against the style of Boucher, and though he never went as far as David, he was looked upon as an illustrious forefather. But, above all, the political worship of Greece and Rome suggested topics to the new artists.

The theory of the school, which, before long, had an æsthetician of its own in Quatremère de Quincy, was a rewording of certain aspects of the doctrine underlying Classicism since the Renaissance. The name *beau idéal* was understood to connote the universal of perfect beauty *sub specie aeternitatis* which matter strives ineffectively to reproduce temporally, but which Art reveals, and which especially Greek sculpture displayed in its sublime austerity. This is what the Italian Canova, the Dane Thorwaldsen, the English Flaxman, tried to realize. Even in painting, the process of artistic abstraction, by conscious rationalism, to obtain the simplicity of the ideal, resulted in sculpturesque effects, a rigidity of attitude conceived to be sublime, uniform or conventional tones to express different ages or emotions, sometimes verging on monochrome. Costume and local coloring were as far as possible eliminated. Clothes were considered a hindrance in expressing the universality of the Ideal, and great characters, even moderns, were, especially in sculpture, preferably portrayed nude, as Greenough did Washington. In historical painting David, obliged to make concessions to accuracy, preferred to paint his figures nude and dress them afterwards. Down to the romantic revolt the *style pompier*, as satirists called it, because its helmets reminded the irreverent of the shiny metal casques of French firemen, was in honor in literature as in the art of David.[1] The *Sabine Women* embodies this method. David's *Serment des Horaces* and *Brutus* had even preceded the Revolution.[2]

[1] The *style pompier* in literature was the turgid and ponderous Empire pseudo-classicism. The local *capitaine des pompiers* of the French semimilitary firemen's service is still the type of "fuss and feathers."

[2] Some of David's obstreperous disciples made themselves rather ridiculous. The *penseurs* or *primitifs* asserted that there had been no true sculpture since Phidias and, like the English pre-Raphaelites, no painting since the Italian

FIREMEN, WITH CLASSICAL HELMETS

The classical school was, however, divided against itself. As in literature, there was a current of Alexandrinism and Anacreontism, in protest against the Davidian rigidity. The vogue of Lantier's *Anténor* was repeated in art. There was a fashion for Ovid, for sensuously sentimental themes such as Psyche (Prud'hon's *Enlèvement de Psyché*), Daphnis and Chloe, Sappho and Phaon. The antiquity of Prud'hon is more poetical and more imaginative than that of David. Even David found it advisable to adopt a pictorial style in works like *Napoleon crossing the St. Bernard Pass*, the *Coronation of Napoleon*, and the imperial *Distribution des aigles*. Under the Directoire, for instance, all the newly rich wanted their own portraits. Napoleon desired the glorification of his military achievements and forced art into heroic eulogy. His taste was crude and self-centered, but by encouraging the representation of spectacular events he reëmphasized costume and background. Thus some of the original school of David, like Prud'hon and Gros (*Pestiférés de Jaffa*) paved the way for the rich coloring and scenic effects of pictorial Romanticism. The crudity of the new classes, eager for heightened colorings, made them turn from an apparently desiccated Classicism to what seemed a realistic presentation of life. To the conservatives this was blatant sensationalism. But the heightened emotions of the age had their effect in breaking down David's static plasticism. By rich coloring, vivid action, pictorial sentiment, and Ossianic reverie men like Gros and Girodet make the transition to romantic art less startling.

As a consequence painters had a much wider range of topics than one is apt to imagine when told that David was preeminently the artist of the Revolution and the Empire. They were not confined to classical heroes of the Revolution or to Brutus and Cato. They gave academic treatment to mythological characters like Adonis, Endymion, Narcissus, and Psyche,

primitives. They wore Greek costumes and sandals and let their beards grow, whence they were called *les barbus*. Their eccentricities anticipated in another form the pink waistcoats and beards of 1830.

or to ancient legends and "anecdotes", such as blind Belisarius. As their sources of inspiration became richer they glorified medievalism, the Carolingian legend and chivalry, Ossianism, the *genre troubadour*, and Biblical episodes influenced especially by Gessner's tragedy, the *Death of Abel*. Modern history was represented by heroic scenes of the Revolution and Empire. Subjects known technically in art as *genre* were frequent: the Conscript's departure; the Soldier's return; a philosopher in meditation near a tomb ("graveyard" theme). Portraits, simple or allegorized, were especially popular;[1] family groups; a wife seeking on a globe whence comes her husband's letter; maidens feeding turtle-doves; a mourning father seated near a table bearing a burial urn and indicating to a son his mother's ashes, while the youth draws near pale and sorrowing.[2]

Napoleon planned to make Paris the center of civilization and the model of architectural magnificence. The shortness of his glory caused most of his schemes to fall by the wayside, but enough was done to show his underlying ideas: imposing thoroughfares, like the rue de Rivoli; commemorative monuments such as the Arc du Carrousel, the Arc de l'Etoile, the Colonne Vendôme, and the Temple of Glory, now the Church of the Madeleine. The architecture of the Empire is ponderous, often lacking grace. It was based on Roman imperialism and frequently took the form of column or arch, or, as a result of the Egyptian expedition, of obelisk. The two chief architects, Percier and Fontaine, were more novel when they applied their

---

[1] Some satirical verses ran like an exercise in the Ollendorff method:

J'ai peint mon père,	Puis au Salon
J'ai peint ma mère,	J'expose ma maison.
Mon fils, mon époux et mon frère.	De ma portière
J'ai pour lui plaire	J'ai peint la mère;
Peint ma grand'mère;	J'ai peint le frotteur, le propriétaire.
Par moi sont peints	Tout locataire
Oncles, neveux, cousins.	Par moi, j'espère,
J'ai peint ma fille,	Doit tour-à-tour
Peint ma famille,	Décorer ce séjour, etc.

[2] These and other subjects are enumerated in Benoît's statistical reviews of catalogues. See Benoît, *l'Art français sous la Révolution et l'Empire*, pp. 377 ff.

ideas to furniture: the heavy products of mahogany and brass, known as Empire, are often clumsy, but they have an individuality and massive strength which harmonize with the militarism of Napoleon. Household decorative art was also softened by the fashionable anacreontic touch and the use of panels, festoons, and medallions with Cupids and pastoral scenes. "This was the period when a divan was called a 'Paphos', and a cheval-glass a 'Psyche'." Josephine made la Malmaison a home of neo-Hellenic mythology and of the style of Pompeii, which had itself borrowed its taste as much from Alexandrian art as from imperial Rome.

CHAPTER V

RESTORATION AND MONARCHY OF JULY.
RELIGION AND POLITICS

WITH the Restoration of Louis XVIII, as after the downfall of the old régime, French political and intellectual life assumes new outward aspects. Freedom of discussion succeeds rigid tyranny. At times repressive censorship looms threateningly in the background, but nevertheless party leaders are more outspoken and, to a greater degree than under Napoleon, ideas are formulated into action. The Restoration brings back political oratory, the *éloquence de la tribune*. Moreover, the relations of religion and politics become, as they still remain, a dominant issue of national life.

Louis XVIII at the Restoration was well intentioned and wiser than one might have expected from a Bourbon. Restored to power by the victorious foes of France, and realizing the enormous impulse of the Revolution toward emancipation, he was not like so many returned *émigrés*, such as Sandeau's marquis de la Seiglière or Béranger's marquis de Carabas, who had "forgotten nothing and learned nothing".[1] He tried to save the face of Legitimacy and was unable to discard completely the pompous and now laughable frivolities of old court etiquette. The song *Vive Henri IV* invoked a frisky George Washington of Bourbonism instead of the Revolution or Napoleon. Nevertheless the king meant to make the new national

---

[1] "There was then seen to burst on Paris a cloud of sexagenarian gentlemen, who came to claim places and positions the very names of which had been forgotten for twenty-five years. Never had such a collection of eccentrics diverted the capital. Uniforms of corps suppressed in the days of the Regency reappeared, to the amazement of our soldiers, who, not knowing what to call these new brothers-in-arms, dubbed them by the comic name of 'Light In-

charter a reality and to give the country at least a semblance of constitutional government. He consequently satisfied neither liberals nor reactionaries; the second Restoration, after the interlude of Napoleon's Hundred Days, saw the cruel retaliations of the White Terror (*Terreur blanche*), as opposed to the Red Terror of '93, and the follies of the reactionary Chamber of

CARICATURE OF THE POLITICAL REACTIONARIES AS "KNIGHTS OF THE EXTINGUISHER"

From Grand-Carteret, *les Mœurs et la Caricature*

Deputies, called the *Chambre introuvable* because it seemed impossible to match, and because it was *plus royaliste que le roi*. Moreover, as Louis XVIII grew with age physically and men-

fantry of Louis XIV' (*voltigeurs de Louis XIV*). [The real *voltigeurs* had been organized only by Napoleon I.] The name 'M. de la Jobardière' [*jobard* = "a person easily deceived"] became the patronymic for all these elderly provincial noblemen, emerging from their old keeps, of which they wished to restore the privileges. Finally, they branded with the title 'Knights of the Candle-extinguisher' (*chevaliers de l'éteignoir*) the people in position, orators and writers, to whom was attributed the intention of bringing us back to the days of ignorance and slavery, in which it had been boldly asserted that peoples were the patrimony of kings."—JOUY, *le Franc-Parleur*, April, 1815

tally flaccid, he let the reactionaries have their way. He fell under the influence of an intriguing woman, Mme du Cayla, agent of the counter-revolutionaries; and a princess of the royal house, the duchesse d'Angoulême, was one of the evil spirits of the Restoration. He became *le Roi cotillon*, or King Petticoat. The murder, in 1820, of the duc de Berry, though it was the personal deed of a fanatic, was used as an argument against liberalism and compromise.

The next king, Charles X, brother of Louis XVIII and of Louis XVI, was the former comte d'Artois, the incarnation of the reckless and selfish pre-Revolutionary aristocrat. Becoming in old age still more stubbornly conservative, and combining with his conviction of the divine legitimacy of the French monarchy a spirit of medieval mysticism, he had himself crowned and anointed at Reims amid obsolete mummeries, and made his reign stand for intolerance. He felt himself to be the elect of God to reëstablish faith in a land given over to the infamies of Voltairianism. Hence the alliance of throne and altar (*le trône et l'autel*). The intransigeance of the White Cockade received short shrift, and in July, 1830, as a result of the popular uprising of the "three glorious days" (*les trois glorieuses*), Charles X went into exile. His rule was followed by the constitutional government of Louis-Philippe, head of the younger, or Orleans, branch of the royal house, the so-called Monarchy of July. But in spite of the reactionary phases of the Restoration, it was, owing to the ferment of new ideas, when literature and art sought to voice political and social problems, a period of remarkable brilliancy and interest. The Monarchy of July was also characterized by the large number of literary men in politics. It is safe to say that, in spite of the contumely heaped on the *bourgeois* monarch and his régime, no more fascinating period exists in the history of modern French society or literature.

In the general clash between Reaction and Liberalism during the Restoration and the Monarchy of July, the aristocracy having for the most part given up its pre-Revolutionary Voltairianism,[1] the alignment of political and religious parties and of philosophical schools was somewhat as follows:[2]

At one end were the conservatives, the Traditionalists and Authoritarians, supporters of the Pope or King. They were in reaction against the Revolution. The extremists were ultramontanes and theocrats in religion, legitimists in politics, readers of the *Quotidienne* and the *Drapeau blanc*, followers of the vicomte de Bonald and of Joseph de Maistre, though the latter, as a Savoyard, was a subject of the King of Sardinia. To Bonald the Revolution had begun with the Declaration of the Rights of Man and was to end with the Declaration of the Rights of God; to Maistre Nature is bad and needs a despot to keep it in check. To the ultras even the government of the Restoration was a bad compromise, and they took issue with any rule derived from theories of a Social Contract or the authority of the people. They wanted a return to the old régime, with at most such concessions to modern times as States-General and Parliaments, and much provincial freedom. The royalism of Maistre and of Chateaubriand harked back to the Middle Ages, and in this they are both precursors of romanticism. The early ultramontane Lamennais separated himself from the legitimists in wishing the *Pope* to lead *Democracy*. Lamennais, in his changes, was always consistent. To him the Kingdom of God was on earth, but

[1] Not entirely, however. We recall the quaint M. de Lessay of Anatole France's *Sylvestre Bonnard*: "M. de Lessay was a Voltairian royalist, a kind fairly common then among bygone noblemen." Some of the *haute bourgeoisie* of the Restoration sympathized with the aristocracy. M. Gillenormand of *les Misérables* was pre-Revolutionary in spirit. He adored the Bourbons and hated 1789. The inheritance of the eighteenth-century man of science lingers in Dr. Minoret, the atheist and encyclopedist of Balzac's *Ursule Mirouët*.

[2] In this discussion the writer has been helped by the analyses contained in Adam's *Philosophie en France* and Weill's *le Parti républicain en France*. As an aid to the reader in understanding the complicated relationships their classifications are here schematized in the briefest and simplest form. *Philosophical and Religious Tendencies:* I. Authoritarians: (1) ultramontanes, theocrats, legitimists; (2) moderates: (a) Gallicans, (b) liberals. II. Rationalists: (1) antidogmatists; (2) spiritualists. III. Pseudo-scientific and scientific school: (1) Utopians; (2) Positivism. *Political Tendencies:* I. Legitimists. II. Doctrinaires. III. Republicans: (1) moderate; (2) advanced.

after his break with Rome he replaced the pope by Humanity, the People, and hence was considered by the theocrats a heretic.

More moderate conservatives than the ultramontanes were, first, the Gallicans, who placed the supreme power in the hands of the king, believed in the episcopacy of the Church in the State, and adopted a somewhat independent attitude toward the pope to show their loyalty; second, those who, believing in the full *religious* authority of the pope, advocated the liberty of the Church in a free state. This group was prominent toward the middle of the century under the name of Liberal Catholics.

At the opposite extreme politically from the legitimists, the two chief defeated parties, Bonapartists and advanced republicans, set up a temporary alliance. Here were the ejected bureaucrats, the shabby half-pay officers, or *demi-solde*, and restless veterans, harping on their poverty, sneered at by the returned legitimists, contrasting the military glory of Napoleon with the disgrace of a government forced upon the country by the foes of France. They sang songs to victory, to glory, to the Vendôme column, as in Emile Debraux's "Ah! qu'on est fier quand on regarde la colonne!" Béranger, who under Napoleon had satirized military adventure (*le Roi d'Yvetot*), encouraged them with his *chansons*. As Balzac's Colonel Chabert incarnates the Grande Armée, so his Philippe Bridau is a rascally example of the former officer. Debraux's roistering *Fanfan-la-Tulipe* kept alive the warlike spirit while the invader still tarried at the gates. The idea of the *soldat laboureur*, the soldier tiller of the soil, allured the ignorant peasant stolidly inured to the hardships of war and peace, and flattered to think that in the past days he could have become marshal of France.[1]

Leagued politically with the Bonapartists in temporary alliance as an opposition party were the heirs of the Jacobins, and the republicans in general. It was they who met the intrigues

---

[1] The *Soldat laboureur* was a well-known *vaudeville* of 1821 and a picture of Horace Vernet. Shops, *cafés*, and taverns were often named after popular plays or literary characters, and even today travelers in provincial France come upon *auberges* dedicated *au soldat laboureur*.

of the ultramontanes with counter-intrigues; who organized the secret political society, the *Charbonnerie*, in imitation of the Italian *Carbonari*; whose anti-Jesuit campaign resurrected Molière's *Tartuffe* as a political document and renewed its neglected prestige, and in the melodrama replaced the villainous monk of Revolutionary plays with the scoundrelly Jesuit. They attacked the somewhat mysterious secret society known as the *Congrégation*, dubbed the *jésuites de robe courte*, which served as a common meeting-place for clergy, aristocracy, and legitimists in general, for intrigue and espionage against the liberals; so that throughout the nineteenth century the term "Congrégation" was used by radicals to designate in general a vague, mysterious party of intrigue conceived to be at work thwarting the emancipation of French thought from religious oppression. Hostility to the clergy was not confined to the mob but was found in the *bourgeoisie* as well, and the antipathy to the *parti prêtre* was such that it was dangerous, in 1830, for a priest to be seen in the streets, and religious establishments like the archbishopric of Paris were sacked. Balzac seeks to embody the evil spirit of the Congrégation in such a person as the abbé Troubert of the *Curé de Tours*. It was for the opposition party that Paul-Louis Courier wrote his virulent pamphlets and Béranger contrasted the evil deity of the ultramontanes with the good-natured *Dieu des bonnes gens*. The piety of the Restoration brought about a return, in well-to-do families, of the *abbé* as a sort of chaplain, secretary, steward, and general friend and adviser, such as we find him in some of Musset's comedies. It was this indirect influence on the young, as well as the open clutch on education, that Béranger attacks in his *Révérends pères*:

> Hommes noirs, d'où sortez-vous?
> Nous sortons de dessous terre.
> Moitié renards, moitié loups,
> Notre règle est un mystère.
> Nous sommes fils de Loyola;
> Vous savez pourquoi l'on nous exila.
> Nous rentrons; songez à vous taire!

RELIGION AND POLITICS

> Et que vos enfants suivent nos leçons.
> C'est nous qui fessons
> Et qui refessons
> Les jolis petits, les jolis garçons.

The advanced republicans, workmen, intellectuals without a ballot, and idealistic democrats, worshiped the Convention and the Jacobins, and deified Robespierre and Marat. The new youthful generation knew but little of the horrors of the Revolution, for Napoleon had discouraged the study of history. So the years 1789-1830 were to the students, especially the brilliant young members of the Polytechnic School, a glorious and mysterious period which had witnessed the birth of liberty and waged war on kings. Their policy was to regain the "natural" limits of France and to spread freedom among enslaved nationalities. Under the Monarchy of July they ranged from historians and theorists, like Louis Blanc, to revolutionaries, like Raspail and Blanqui, organizing secret societies, carrying on propaganda in prisons, and advocating regicide. Weill, in his *Parti républicain*, illustrates one type of advanced republican by the *Bonhomme Système* of Renan's *Souvenirs d'enfance et de jeunesse*.

If the advanced party may be described as one of destructive rationalism, contrasted with the traditionalists, the latter were also faced by more moderate antidogmatic rationalists, and even by spiritualists like Royer-Collard or Victor Cousin. At first, between the two extremes of authoritarianism and its enemies, the governmental party of Louis XVIII strove, though with a natural conservative bias, to keep a balance. But there was a new group of moderates, verging toward the liberals; these were at first largely theorists, but they were in quest of a practical policy of government through conciliatory justice. These were the *Doctrinaires*, sometimes aided by the moderate republicans. They wanted to transform into a positive doctrine the philosophy of the charter of Louis XVIII, and to reconcile royalty and liberty. They tried to draw lessons from past historical experience as a basis for a constitutional party of progress.

They were admirers of England and the Whigs of 1688 and thought Louis-Philippe would be a French William III. But the *doctrinaires* wanted civil liberty more than political liberty; they emphasized the rights rather than the duties of man. They wanted, above all, to consolidate their own privileges, distrusted the sovereignty of the people, and despised the proletariat. During the Monarchy of July under the leadership of Guizot they formed the parliamentary Center, as opposed to the conservative Right and the advanced Left. They made money the guaranty of the aptitudes of the electorate to make use of the ballot.

Their allies against the ultras in both directions, the moderate republicans, were for the most part disciples of the Ideologists. Without absolute identity of ideas they corresponded somewhat to the intellectual temper which we find in a theorist like Thomas Jefferson. La Fayette, an admirer of the United States, wanted a conservative republic, on the model of the Constituent Assembly, with a President instead of a King, but accepted Louis-Philippe as a compromise, with the rather specious excuse that the constitutional monarchy was "la meilleure des républiques".

Considering the opponents of the counter-revolutionary theocrats and ultramontanes more from the point of view of thought than of political strategy, we find at the opposite extreme among the rationalists the pronounced antidogmatists. They were usually advanced republicans and nonreligious Utopians, sometimes absolute skeptics but often deists; but they are conveniently grouped together under the general name of neo-Voltairians. They thought that religion was merely good for the control of the lower classes: "God is useful for scaring servants." Voltairianism was often merely a tone or method of critical attack, and replaced religion by a sort of *morale publique*. Balzac, in *la Muse du département*, speaks of

good sense, the law of social proprieties, family interests, all the elements of what was called under the Restoration *la morale publique*, through hatred for the term "Catholic religion".

RELIGION AND POLITICS

Just as Royer-Collard was one of the founders of political liberalism, so Victor Cousin, before he became under Louis-Philippe the semiofficial philosopher of the French *bourgeoisie,* was in philosophy the liberal moderate. Cousin was at first a romanticist in temperament; he revealed German metaphysics to the French and was originally headed for a vague pantheism,

LE VENTRE LÉGISLATIF
Daumier's satire of smug middle-class rule

but became later the cautious philosopher of the *bourgeoisie*. He founded Eclecticism, culled from past systems, which became practically the official doctrine of the state schools. He evolved a compromise theory of thought, based on the unity and authority of reason, dealing with the laws of the intellect and the different manifestations of the divine in the human mind. He hoped to create a system at once satisfactory to the non-ecclesiastical liberals and sufficiently idealistic to hold the sympathy of the theocrats and of the young liberal Catholics who were rallying to the cause of constitutionalism, and who were prepared to discard the theories of Bonald and Joseph de Maistre, and even the spirit of Gallicanism, which they carried back beyond Napoleon and the Revolution, and conceived as leagued with Bossuet and the political absolutism of Louis XIV.

Under the Monarchy of July, as compared with the Restoration, the relative values of the parties shifted. Literature, art, politics, and manners grew more democratic. The theocrats and legitimists were relegated to the background. Political discussion was intense, and theories of social reform became acute in a community more and more industrialized. Power passed more than ever into the hands of the *rich* middle classes. The policy of the government was to minimize the Revolution and consider the new dynasty merely as indicating progress instead of reaction. The idea of royal legitimacy was now replaced by that of a contract and of a monarchy bestowed on the king by the people. Middle-class virtues, typified by the term *ordre*, ruled supreme. The respectable Guizot punctiliously interrupted affairs on stated days to walk out with his aged mother. The national ideal which under the Empire had been military conquest, and under the Restoration a modified Christian feudalism, was now wealth, success, position, and influence. But the king, backed by Guizot, was unwilling to go as far as the times required, and his policy of blind resistance brought about his downfall in 1848. The opposition, whether constitutional liberals or republicans and socialists, attacked in varying degree the meddling interference of the king, grown stubborn with age, the number of bureaucrats, and the want of official sympathy for liberalism in other European countries and for popular aspirations abroad to escape from tyranny. The French were especially offended by the emphasis placed on wealth for the electoral franchise, and the opposition of the king and Guizot to the so-called *adjonction des capacités*, namely, the bestowal of the ballot upon the intellectual *élite*, doctors, lawyers, and professors, who could not qualify in a financial sense.

The Revolution of July, presumably a democratic step, though it broke the legitimists, resulted, therefore, in an intensified antipathy between the "haves" and the "have-nots". As early as 1842 Mme de Girardin says that the antithesis is between *propriétaires égoïstes* and *prolétaires envieux*. The self-satisfied moneyed class became more domineering. The spirit of caste was greater than ever and was accentuated by the fact that the blouse and cap were more generally worn by the working classes then than they are today. Disregard for the hygiene and social welfare of a vast population, drawn by the growth of industrialism from the country into congested districts, and obliged to work from ten to sixteen hours a day for starvation wages in a position of perpetual legal inferiority to the employer, embittered the hostility. As early as 1831 there was an uprising of workmen at Lyons to get a decent livelihood, proclaiming the right to "live working or die fighting".

The smug Voltairian deism or semiofficial Gallicanism of the *bourgeoisie*, and the docile eclectic religiosity of Cousin's idealism, were faced by all the emotional impulses, political, spiritual, social, or merely literary, that were dissatisfied with the order of things.

The literary Revolution is what we know as Romanticism, and it reaches its height in the early years of the Monarchy of July. Much of the early notoriety of the romanticists came from political entanglements. Literature and art were in time conceived as having a social purpose to express ideas of justice and political emancipation. The poet was a prophet and high priest. Hugo and Lamartine were inspired to bring about social regeneration. Even the hermit poet in his ivory tower was a leader (Vigny's *Moïse*). George Sand transmuted Mme de Staël's superior woman, Corinne, into the artistic genius Consuelo, playing a mystic sacerdotal rôle.

In a political sense there was a revival of democratic idealism by which the sins of the old Revolution were forgotten or explained away as a necessary stage of human progress. Intuitive myths were built up, historically and economically false, but which helped to formulate a creed and exerted an influence on posterity. Historians conceived nations as having a mystic, "pantheistic" soul, expressed in the upward impulse of the people, breaking the bonds of oppression. Michelet glossed over Revolutionary crimes in the name of liberty, and Lamartine idealized the Girondists. Democracy was linked with propaganda and romantic political humanitarianism called for the relief of oppressed nations.[1] The poor were extolled, even deified, by agitators as the downtrodden depositaries of honor and virtue, oppressed by the scheming rich, whose education and privilege had merely taught them hypocrisy and selfishness. George Sand's "sociological" novels[2] represented the people as the revelation of the true, the beautiful, and the good. Class hostility was engendered and encouraged.

Spiritual impulses were entangled with the political and social ideas. There was the important movement of Liberal Catholicism, when the term "liberal" is applied not to religious belief but to political and educational freedom. It contained in its ranks at first ultramontanes and Jesuits. There were the social Utopians who reorganized society and deified Humanity, ranging from materialists like Fourier to mystics like Pierre Leroux.

---

[1] The present close military union of France and Poland against Germany has abundant precedent in political humanitarianism of the last hundred years. "Vive la Pologne" was heard in 1848 almost as much as "Vive la République". People danced the mazurka and dressed their children on holidays as National Guardsmen or Polish lancers. There are Poles in Balzac's pictures of the times (for example, *la Fausse maîtresse* and *la Cousine Bette*) and Balzac married a Polish woman. He likens the Poles to the French and calls them the "Français du Nord". The indifference of Louis-Philippe's *bourgeois* monarchy to the enslavement of Poland, and the callous use by Marshal Sébastiani, in 1831, at the fall of Warsaw, of the catchword of *bourgeois* respectability, "l'ordre règne à Varsovie", contributed to the unpopularity of the Monarchy of July. The Polish poet and orator Mickiewicz, an exile in France, roused many to frenzy by his eloquent portrayal of Poland in the part of Christ suffering for humanity, and playing a Messianic rôle, destined to be spiritually resuscitated. Napoleon III, who had been in youth a mystical socialist, carried out the idea of the relief of oppressed nations in the war of Italian liberation. The politician Charles Floquet won his first notoriety by insulting the Czar of Russia with the cry "Vive la Pologne, monsieur", at the exposition of 1867.

[2] The *Compagnon du tour de France*, the *Meunier d'Angibault*, the *Péché de Monsieur Antoine*.

There were the more specially religious or "Messianic" theorists, creators of new theologies. The reaction from eighteenth-century rationalism brought a craving for worship. Eccentric creeds sprang up and private religions flourished.[1] Schemes for political and social hierarchy took on a mystical symbolism and sacerdotal priesthood amid the utopian theories. There was the abbé Châtel, founder of the unsuccessful *Eglise française*, a vague rationalism tinged with pantheism, advocating the suppression of confession for the laity and of celibacy for the priesthood. On the walls of his church were incongruous names such as Confucius, Parmentier, who introduced the potato, and the banker Laffitte. Maurice Barrès, in his *Colline inspirée*, has recalled the religious utopian Vintras. The "crank" *le Mapah* (signifying *maman* and *papa*) wandered through Paris in a queer sacerdotal garb teaching the "Evadian" religion of Eve and Adam. The Saint-Simonian religion had a ritual, a hierarchy of "fathers" and "mothers", and a *père suprême*, and Enfantin posed as an apostle and thaumaturgist.[2] The times, indeed, were full of the crudest forms of mysticism, such as theories of spiritualism and magnetism, as Balzac testifies in many of his novels, especially *Ursule Mirouët*.

The great figure of religious romanticism is Lamennais, a man persecuted by his enemies and long banned from "right-thinking" books, but who must be considered one of the most important influences in the democratization of French religion. His own evolution admirably illustrates the changes in his time.

Lamennais began by being an ardent ultramontane. He was angry that royalty had compromised with the Revolution, and

---

[1] On Romantic "Messianism" and George Sand's *Spiridion*, see interesting passages in Thackeray's *Paris Sketch-Book*.

[2] In a caricature by Daumier, Robert Macaire says to Bertrand: "The days of limited liability companies are over; let us be busied with what is eternal. What if we were to make a religion?" "A religion, that is not easy", answers Bertrand. "You make yourself Pope, you hire a shop, you borrow some chairs, you make sermons on Napoleon, on Voltaire, on the discovery of America, on anything. There you have a religion. It is no more difficult than that."—Guex, *le Théâtre et la société française*, p. 106

called the French Gallican clergy "tonsured lackeys" begging favors at the Tuileries. In the face of the hostility of the French clergy and of individual enmities he went to the other extreme. He now wanted the freedom of the church, united its cause with that of the Revolution, and wished the pope to become a popular leader and take the part of oppressed nationalities. By so acting he proved more Catholic than the pope, as the *Chambre introuvable* had been more royalist than the king. The pope did not desire to be on bad terms with the French clergy; he was predisposed to authority and was himself attacked by Italian liberals. He made no allowance for Lamennais's orthodoxy and condemned his liberalism. Falling into increasing disfavor between 1830 and 1833, his periodical *l'Avenir* was put under the ban. Forced to choose between the church and democracy, Lamennais took the latter. In 1834 he published the *Paroles d'un croyant*, a striking example of apocalyptic religious prose in rhythmic phrases, of which the emotional poetic language had a great effect on the style of the young romantic democrats and humanitarians. Because of its extraordinary vogue it is entitled to rank as one of the paramount works of the French nineteenth century, and Lamennais is one of the founders of Christian Socialism.

The third stage of Lamennais's evolution made him lose all religious authority and enabled his foes to class him with free-thinkers or the actual enemies of the church,—Michelet foaming against the Jesuits; Quinet, who thought Catholicism incompatible with liberty and would have liked to see France become Protestant; social humanitarians like Pierre Leroux; and many others. He died unreconciled with the church, and without political power, but as a literary and moral force on French democracy his influence was extreme.

Tactically a wiser course was played by Lacordaire and Montalembert, who succeeded in making the party of Liberal Catholics a reality. Lacordaire, the "romanticist of the pulpit", was an ally of Lamennais, but, breaking with him, he submitted to Rome.

The effort of the Liberal Catholics took the form of endeavors to secure schools free from the monopoly of the state educational system, or "University". They went halfway to meet the *bourgeoisie*, among whom many were tiring of Voltairian deism or free thought. They brought the church to the people, dealt with questions of the day, attacked together the Gallicans and the partisans of the University, where the official eclecticism of Cousin was taught, and posed as the "sons of the crusaders" against the "sons of Voltaire". Victory was finally won by the famous Falloux law of 1850, which enabled the Catholics to parallel the state secondary educational system. This measure was the great object of attack when, half a century later, the French radicals, hostile to all clericalism, sought to restore, as a lay measure, the monopoly of the state in education. The Restoration of 1830 was largely anticlerical; by 1848, through the wise tactics of some of its members, the church had again made itself powerful.

CHAPTER VI

RESTORATION AND MONARCHY OF JULY. DEMOCRATIC MYSTICISM. POSITIVISM. THE NAPOLEONIC LEGEND

THE great emotional wave of the early nineteenth century which merged humanity with the divine, and which critics have rather vaguely designated as a form of pantheism, found particular expression among philosophical or pseudo-philosophical interpreters of history and those who drew lessons from the past to teach democracy. The most noteworthy of such men, because of the influence of their books and lectures, were Quinet and Michelet. Quinet had in youth fallen under the spell of theories of historical dynamism and Herder's development through successive transformations. He used them to explain the history of humanity as the growth of the self from the oppression of external forces. The annals of humanity are permeated with the divine spirit working through the ages in peoples. This spiritual progress is destined to culminate in the sway of free democracy. Toward this ideal Revolutionary France is the leader. She is the beacon light to oppressed nations and the incarnation of justice and of democracy. When Quinet lectured at the Collège de France, nominally on southern literature, in reality on the Jesuits, ultramontanism, and democracy, his words were followed by rapt audiences of men and women from every European country, to whom his teachings seemed inspired. Occasionally, we are told, a listener in the gathered throng might be seen kneeling, as if in reverent worship of the speaker's words. Hostile to dogmatic religion, especially Catholicism, Quinet wanted a humanitarian republic governed by the spirit of rational morals and civic duty, and his aspirations anticipated much that the Third Republic carried out in the establishment of lay education.¹

Michelet, who had also undergone the influence of German historical transformism and the theories of the Italian Vico, shared Quinet's transcendent ideas with an even greater pantheistic and messianic urge. A more vivid and picturesque writer, he composed his history of the French people in a mystic passion. The people became a potent, anonymous, and multitudinous force, ascending to freedom and democracy, noble, generous, and infallible.

Men like Quinet and Michelet were, therefore, idealists, preachers of progress and liberty, of moral and intellectual upward striving, who replaced the spiritualism of religion by the mystic spiritualism of a divinized humanity. Like all their compeers in contemporary movements toward social regeneration, Quinet and Michelet believed too much in the goodness of human nature. They based their views on theory rather than on facts, and confidently applied to future times laws of history that were not supported by evidence.

The interpretative visions of Quinet and Michelet had counterparts in the humanitarian optimism of the contemporary Utopians. The latter had supreme confidence in the ability of humanity to remedy its evils through association and solidarity, or what was later called socialism. They felt that the divinity of the people was no less able than the divinity of revealed religion to evolve technical schemes, and were ready to help with their own suggestions.

---

¹ Quinet's ideas underwent many variations, especially after Napoleon's *coup d'état*, and it is impossible to state them consistently; but he is considered a patriarch and prophet of modern French democracy, by his program of the separation of church and state, obligatory lay instruction, and the realization of liberty, equality, and fraternity. Seillière, in his book (*Edgar Quinet et le mysticisme démocratique*), says that, if Quinet had not died in 1875, he might well have become President of the Republic after May 16, 1877, and the triumph of the men who followed his ideals,—Gambetta, Ferry, and Floquet. A warship of the modern French navy is called the *Edgar-Quinet*, just as another one is the *Jules-Michelet*.

The socialism of the first half of the nineteenth century was, in part, a reaction against the treaties of 1815, and a struggle for the liberation of oppressed peoples. It strove to carry abroad the fruits of the French Revolution, but was not destructive of patriotism, like later international socialism and communism. Intellectual Europe was aglow with sympathy for oppressed Greeks, Poles, and Italians. Much more significant, however, because more immediately vital, was the desire, especially under the Monarchy of July, to remedy the inequality of fortunes and to correct the injustices of the new industrial age.

After the conspiracy of Babeuf, source of revolutionary socialism, direct action was for a time replaced by theories of peaceful reform. Civil and foreign wars were too fresh in memories to make anything welcome but doctrines. The social theorists continued the abstract reasoning dear to the French temperament. They isolated man from his environment, conceived a sort of man in himself endowed with pristine goodness. Or, vaguely recalling the brotherhood of the early Christian Church, they imagined that, by removing man from a faulty civilization and plunging him into new social conditions of their own devising, they could solve the problem of happiness. These dreams, they hoped, would in time be actually realized and would replace the unhappy conditions of the industrial revolution. They relied on argument and persuasion, without the appeal to force or the arrayal of class against class, which we find in Marxian socialism. But though the utopians preached peace, the workingmen built barricades. Moreover, the spirit of revolt and of secret conspiracy passed, through the teachings of Babeuf's follower Buonarroti, to professed agitators like Auguste Blanqui, Barbès, and Raspail. These men, once objects of vituperation to every respectable Frenchman under Louis-Philippe, are now, in the days of radical Municipal Councils in Paris, honored by having public thoroughfares named after them. The fiasco of the Republic of 1848 drew the class war perceptibly nearer.

Saint-Simon was the first important modern French utopian. He was one of the most moderate and, though personally an unpractical visionary, his ideas contained much common sense. His influence was felt more specifically by intellectuals, and after the days of Saint-Simonism many of his young followers, grown to maturity, were eminent men of affairs. Saint-Simon believed in progress toward perfectibility. He wished, however, to transfer the object of religious effort from Heaven to Earth, and dreamed of a new religion of human morality, based on brotherhood and helpfulness to the poor, so as to do away with ignorance, poverty, and inequality and to return to the ideals of early Christianity without ecclesiasticism. All men should work, intellectually or physically, and each should love his neighbor. Society can regulate individual conduct for the general welfare. The guiding principle should be *distributive justice* rather than egalitarianism, or, according to the motto of the *Globe*, which in 1830 became an organ of Saint-Simonism: "A chacun suivant sa capacité, à chaque capacité selon ses œuvres." Man was no longer to exploit man, but man was to unite with man to exploit nature. The consequences of Saint-Simonism were chiefly economic. There was at first no idea of collectivism or communism, and the tribute which it paid to intellectual merit and the kingship of philosophers caused it to be looked upon as an industrial aristocracy. It was a scheme of capitalistic reorganization, assuming in human nature a desire for justice, sympathy, and brotherly love.

Saint-Simon died in 1825, but his school belongs to the period of 1830. His disciples, few in number, included brilliant thinkers, clever mathematicians from the Polytechnic School, like the future economist Michel Chevalier, philosophers like Auguste Comte and Pierre Leroux, the composer Félicien David, and the historian Augustin Thierry. They were all fired with enthusiasm for the betterment of humanity, and gradually their ardor became more religious and mystical. The two leaders of the Saint-Simonian school after Saint-Simon were Enfantin and Bazard. They went on toward socialism and, after a quarrel, the former organized, at Ménilmontant on the outskirts of Paris, a fraternal community, in which advanced views on the relations of the sexes brought about police intervention. By 1832 organized Saint-Simonism fell to pieces, but in the incoherent ideas of its founder or of his enthusiastic but immature young disciples are found the germs of many important reforms of the nineteenth century. The Saint-Simonians have been called "apostles of industrialism, foreshadowers of socialism, knights of pacifism, builders of railroads, advocates of interoceanic canals (Suez), creators of banks, popularizers of education, champions of the emancipation of woman and believers in her equality with man." It was, unfortunately, the extreme to which the brilliant but sensual Enfantin carried theories of sexual relations that was partly responsible, together with Fourierism, for the charges of immorality brought against early socialism,—a prejudice which underlies the hostile criticism of novels of the social emancipation of women.

As Saint-Simonism, founded by an aristocrat, had an aristocratic tendency in its organization, so Fourierism was the vision of a new world for the common man. Fourier, more unpractical even than Saint-Simon, at times even mentally unbalanced, and influenced by his musical temperament, replaced Civilization by Harmony. Fourier asserted that man's natural Love of Work, when confronted by the form of labor most attractive to him, would prove a sufficient incentive. By gathering people in moderate-sized "phalanxes" of three hundred families, dwelling in uniform community groups, called *phalanstères*, it would be possible to rebuild society. The ideas of Fourier became grotesque when he expounded "gastrosophy" and "phanerogamy".[1]

---

[1] The fantasies of Fourier lent themselves to satire. Mockers twisted chance suggestions of his that somehow or somewhere human beings might develop new organs and keener human senses by the improvement of physical and moral conditions. Before long caricaturists began to represent socialists with long tails for ornament and as defensive weapons. Each tail terminated in an enormous eye. See the chapter entitled *les Queues promises à l'humanité*, in Louis Reybaud's *Jérôme Paturot à la recherche de la meilleure des républiques*.

Fourierism did not attack capital. The phalanstery was rather a coöperative profit-sharing organization, based on the false assumption of the attractiveness of labor and admitting as members both rich and poor, but, as it seemed to the individualist, involving the violation of personal rights.

Fantastic as much of Fourierism appears, it had some successful partial applications. Fourier's ideas on profit-sharing anticipate modern coöperative societies. The *familistère* of Guise in France, founded by Godin, had years of successful activity. The famous American community at Brook Farm, connected with the names of Emerson and Hawthorne, was based on Fourierism. Eugène Sue is a literary Fourierist in some of his novels, and Emile Zola, as late as his *Travail*, preaches a form of Fourierism.

Successors of Fourier like Victor Considérant and Etienne Cabet tried to plant colonies in Texas.[1] Cabet wished to put into practice the ideals of his romance, the *Voyage en Icarie*, published in 1840. In 1848, with the sympathy of the English socialist Robert Owen, he sent out a colony of "Icarians" to settle in Texas. The last Icarian settlement of the United States, in Iowa, was not dissolved until 1898. It is pathetically sad to read of the tribulations of Cabet, the visionary who wished to make men happy, and of the struggle which he made against financial difficulties, bickerings, jealousies, and disease in Texas and at Nauvoo, Illinois, on the site of the abandoned Mormon settlement, to which the colony moved, until his death in 1856, at St. Louis, where his neglected tomb may still be found.[2] The

[1] Texas seemed to have a romantic attraction for the French as a virgin soil for experimentation. As early as 1817 General Lallemand led a band of veterans to the *Champ d'Asile* on the Trinity River. The Spanish claimed the place, and the colonists went to Alabama to join another French colony where were to be found such names as Demopolis, Aigleville, and Marengo. Demopolis and Marengo County still exist in Alabama. On General Lallemand's venture see Béranger's song, *le Champ d'Asile*.

[2] Nothing gives a better idea of the transitoriness of renown than to read how, in his old age, Considérant, once a Representative and a leader of a colony, lived with his wife in modest rooms, eating at cheap restaurants and becoming one of the nameless habitués of lectures at the Collège de France.

Icarian communities were despotic communisms, except for family relations, and sinned chiefly by their deadly monotony.

Pierre Leroux was one of the first actually to use the term "socialism". He was an incoherent mystic, who wished to reconcile religion with philosophy, or to replace Christianity with the religion of Humanity or Humanitarianism, a pantheistic spiritualism based on the principles of Perfectibility in time and Solidarity in space. Man is a part or manifestation of the great soul of humanity. Leroux had considerable influence on the mystical fiction of George Sand: *Spiridion, les Sept cordes de la lyre, Consuelo, la Comtesse de Rudolstadt*. Her Spiridion is meant to be a composite of Leroux and Lamennais.

Louis Blanc was an advocate of state socialism. He wished to do away with competition and to have the state guarantee work to the unemployed. It was to be the capitalist and depositary of wealth, distributing work and reward to the toilers, regulating production and consumption. The National Workshops of 1848, the failure of which led to the bloody insurrection of June and the end of utopian socialism, were, however, a malicious attempt to discredit the theories of Louis Blanc and make them fail in their practical application.

Constantin Pecqueur, a now nearly forgotten theorist, was the real founder of modern French social-democratic "Collectivism" and the formulator of conceptions for which others have received credit. He combined the idea of state socialism, as with Louis Blanc, with that of communism of instruments of production. He first emphasized what has become a fundamental assumption of modern communists, namely, the *hour of labor* as a common unit, regardless of differences of productive capacity among toilers, the modern notion being reduction to the average of the least competent workman. Pecqueur wanted the state to be the only capitalist, with everybody employed at approximately equal pay.

The theories of Pecqueur thus anticipate many of the important ideas of Proudhon and of Karl Marx, both of whom proclaimed the unit of value to be founded on the hour of work;

but, in common with nearly all French theorists down to the middle of the nineteenth century, and as opposed to Karl Marx, Pecqueur preached a reform by peaceful means. His collectivism was humanitarian, and not, like that of Marx, founded on class warfare and revolutionary methods.

Almost without exception the utopians had been optimists. Their enthusiasm made them fail to realize the difficulties in their way. Pierre-Joseph Proudhon was the pessimist, hostile not only to the state of things but to the remedies suggested. The industrialism of Saint-Simon, the *phalanstère* of Fourier, the Icarian community of Cabet, the state socialism of Louis Blanc are all forms of governmental despotism, and as unjustifiable as the servitude of Rousseau's social contract or the Jacobin tyranny of Robespierre. Proudhon believed in governmental nihilism, or an-archy, signifying the elimination of externally imposed authority, the eradication of the governmental (not the economic or social) order. In this sense Proudhon, though an "anarchist", was also a believer in pacific methods, in spite of the bloodthirsty practices employed by followers who exaggerated his teachings. His influence was to a great degree exerted *after* 1848, and is still vigorous among the French proletariat.

Proudhon belonged to the class of peasant laborers working with their hands. In character and theory he illustrates the stubborn, hard-headed, argumentative, and in some ways intensely conservative individualist that forms so important a part of the French nation. Sainte-Beuve says that his epoch-making question of 1841 (*Qu'est-ce que la propriété?*) would, he hoped, begin an era in economics, as Sieyès's query about the Third Estate marked one in politics. But his answer, that "property is theft," was not meant to imply that property should be destroyed. He objected to the invasion of the freedom of the individual cultivator of the soil in the shape of rents, profits, tenant dues, and the like. Proudhon's ideal of happiness was the prosperity of the *cultivateur* and *petit bourgeois*. He believed in the family and thought that each family should have its own little plot of land to occupy and cultivate; that effort should be equally remunerated, regardless of quality or effect, in terms of the expenditure of effort and the hour of labor; that every governmental obstacle to individual freedom should be removed. He objected to governmental socialism and communism. The state, so far as it existed, should be merely an industrial mutualism based on Justice, or righteousness in the exchange of products. By a gradual process of education and increased skill the inequalities in the rate of production were to diminish, and the state would be unnecessary, because contracts would be respected and mankind would thrive in universal brotherhood. Thus Proudhon's political ideal was a loose federation of the tiny units called in France *communes*, his economic ideal an anticommunistic mutualism.

Consequently, Proudhon, the anarchist, was not the bloodthirsty destroyer that the word "anarchy" now usually implies. He was a reformer, and even in his pessimism over the evils of civilization he had an optimistic, utopian vision of the future; but the fertility of his ideas, and his many inconsistencies and contradictions of detail, made his followers often play him false. Proudhon was ill served by those whom he inspired.

In spite of the detailed attention given in the preceding pages to the utopians and democratic mystics, because of their literary influence, the positivism of Comte represents the most important scientific advance of the first half of the nineteenth century in its intellectual consequences. On the foundation which he laid rests much of the materialistic philosophy of the following generation. He discarded as past history the theological and metaphysical schools, and undertook to construct a new philosophy dealing only with what is contributed by scientific observation. The positivism of Comte is a form of relativism. It aims at constant progress and culminates in sociology, or study of the laws of human society. It had its influence abroad as much as in France. Littré, G. H. Lewes, and Frederic Harrison have been noted positivists, and John Stuart Mill was influenced by positivism.

DEMOCRATIC MYSTICISM

Comte was not free from the prevailing social mysticism, for in time, after 1848, he tried to superimpose on his scientific philosophy a new dogma, and to create the religion of humanity. This new religion, with its elaboration of sacerdotalism, could not appeal to those who had just rejected theocracy, and except with a select band of faithful disciples it remained a curiosity, especially in the cult of Clotilde de Vaux, the young woman whose memory he ardently worshiped. Comtism of the latter sort has had more success in Brazil than elsewhere. None the less, the commemorative worship of the great and noble men of history in place of the saints of Catholicism, a custom of the great Revolution, probably owes some of its continued popularity to Comte. Perhaps his example helped to make such celebrations lose their political and revolutionary significance, and fostered our modern passion for the celebration of centenaries of men like Dante, Shakespeare, and Molière.

The emotional upheaval of the age was reflected in discussion about a matter which had been unknown to previous generations,—feminism. Most women in France were then, as now, on the whole satisfied with their lot, and did not care for the ballot, unless it were individual agitators, like the socialist Flora Tristan, grandmother of the painter Gauguin. But George Sand, in demanding pity for the *femme incomprise* (the misunderstood woman), forced into unhappy marriage, and in calling for the equality of the sexes and the privileges of men, especially in the presence of love, was reflecting the new theories, like those of Pierre Leroux. Women who wanted equal rights in government, like those who demanded that Louis-Philippe be designated "King of Frenchmen and Frenchwomen", instead of "King of the French", were rare. Even when universal suffrage was conferred in 1848, not many women asked to share it. The few who did were laughed at as *Vésuviennes*.

The utopians were therefore considered daring in their suggestions. The equalization of the sexes of the Saint-Simonians and the "sacerdotal couple" were called licentious; Fourier's theories of "phanerogamy" and "butterfly-love" seemed to favor polyandry and prostitution. But a not unnatural consequence both of the expansion of human sympathy and of the question of the equalization of the sexes was pity for the fallen woman. "N'insultez jamais même une femme qui tombe", wrote Hugo, and literature in time became familiar with the theme of the repentant Magdalene. She is no worse than others, or rather more sinned against than sinning, and is usually the victim of poverty, injustice, and the hardships of the social system.

Preceding pages have described the evolution and growth of the mystical, pantheistic myth of humanitarianism, the Legend of the Goodness of Democracy, and of perfection immanent in the people. There is another outgrowth of the Revolution no less striking, though it centers about a single name,—the Napoleonic Legend. This concept, after Napoleon's death, was one of the impelling forces of literary romanticism; it affected French civil and military policy, and in time brought about the Second Empire.

Napoleon had not been popular in France during his reign, when people had suffered from tyranny and economic hardships, and the manhood of the country had been sapped by countless deaths on the battlefield. Yet no sooner was he an exile on an island in the mid-Atlantic than an atmosphere of mystery began to enwrap him like an Ossianic mist, and he seemed a Promethean figure on a distant rock suffering for France. Napoleon had come on the scene in time to turn to his advantage the outgrowth of the Revolution, patriotism, which considered provinces no longer the personal property of princes, but self-conscious peoples; though he himself, as emperor, unblushingly violated this principle. He capitalized the victories of the Republic to his advantage and aroused a martial neurosis by the sound of bugle and drum, by the rhythmic tread of marching hosts, by glittering uniforms and the gigantic troopers of the *vieille garde*. But Napoleon entered history largely by way of St. Helena and the writings of those who followed him into exile, especially Las Cases and his *Mémorial de Sainte-Hélène*, that Bible of Stendhal's Julien Sorel. In his recorded conversations

THE *VIEUX SERGENT* OF BÉRANGER
Illustration by Charlet

Napoleon slurred over his days of tyranny except as a glorious period marked by proud victories, Austerlitz, Jena, Friedland, Wagram. On the other hand, he posed as the representative of the ideas of '89, the crowned Washington dictator by necessity, a lover of peace driven from the humane task of emancipation by hostile countries, and the supporter of the principle of free nationalities.

Thus Napoleon's sins were forgiven, and he loomed before peasant, workingman, and *bourgeois* alike as a great liberator from the injustices of the old régime. He was transmuted into a champion of liberalism. So Quinet portrayed him as coming from the people, a precursor of triumphant democracy, and the soldier-missionary of human fraternity. Poets like Hugo wrote of him:

> Toujours lui! Lui partout!—Ou brûlante ou glacée,
> Son image sans cesse ébranle ma pensée.

Song-writers like Béranger popularized his memory; artists and draftsmen like Charlet and Raffet portrayed him and the imperial trooper; above all, historians like Thiers and the now forgotten but once popular Norvins built up the Napoleonic tradition. Even the crudely colored woodcuts called *images d'Epinal* contributed to the same end. Louis-Napoleon in time reaped the benefit of this falsification of fact, and was accepted by the French people as Napoleon III, heir of the traditions of liberalism.

The martial spirit too was flattered. The fierce talk of an imperial veteran, named Nicolas Chauvin, became a byword for patriotic jingoism; and his name, especially after he received artistic consecration in the illustrations of Charlet, and a play of 1831 called *la Cocarde tricolore,* has been perpetuated in the modern term *chauvinisme.* The spirit of Napoleonic militarism gets its glorification in the type of the veteran of the *Grande Armée,* the *vieux grognard,* whom Rostand has recalled in Flambeau of *l'Aiglon.*[1]

---

[1] Per contra, Alfred de Vigny poeticized the officer into a gentle, high-minded, and melancholy being (*la Canne de jonc*).

During the Monarchy of July, Napoleon was in the plays of every theater. In 1838 Heine records, in his correspondence from Paris, that when a play at a boulevard theater brought in

MAYEUX DETECTS HIS LIKENESS TO NAPOLEON

Drawing by Traviès

the emperor or an imperial episode, it was acclaimed, however poor it might be. People were roused to excitement and tears by the words "French eagle", "sun of Austerlitz", "Jena", "the Pyramids", "the *Grande Armée*", "honor", "the *vieille garde*", "Napoleon":

Enthusiasm reaches its climax when the man himself, THE MAN, arrives at the end of the play, like the *deus ex machina*. He always wears the magic hat, has his hands behind his back, speaks as laconically as possible, but never sings. I have never seen a *vaudeville* in which Napoleon sings. All the others sing.

It is not surprising, then, that current mystical emotionalism soon developed the idea of the Titan, or, as we now say, "Superman", and deified energy and power. When Romanticism is described as "literary Napoleonism",[1] it means the glorification of unrestrained self-will, and we understand why critics like Seillière define the romantic impulse as imperialism. We have the literary superman: Hugo, Balzac, Dumas were devoured by all-conquering lust for literary domination. Characters in fiction become the incarnation of unbridled desire: Julien Sorel wants to be Don Juan or Napoleon; Balzac's men must conquer society at all costs. The Titan merged into the Genius, then naturally into the Lawgiver, the Prophet, the Messiah, the High Priest. So we are helped in understanding the inspired tone assumed by poets like Hugo or Vigny, preachers and exhorters such as Michelet, Quinet, Lamartine, utopians such as Pierre Leroux, even hierophants like the Saint-Simonian leaders or the contrivers of eccentric cults.

Louis-Philippe tried to counter the charges of materialistic sloth brought against his *régime* by the conquest of Algeria, by creating at Versailles a great picture gallery in honor of the military glory of France, filled with victories painted by the square meter, and by the false step of encouraging the cult of Napoleon and bringing back his remains from St. Helena to France. The *retour des cendres* was fatal. The great hero was now again on the banks of the Seine, among the French people he had "loved so well." The contrast of militarism and pacifism was disastrous to the latter. Even the picture of the gay young soldier, the *tourlourou*, waging war for France in Algeria and

[1] Félicien Pascal, quoted by Dechamps, *Sainte-Beuve et le sillage de Napoléon*, p. 61.

cheerily singing *la Casquette du Père Bugeaud*,[1] did not satisfy, and the figures of Dumanet, the conscript, and of M. Prudhomme, in his costume of officer of the National Guard, were an anticlimax to that of the *vieux grognard* or to memories of the hero himself:

> On parlera de sa gloire
> Sous le chaume bien longtemps.
> L'humble toit, dans cinquante ans,
> Ne connaîtra plus d'autre histoire.
> Là viendront les villageois
> Dire alors à quelque vieille:
> Par des récits d'autrefois,
> Mère, abrégez notre veille.
> Bien, dit-on, qu'il nous ait nui,
> Le peuple encore le révère,
>   Oui, le révère.
> Parlez-nous de lui, grand'mère;
>   Parlez-nous de lui.
>
> BÉRANGER, *les Souvenirs du peuple*

[1] During the African campaigns, on the occasion of a night alarm, the commanding officer, Marshal Bugeaud, appeared in his nightcap. Immediately there sprang up among the troopers a popular song which has remained until fairly recently a favorite bugle call in the French army:

> As-tu vu
> La casquette, la casquette,
> As-tu vu
> La casquette du Père Bugeaud?

CHAPTER VII

RESTORATION AND MONARCHY OF JULY. SOCIETY. SOCIAL AND LITERARY TYPES

THE society of the Restoration was as sentimental as that of the previous age, and Mme Cottin appeared to it one of the first writers of modern times. Women delighted in novel-reading, as before; but feminine sensibility took on also an idealistic phase, sometimes of poetic mysticism, sometimes of vague religiosity. The imperial Juno or female dragoon was transformed to the "angelic" *femme frêle* with a *visage de keepsake*,[1] dressed in soft muslins, vaporous laces, and dainty shawls,[2] with virginal yearnings for ideal poet and lover, dreaming over the *Méditations* of Lamartine, and fading away with consumption.[3] "She bowed in exquisite languor like a frail reed before the breath of love." Some women, otherwise sturdy, drank vinegar to look pale and delicate, and became incidentally

---

[1] Keepsakes were annual gift books containing stories, poems, and sentimental pictures. They were very popular in France, England, and America.

[2] From the days of the Directoire the shawl was as useful for coquetry as the fan to the *señorita*. Society beauties displayed their grace in an interpretative *danse du schall*, as modern girls show off in eurythmics. Mme Récamier was famous in the *danse du schall*, and Corinne first appeared to Oswald in a shawl turban, "dressed like the Sibyl of Domenichino, an India shawl twisted about her head, and her hair, of the most beautiful black, entwined with this shawl." The *Ermite de la Chaussée d'Antin* records a letter, dated October 28, 1811, in which the writer says to him: "Thanks to you I have returned to my paternal home before my education was completed, without having learned the Russian Step and the Shawl dance, without knowing how to play the tambourine or the castanets." A Cashmere shawl was a conventional part of a wedding outfit until the Second Empire.

[3] Mme de Girardin wrote in her *Lettres parisiennes* in 1836: "Under the Empire the women were all beautiful, then there came an interruption. Under the Restoration the pretty face and irregular features took precedence."

tuberculous. Even young men wanted to be cadaverous. It gave them *l'air fatal, byronien, giaour,* wrote Théophile Gautier in his history of Romanticism, as though they were devoured by passion and remorse. All this is reflected in the *genre poitrinaire,* or Consumptive School, of poetry, which, however, need not be treated too cynically. The moral and physical reaction from the Revolution and the Empire had created a special neurosis both in men and women.

Such a characterization must not be too general. All women were not melancholy, and the frantic dancer coexisted with the *femme frêle.* Many women were intellectual; they were impassioned for the orators and philosophers; and *salons,* political and literary, flourished as before and after. Yet the glories of the Empire were gone. Showy uniforms were seen, not so much on real officers as on fat grocers serving as militiamen in the national guard, or by the strutting shopkeeper's clerk, M. Calicot,[1] feigning a swashbuckler style of costume and speech. Now it is the *rentier* of the Marais quarter, living on his income, or the shopkeeper (*boutiquier*) who sets the tone: M. Gillenormand of Hugo's *Misérables* or Désaugiers's Monsieur and Madame Denis. The *bourgeois* was apt to be, in religion a Voltairian, in politics an Orleanist or liberal, in literature a classicist. Hence, in part, the favor which Romanticism encountered in both artistic society and among rebels against convention, like artists, students, and *grisettes;* hence, in part, the reason why *bourgeois* and *artiste* were antithetic insults.

The *bourgeois* of 1789 represented a class. From the social conflicts which succeeded for so many years he emerged victor,

---

[1] M. Calicot, the martial tradesman's clerk of Scribe and Dupin's *Combat des montagnes* (1817). The *commis* of Paris were ready for a riot against this insult to their pride, but the designation still remains for a salesman in a *magasin de nouveautés.* The strutting *garde national,* the assertive *gendarme,* even the modest rural *garde champêtre,* with his cocked hat and peasant's blouse, have been types of authority borrowed from the uniform. For the respect for the uniform see Sardou's *Nos bons villageois* and Nadaud's famous Pandore in the *chanson* so popular during the Second Empire, with its refrain "Brigadier, vous avez raison."

and under the Monarchy of July he reaped his reward in influence and prosperity. Forthwith he became the object of jealous

A *VISAGE DE KEEPSAKE* (THE *FIANCÉE*)
From a *Keepsake* of 1830

envy. By the workingman he was looked upon as a selfish and heartless employer, by the impecunious young romantic artist and rebel as the incarnation of prosaic and thick-headed stupidity. Thus there has been created in modern civilization the

Great Bourgeois Bugaboo, the meaning of which varies to fit the vituperations of each different malcontent. Everything *bourgeois* is wrong, and everything that the objector dislikes is *bourgeois*. To Flaubert the term meant vacuous Philistinism; to the Bohemians of Murger it meant paying one's bills; to the jazz age it means respectability. Marxism and the class war in time so intensified the opposition between capital and labor that whereas Gautier described the specimen as a fluid vacuum (*un néant fluide*) and Flaubert as *celui qui pense bassement*, implying not so much a class as a type of mind, the modern Russian Bolshevik applies the epithet *burzhuy* to the intelligentsia! To the French proletarian nothing is more hateful than the *sale bourgeois* who keeps his clothes clean.

During the Restoration and the Monarchy of July the Paris well-to-do classes lived in fairly distinct quarters, each of which had its separate characteristics.[1] Because of the drastic reconstruction of Paris under Napoleon III the reign of Louis-Philippe has received less credit than it deserves for the improvements of the capital, improvements which did not, like those of Haussmann, destroy the picturesqueness of the city. They included new quays, gas instead of lamps, wider streets, better pavements, and the *galeries couvertes*, or covered arcades for shops, which still remain as pathetic examples of shabby gentility. But the by streets were quaint, and before the rise in the value of real estate made the cost prohibitive, walled gardens with trees and foliage in many neighborhoods made the city seem less like a caravansary.[2]

Among the quarters there was the faubourg Saint-Germain,

---

[1] The comedy of Mazères and Picard, *les Trois quartiers* (1827), portrays the petty *bourgeoisie* of the rue Saint-Denis, the financiers of the Chaussée d'Antin, and the aristocracy of the faubourg Saint-Germain. For a picture, in recent fiction, of the lot of the peasantry under the Restoration, see the excellent *Jacquou le croquant* of Eugène Le Roy.

[2] Balzac, in *la Fausse maîtresse*, writes of the development of apartment houses, due to the rise in the value of real estate: "All fortunes in France are becoming constricted; the stately city dwellings of our fathers are constantly pulled down and replaced by something like phalansteries [cf. p. 90],

then as now the home of the aristocracy and of the old families, unwise in their policy as *boudeurs*, sulking against the Revolution of July and withdrawing from politics and business,[1] but with traditions of chivalry and dignity. Balzac, in *la Duchesse de Langeais*, writes of

> that high aristocracy which wished to die or remain untouched, which deserved as much praise as blame, and which will always be imperfectly judged until a poet has shown it happy to obey the king by perishing under Richelieu's axe, and scorning the guillotine of '89 as a dirty act of vengeance.

The faubourg Saint-Germain had its somewhat less perfect, because more liberal, counterpart in the faubourg Saint-Honoré on the other side of the Seine. On the north bank of the river, too, was the Chaussée d'Antin, now a retail shopping street, but then a quarter of prosperous merchants and capitalists. Jouy's *Ermite de la Chaussée d'Antin*, a sort of French counterpart of Addison's *Spectator*, depicting Paris of the Empire and early Restoration, takes its name from this street.

The faubourg Saint-Germain and the Chaussée d'Antin were the two rival quarters, embodying two different conceptions of government and of social life. But there were also the quartier Saint-Denis of small tradesmen; the faubourg Saint-Jacques in which the peer of France of the Monarchy of July lives on the third story above a wealthy quack." But even in modern Paris the wanderer is surprised to come upon private gardens in closely built-up quarters. The phrase "entre cour et jardin" is conventionally used to designate the ideal location of a dwelling, with a courtyard in front and a garden in the rear. Boileau, in his sixth satire, speaks of the gardens of Paris in the seventeenth century:

> Paris est pour le riche un pays de Cocagne :
> Sans sortir de la ville, il trouve la campagne ;
> Il peut dans son jardin, tout peuplé d'arbres verts,
> Recéler le printemps au milieu des hivers,
> Et, foulant le parfum de ses plantes fleuries,
> Aller entretenir ses douces rêveries.

---

[1] *Les Boudeurs* of Longpré (1835). Better remembered is the picture of the (provincial) *boudeurs* in Jules Sandeau's *Sacs et parchemins*, and especially in the Gaston de Presles of *le Gendre de M. Poirier*, which Augier drew from Sandeau's novel.

and the Latin quarter, where youth studied and disported; the old Marais, already beginning to fall from its high estate and become industrialized, but still the home of some of the *bourgeoisie*

FASHION UNDER LOUIS-PHILIPPE

who had not yielded to the seductions of money-making. Under Louis-Philippe and Napoleon III the great boulevards were the common sauntering-place of fashion and the home of Parisian wit. Under Louis-Philippe, too, other districts are noted: the workingmen's quarter, the faubourg Saint-Antoine, which read Eugène Sue and prepared the Revolution of 1848; and the new quarter of Notre-Dame-de-Lorette, so frequented by devotees of Aphrodite that during a good part of the Monarchy of July the fast woman, that degeneration of the *grisette* in time called a *cocotte*, was known as a *lorette*. Escorted by her "Arthur" or "Dodolphe" (Adolphe), that is to say her "Charley" or "Johnny", the *lorette* was a familiar type, portrayed in the novels of Paul de Kock and the sketches of Gavarni.[1] The Goncourts wrote a youthful book on the *lorette*. The fast woman on a more magnificent scale, such as we find in *la Dame aux camélias*, is prominent toward the end of the Monarchy of July and foreshadows the manners and morals of the Second Empire.

Under Louis-Philippe, with the increase of financial prosperity, the Parisian turned more openly to enjoyment and self-indulgence. The rich *bourgeois* furnished his home with heavy furniture (which he thriftily protected with canvas coverings, or *housses*), lavish draperies, glass chandeliers, gilt-framed mirrors, and endless knickknacks. Without the house the pleasure-seeker would air himself on the boulevard in a "tilbury" with a groom, loiter at a club, and eat an ice at Tortoni's or chew a toothpick[2] while watching the women go by, indulging in the idle pursuit of enjoyment, for the beginnings of which the reign of Napoleon III has been too exclusively blamed. There grew up that peculiar form of French wit known as *la blague*. Smart

[1] Of individual streets near Notre-Dame-de-Lorette the one most often mentioned was probably the rue Bréda, steeply ascending toward Montmartre, which the Anglomaniac dandy, though he might never have left Paris, would call "Bréda Street". In recent times, to spare its inhabitants' injured feelings, the street was renamed after Henry Monnier, the inventor of the supreme caricature of the *bourgeois*, M. Prudhomme!

[2] Women also chewed toothpicks. The Goncourt brothers (*Charles Demailly*, chap. xxviii) describe a house with a woman and a toothpick at every window: "At the back, the house, illumined by the rosy reflection of a setting sun, displayed at every window women resting on their elbows, like portraits of women in a frame, chewing a toothpick, and greeting below, on the right or the left, some memories of the past, or of yesterday."

successor of the *esprit* of Voltaire and Piron and the brilliant wits of the eighteenth century, it was incisive, cynical, and paradoxical. It turned its ridicule on respected morals and conventions, and winked at successful turpitude. It was more clever than kind, and perhaps by its tone had something to do with the increasing acceptance in novel and drama of adultery and illicit love, the *ménage à trois*, as the natural sequel of marriage. The new journalism and the *chroniques* of the boulevards reflect this spirit. The reign is one of caricature, of clever memoirs, character studies, and descriptions.[1]

The Parisian of Louis-Philippe's day was not only a sauntering *flâneur*; gilded youth (the *jeunesse dorée*) danced as well. The student disported himself in polka, mazurka, or galop with Mimi and Musette at the *Bal Bullier* or *Closerie des Lilas*. *Galop infernal* and *valse échevelée* are stock terms of description. The *bourgeois* on a spree went to the tavern of the *Vendanges de Bourgogne*, to the *Bal Chicard* or the *Bal Musard*, or to the *Jardin Mabille*, where la Reine Pomaré danced the polka and Céleste Mogador in the *cancan* kicked hats from her partners' heads. Gustave Nadaud wrote, with sublime disregard of the value of adjectives:

> Pomaré, Maria,
> Mogador et Clara,
> A mes yeux enchantés
> Apparaissez, chastes divinités.

These bacchantes are commemorated in poems like Banville's *Mascarades*, in his *Odes funambulesques*, and particularly in such lines as the following by Alfred Delvau:

> C'est notre Pomaré dont la danse fantasque,
> Avec ses tordions frissonnants et penchés,
> Aiguillonne à présent comme un tambour de basque
> Les rapides lutteurs à sa robe attachés.

---

[1] The *Français peints par eux-mêmes*; the *Guêpes* of Alphonse Karr, the *chroniques* of Nestor Roqueplan. More delicate are the sparkling *Lettres parisiennes* of the "vicomte de Launay", that is, Delphine Gay (Mme de Girardin).

> Quand sa vive polka frémit dans la cadence,
> Ses plus chauds amoureux se battraient pour mieux voir
> Ses pieds tourbillonnants entraînés par la danse,
> Et tous se damneraient pour les baiser le soir.

Masked balls, private and public, were all the rage, to which men went disguised as postilions and women as street urchins (*titis*) or wharf-laborers (*débardeurs*) in loose trousers and *casquettes*.[1] Carnival was for some years the wildest Saturnalia, and in the early forties the riotous *mardi gras* parade at early dawn from the heights of Belleville, known as the *descente de la Courtille*, including all classes from dandies and duchesses in dominos to *bourgeois* and courtesans in travesty indulging in wild banter, was an occasion of rough pandemonium, in neglect of wonted proprieties.

Under such circumstances it is not surprising that types and fashions change.[2] The *femme frêle* was less predominant. By the side of the Romantic *âme méconnue*, yearning maiden, unappreciated wife, or lonely widow there was the emancipated woman like George Sand, just as romantic in her passions, smoking one of those quaint new-fangled cigarettes, or even a cigar; receiving men in her boudoir; declaiming against outworn conventional morals; preaching socialism, and posing also as a *femme incomprise*, with a "right to happiness".

The examples of smart fashion in the forties were the *lion* and the *lionne*, the latter a fit companion for the masculine combination of Anglomania and elegance. It has ever been the pleasure of the English and the French to make fun of each other. Under

---

[1] Vogue of the comic opera, the *Postillon de Longjumeau*, and of Gavarni's sketches of *titis* and *débardeurs*. A frequenter of cheap masked balls was a *badouillard*. Thackeray's *Paris Sketch-Book* has a description of carnival balls and the riot of dancing. Flaubert's *Education sentimentale* introduces a masked ball as an important episode. This book is one of the best for a description of Paris life in the forties.

[2] Mme de Girardin notes incidentally in 1844: "Another passing mode, more amusing and less dangerous, the faintings. People faint a good deal this year. Under the Empire people fainted readily for a word, a look, a mere trifle; then, under the Restoration, they suddenly stopped fainting. Now they are beginning to refaint."

A MASKED BALL AT THE OPERA IN 1843

the Restoration there was some consolation in lampooning the victor.¹ It was *la revanche de Waterloo*. But his ways were imitated none the less. With the advent of Byronic Satanism in literature and traditions of Beau Brummell in fashion the French also had their type of *le dandy*. The dandy was a "gentleman", like Bulwer's Pelham. Well groomed and corseted, with magnificent cravats, he viewed the passing flux haughtily and impassively, his thumbs hooked in the armholes of his waistcoat, as he warmed his back at the open fire.² He was impeccable in bearing, yet different from the ordinary man in his eccentricities, his paradoxes, and his skepticism. His pastime was to scandalize the *bourgeois*. He was a cynic who talked of horses and women, and believed in the former more than in the latter. It was easy, wrote Mme de Girardin, to be

---

¹ Cf. *les Anglaises pour rire* (1814), of Sewrin and Dumersan, representing "fake" Englishwomen, that is, men in pursuit of a love affair masquerading as Englishwomen. The English thronged to Paris at the Restoration and have done so ever since (cf. Boutet de Monvel, *les Anglais à Paris, 1800–1850*). The English actors who came to Paris in 1822 were hooted for political reasons. A second visit in 1827 created a furore. French writers of farces liked to bring into their plays a "M. Bifteck" or a "M. Goddam". The stage Englishman, such as the *milord* in Auber's *Fra Diavolo*, persisted in farces and comic papers until recently in the shape of a red-headed individual with enormous teeth, a loud checked suit and gaiters, a sun helmet with a white scarf, constantly ejaculating *âoh, shocking!* Later came the Cook's tourist with his guide book, and after the World War Colonel Bramble, the phlegmatic officer, was created by André Maurois. "You know that splendid mine for French caricatures, the eternal vaudeville, the traveling Englishman!" (*Charles Demailly*, chap. xxix.)

² "This magnificent specimen of the Portuguese race in Brazil established himself with his back to the fireplace in a posture showing acquaintance with Parisian ways. His hat in one hand and his arm resting on the velvet-covered mantelpiece, he went towards Mme Marneffe to talk with her in an undertone quite heedless of the horrible *bourgeois* who, in his opinion, very unsuitably encumbered the drawing-room" (*La Cousine Bette*). Readers of Anthony Trollope's *Barchester Towers* will recall how the elegant gentleman, Mr. Arabin, conversed with a young lady, warming his back at the fire, holding his coat tails apart and draped over his arms. Contemporary pictures show numberless gentlemen leaning against the mantelpiece and carrying their hats. The distinguished position was to hold the hat by the brim with the crown against the leg, revealing the lining and the immaculate inner band.

DESCENTE DE LA COURTILLE

disenchanted, to be unable or unwilling to love, to lie comfortably on a sofa with a bored air and wait for "ready-cooked consolations" (*des consolations toutes rôties*) to drop from heaven.[1]

The dandy aped the language and traditional phlegm of the Briton and was glad to marry an English heiress.[2] Mérimée was an impeccable "gentleman", Alfred de Musset ("Miss Byron") was a dandy when not too drunk. Barbey d'Aurevilly, who died in 1889, has often been spoken of as the last shabby, moth-eaten, romantic dandy, outliving his generation, but the eccentricity of intellectual dandyism has been repeated in contemporary France in such specimens of what is now called *snobisme littéraire* as Robert de Montesquiou-Fezensac and Marcel Proust.

The vocabulary of English sports, particularly racing, came into vogue. The Jockey Club, still fashionable today, was founded in 1833, and everybody talked of *raout, turf, gentleman-rider* and *steeplechase*.[3] The elegant *gandin,* or stroller on the boulevard de Gand (former name of the boulevard des Italiens) during the Restoration, was now not only *un dandy* and *un beau,*

[1] Allusion to the saying concerning a lazy person: "Il attend que les alouettes lui tombent toutes rôties dans le bec."

[2] English girls seem to have been sincerely admired, and marrying a rich Englishwoman was an ideal way of having one's "ship come in". It was as satisfactory as the inheritance from the mythical *oncle d'Amérique* of later years. Alfred de Vigny married an Englishwoman; so did Lamartine, and spent her money in showy Oriental travels. "'A young man dressed like this, Lucien de Rubempré hears himself told, once in new clothes, can go and stroll in the gardens of the Tuileries. He will marry an Englishwoman by the end of a fortnight.' Balzac recurs elsewhere to the subject of his rich Englishwoman; and, like him, all the contemporary novelists come back to this interesting question, all the more so that, if one is to believe them, their Englishwomen abounded in Paris" (Boutet de Monvel, op. cit. p. 162). In the *Peau de chagrin* Balzac describes an English girl as follows: "An Englishwoman, white and chaste etherial shape, come down from the clouds of Ossian, seemed like an angel of melancholy, a remorse fleeing from crime." One would scarcely imagine, from this description, that she was really a wild reveler at an orgy.

[3] Avez-vous jamais vu les courses d'Angleterre?
On prend quatre coureurs,—quatre chevaux sellés,
On leur montre un clocher, puis on leur dit: Allez! etc.
  MUSSET, *A quoi rêvent les jeunes filles*

but *un fashionable*,[1] aspiring to rival those composites of British and French sport or fashion, Lord Henry Seymour (*milord l'Arsouille*) and Count d'Orsay.

All young men of fashion were not, however, of the *blasé* type. Balzac, in *la Fille aux yeux d'or*, writes of elegant youths "perfumed with musk, with elaborate cravats, booted, spurred, sporting horse-whips, walking, talking, laughing and giving themselves over to all the devils". But the *lion* (occasionally the *furieux*) of the Monarchy of July is the outgrowth of the dandy, filled with a still more Byronian and Don Juanesque disenchantment. Do not confuse too much the dandy and the lion, wrote Mme de Girardin. The dandy is "celui qui veut se faire voir", the lion is "celui qu'on veut voir". The lion has exhausted all the mild pleasures of life; love is a worn-out term, and he seeks excitement in illicit passion, in emptying magnums of champagne, and in reckless riding through the Bois. He often cultivates a tone of rude bluster and takes it for granted that every woman can be his victim.[2]

The dashing and unconventional woman was the *lionne*. Snapping her fingers at *bourgeois* conventions, riding on horseback or in a landau, or *milord*, outspoken in speech and with something of the romantic rebel in her pose, she prided herself on being as disenchanted as the *lion* and as free to live her life. There might be the sporting lioness, the society lioness, the political lioness, or the literary lioness, like George Sand. Sometimes the *lionne*, or *panthère*, was no more than a glorified courtesan, and Augier, in *les Lionnes pauvres*, shows to what love of money and luxury leads. Musset wrote in his *Andalouse*:

> Avez-vous vu dans Barcelone
> Une Andalouse au sein bruni?
> Pâle comme un beau soir d'automne;
> C'est ma maîtresse, ma lionne!
> La marquesa d'Amaëgui.

[1] Also *un mirliflore*, or *mirliflor* (cf. above, p. 54). Eugénie Grandet's dressy Parisian cousin in Balzac's novel is described as a *mirliflore*.
[2] The word *lion* covers a wide range between Frédéric Soulié's *Lion amoureux* of 1839 and Ponsard's *Lion amoureux* of 1866, a warrior of the Directoire.

The playful sentiment of the Restoration and of the Monarchy of July revolves around that precursor of the modern *midinette* known as the *grisette*. The term, as designating a young working-girl, originated before the nineteenth century and is found in Mercier's *Tableau de Paris*, but the development of industrialism and of handicrafts caused a great increase in the number of people who went out to work. The life of the laboring classes was dull and sordid, but there is always a happy-go-lucky type which meets troubles cheerfully. There was enough of fact in the literary portraiture of the *grisette* to make it not entirely an impossible idealization. The *grisette*, then, was the irresponsible, thoughtless city girl, who worked all the week as *couturière* or *brodeuse* and had a good time on holidays, taking life, said Jules Janin, as an impromptu. Unmoral rather than immoral, she was a companion and helpmate in the good fellowship of student loves and intimacies not destined to endure, but joyful while they lasted. She was the improvident and sometimes fickle sweetheart of youth that lives without thought of the morrow. She is portrayed as a winsome figure with her pretty harum-scarum features, her *minois chiffonné*, tripping through the streets, a little basket, or *cabas*, slung over her arm, wearing a pretty *fichu*, a black apron, a nosegay of *giroflées*, and *brodequins*, or shoes without heels, like sandals, laced around the ankle. She was not ambitious, and her pleasure, after working all the week, was to go riding on donkey back or swing in an *escarpolette* on Sundays at Saint-Cloud, Montmorency, or Romainville, while the height of luxury to her was a ride in a *milord* and a lobster salad! The *grisette* is ubiquitous in the frisky novels of Paul de Kock; she is glorified in the sentiment of such songs as Béranger's "Dans un grenier qu'on est bien à vingt ans", and gets a permanent name in his Lisette and Frétillon, or in the Mimi Pinson of Musset. But the writer who did more than anybody else to idealize the *grisette* was Henry Murger, author of *la Vie de bohème*, inventor of Mimi and Musette and their artist lovers. Murger concealed the sordidness of bohemian existence, which

THE *GRISETTE*

From a drawing by Gavarni

appears with more grim realism in the now-neglected writings of Champfleury; he surrounded with whimsical gayety the hardships of attic life and meals in cheap eating-places (*gargotes*). He created, in Rodolphe and Schaunard, the *poncif*, which has lasted ever since and has been imitated in real life, of the bohemian art student and his mistress, with beard, round *béret*, or broad-brimmed hat, short jacket, and baggy trousers. The latter's pose of eccentricity and scorn for the Philistine harks back to the early days of Théophile Gautier and his wild associates who fought for *Hernani*, and the *blague* of the modern studios perpetuates the jargon, part slang, part preciosity, part parody of the noble style, which, as Bouvier points out in *la Bataille réaliste*, is the style of Champfleury's bohemian stories and of Murger's *Vie de bohème*.[1]

Near the *grisette* was the *lorette*, already alluded to in previous pages. The *lorette* was the girl who had given up regular employment and was frankly dependent on temporary *liaisons*. With financial ups and downs, money is her aim, and the *lionne* her ideal. But she is never presented to us in the grim hideousness of the modern prostitute, and she is usually portrayed as an attractive creature in her cheery recklessness. Nestor Roqueplan was credited with the invention of her name. Théodore de Banville wrote, in *l'Amour à Paris*:

> La grisette! Il revoit la petite fenêtre.
> Les rayons souriants du jour qui vient de naître,
> A leur premier réveil, comme un cadre enchanteur,
> Dorent les liserons et les pois de senteur;
> Une tête charmante, un ange, une vignette
> De ce gai reposoir agace la lorgnette;

---

[1] "Oh! the sweet songs of youth! The happy times of gingham dresses and barège shawls! The *bals* of the Chaumière, the dinners of the Moulin-Rouge, that first mill over which one throws restraint to the winds" [cf. the expression "jeter son bonnet par-dessus le moulin"].—*Le mariage d'Olympe*, Act II, Sc. xiv. The *grisette* and the costumes of the reign of Louis-Philippe have been recalled to popularity during the last generation by the delightfully melodious operetta of André Messager, *Véronique*, in which a high-born maiden disguises herself as a *grisette* to win her lover's affections.

> En voyant de la rue un rire triomphant
> Ouvrir des dents de perle, on dirait qu'un enfant
> Ou quelque sylphe, épris de leurs touffes écloses,
> A fait choir, en jouant, du lait parmi les roses.
> . . . .
> La grisette, doux rêve ! Elle avait ses apôtres,
> Balzac et Gavarni mentaient comme les autres ;
> Mais un jour, Roqueplan, s'étant mis à l'affût,
> Dit un mot de génie et la *Lorette* fut !

In spite of the popularity of the *grisette* it should not be imagined that the pure and honest working girl had no Homer. There was Fleur-de-Marie, the chaste maiden of Eugène Sue's *Mystères de Paris*, amid an environment of crime, and especially Jenny l'ouvrière at her window garden:

> Voyez là-haut cette pauvre fenêtre
> Où du printemps se montrent quelques fleurs;
> Parmi ces fleurs vous verrez apparaître
> Une enfant blonde, aux plus fraîches couleurs . . .
> Voyez là-haut cette pauvre fenêtre
> Où du printemps se montrent quelques fleurs.
> C'est le jardin de Jenny l'ouvrière,
> Au cœur ardent, content de peu . . .
> Elle pourrait être riche et préfère
> Ce qui lui vient de Dieu.[1]

---

[1] *Jenny l'ouvrière*, a *romance* of 1847, words by Barateau, music by Étienne Arnaud.

CHAPTER VIII

RESTORATION AND MONARCHY OF JULY. SOCIAL AND LITERARY TYPES (CONTINUED)

THE dominating social type of the reign of Louis-Philippe was the *bourgeois*. We have already touched upon the political manifestations of class feeling which found expression in the theories of the *doctrinaires*. We are here concerned with the *bourgeois* as example and product of materialistic industrialism, replacing in power the old aristocracy.[1] The *bourgeois* is the embodiment of "honest respectability", desirous of commemoration by others for his domestic virtues and commercial rectitude; as Balzac expresses it in *la Grande Bretèche*, like the epitaph of a grocer in the Père-Lachaise Cemetery, "good father and good husband". The expression *grande bourgeoisie* is often used to designate the influential capitalist order in control of authority. The dramatic incarnation of the smug moneyed class is the M. Poirier of Augier's comedy. A little lower in position and of more farcical treatment are Labiche's M. Perrichon, and the Malingear and Ratinois of his *Poudre aux yeux*, though these plays belong to the Second Empire. Musset's Dupuis and Cotonet and Flaubert's Bouvard and Pécuchet[2] satirize the crassness of *bourgeois* mediocrity, apart from wealth and station, as found in clerks and provincial townsmen. In real life one might take, among many, that *bourgeois de Paris*, as he called himself, Dr. Véron, newspaper manager, director of the Opéra, and man about town, with his big cravat, the delight of caricaturists:

---

[1] In 1847 we have the comedy of Etienne Arago, *les Aristocraties*, that is, of birth, of the sword, of money, and of hard-working toil.

[2] The incomplete *Bouvard et Pécuchet* is of 1881, but Flaubert had had the work on the stocks for many years.

—tout ce que calfate
La cravate.[1]

The *bourgeois* long kept his face smooth in aversion to the hirsute romanticists and republicans; but gradually little *nageoires*, or fins, on the cheeks in front of the ears were stamped with the approval of the army and even of royalty, and in time developed into full-fledged "mutton-chops". Countless drawings and descriptions enable us to visualize the solemn *bourgeois* in collar and choker, with arm tucked in the front of his waistcoat, perorating on the "Car of State". M. Prudhomme, of whom we shall have more to say later, was of the opinion that "the Car of State is sailing upon a volcano" ("le char de l'Etat navigue sur un volcan"). To the sarcastic, *bourgeois* pompousness seemed a vulgar imitation of aristocratic dignity. In 1840 Mme de Girardin could maliciously write words in which M. Thiers, with his diminutive stature, piping voice, and southern accent, is made an unfair antithesis to the nobleman:

In an age like ours it is a great misfortune to have a noble birth, a noble bearing, noble manners. That is the misfortune of M. de Lamartine. It is, on the other hand, a very lucky thing to have a common birth, a common bearing, common manners. That is the good luck of M. Thiers.

The policy of the Monarchy of July was to preserve peace but to humor male vanity and the martial spirit by the *Garde nationale*, or militia. Service in this citizen soldiery permitted the *bourgeois* to reconcile the pursuit of gold with the display of showy costume, and to make him believe himself the patriotic support of national prosperity. Wealth helped in the *Garde nationale*, especially as members supplied their own uniforms, and when, under the Republic of 1848, certain crack regiments in bearskin shakos protested against the admission to their

[1] Théodore de Banville, V—— *le baigneur,* a parody of Hugo's *Sara la baigneuse.* Roger de Beauvoir boasted of addressing a letter "A Monsieur Véron, dans sa cravate, à Paris".

UNIFORMS OF THE PARIS NATIONAL GUARD OF 1848, WITH THE
BONNETS A POIL

ranks of the proletariat (the *manifestation des bonnets à poil*), their motive was the snobbishness of caste and of money.[1]

The vaudevilles, especially of the Restoration, gave light silhouettes of petty shopkeepers and their wives, of *coiffeurs*,

[1] As early as 1815 Scribe, by his famous M. Pigeon of *Une nuit de la Garde nationale*, had portrayed the proud militiaman even in plain clothes, with belt and accouterments over his civilian's coat: "On peut bien aimer son roi sans être en uniforme."

cuisinières, ravaudeuses, and of Henry Monnier's famous *roman chez la portière*.[1] The comedies of manners and the novels show innumerable types and characters,—merchants, financiers, landed proprietors,—and frequent subjects are money-making by speculation or marriage, and success in politics or the professions. The comedies of Scribe, discarding the shepherdesses and bucolic swains of the eighteenth century, are full of brisk young officers in quest of rich widows. A *position sociale* was all-important in those days, and it depended on money. Hence both the pursuit of the rich woman, irrespective of love, and the partial justification of George Sand's revolt against marriage. Thackeray, in his *Paris Sketch-Book*, records a quaint type, not merely of literature but of life, the *veuve de la Grande Armée*, a successor of the lady of the Directoire period who had been "ruinée par l'émigration":

La Grande Armée has been a father to more orphans, and a husband to more widows, than it ever made. Mistresses of *cafés*, old governesses, keepers of boarding-houses, genteel beggars, and ladies of lower rank still, have this favorite pedigree. They have all had *malheurs* (what kind it is needless to particularize). They are all connected with the *grand homme*, and their fathers were all colonels. The title exactly answers to the "clergyman's daughter" in England—as "A young lady, the daughter of a clergyman, is desirous to teach", etc.; "A clergyman's widow receives into her house a few select", and so forth.

[1] "There are fashions in humor as there are fashions in dress. Under the Restoration people enjoyed the performance of scenes in the cheap neighborhoods by the city gates and suburban eating and drinking resorts; they were amused by the drunken types of Pigal. The popular theatre, the Variétés, played only vaudevilles of chair-menders and cooks. Under Louis-Philippe, the upper and the middle *bourgeoisie* passed under the eyes of Balzac and of Henry Monnier. The Second Empire thought it was raising the comic a degree higher by joining satire to luxury. Money circulates freely and is more easily spent. The theme of the dissolute woman enters comedy to an important degree. People ask of it less wit and sentiment, and more toilets."—CHAMPFLEURY, *Henry Monnier*, p. 257. The *roman chez la portière* is synonymous with a pandemonium of irrelevant topics and talk. The novel that the *portière* was trying to read, amid all the interruptions, was "Co-élina, ou l'enfant du Ministère"! This is again evidence of the great vogue of Ducray-Duminil's *Cœlina*. Cf. p. 64.

But it is especially in the *Comédie humaine* of Balzac that we get the cruel criticism of the age, as expressed in its noted types, the *roués* of the reign of Charles X, the money-makers of that of Louis-Philippe. Here are shopkeepers, financiers, brokers, proprietors, officeholders, and journalists, all devoted to the creature comforts and the *stratégie des intérêts*: the baron de Nucingen, representative of high finance; nineteenth-century *condottieri* and soldiers of fortune, such as Lucien de Rubempré, making his way by women (an interesting type between the elder Dumas's Alfred d'Alvimar of *Angèle* and Maupassant's Bel-Ami) or Rastignac, whom Thiers's enemies thought he resembled, the political climber and lover of money and power, ready for the conquest of Paris ("A nous deux maintenant!"), or Maxime de Trailles, the debauched adventurer, erecting selfishness into a principle; Henry de Marsay, the skeptical dandy and shifty politician, the *roi des viveurs*; Valérie Marneffe, depraved middle-class courtesan; Vautrin, ex-convict and social rebel, the genius of crime;[1] the misers Grandet and Gobseck; old man Goriot, Balzac's Lear, neglected by his pleasure-loving daughters; Baron Hulot, a specimen of the long-ridiculed "vieillard amoureux", become *gâteux*, or imbecile; the "*illustre*" Gaudissart, loquacious commercial "drummer". In the comedy *Mercadet* is another of Balzac's famous types, the self-satisfied and overconfident speculator and promoter. Balzac's honest people are generally the victims of intriguers: for example, his *curé* of Tours, or César Birotteau, the tradesman. The "hero" of Balzac is, then, a famous character of French literature, and it has been pointed out more than once that he helped to *create*, even more than to *record*, social types. In real life the selfish and merciless adventurer and climber was even more characteristic of the Second Empire than of the earlier part of the century. In this sense fiction was partly a model for life in the following generation.

In another way Balzac made fiction richer by being what

[1] Rastignac and Vautrin are half-romantic, Napoleonic characters in their symbolism. Vautrin is a forerunner of Jean Valjean.

Jules Janin called the "Christopher Columbus of the woman of forty". Hitherto novels had described the loves of young girls. Balzac showed that a woman of thirty or forty can still have emotions. Mme de Girardin, in 1836, quotes Janin as saying that Balzac makes answer to the girl of sixteen: "We are busy with your mother; come back in twenty years and we shall see what we can do for you."[1]

Thus conditions have changed radically since the days when, as recorded in a previous chapter, virtue was derived from goodness and sensibility. At the time when the misguided utopians were struggling to base society on altruism, Balzac declares that there is no absolute virtue, there are only circumstances. Vautrin announces, "La vertu, c'est l'argent." The society of the reign of Louis-Philippe that counted is portrayed as largely composed of people devoted to self-advancement whether by individual effort or by mutual-admiration societies of political and literary climbers.[2] At the same time all classes were convinced of their own rectitude and satisfied with their achievements. The journalist thought it in his power to make and unmake reputations; the officeholder, or *fonctionnaire*, felt a security of tenure which made him contemptuous of the penniless aristocrat; the money-makers grew more vain and rubicund as their fortunes multiplied. They felt that they owed their prosperity to their own cleverness. Often their religion had no higher idealism than Béranger's *Dieu des bonnes gens* or the irreverence of his song "Le bon Dieu avait mis le nez à la fenêtre."

At the bottom of the ladder were the unhappy and dissatisfied working classes; but they were by no means without spokesmen and defenders. As early as 1830 Barbier's fierce *Iambes* goaded them to rebellion against the existing order, and such poems as his *Lyre d'airain* described the misery caused by industrialism and the introduction of machinery. The utopians, Lamennais,

---

[1] But in comedy the rivalry of mother and daughter dates back to Dancourt, and under the Restoration the plays of Casimir Bonjour and of Mazères deal with the woman of thirty and forty.

[2] Cf. Scribe's *la Camaraderie* and *le Puff*.

Lamartine, Hugo, worked for the toilers. The "bards of democracy", like Pierre Dupont, with his *Chant des ouvriers* and his *Chant du pain*, at the time of the famine of 1846–1847, foreshadowed the revolution of 1848:

> On n'arrête pas le murmure
> Du peuple, quand il dit: J'ai faim!
> Car c'est le cri de la nature:
> Il faut du pain!

Hégésippe Moreau was made by the malcontents an occasion for attacks on the state of things. He was one of the most talented and promising poets of his time, but essentially the man with a grievance, a sort of unsuccessful Rousseau, a "Rousseau manqué", who died of poverty and privations at the public hospital in 1838 at the age of twenty-eight. He was compared with Chatterton, the *Poète mourant*, and the unsuccessful geniuses of literature.

Above all, the cause of the submerged classes was upheld in melodramas, and in *romans feuilletons* running as serials in the newspapers. These are not considered today to have much literary value, but some of them had extraordinary vogue in their time and were potent causes of the unrest which culminated in the Revolution of 1848. Their conventional method was to portray heroism in an environment of crime, poetry in the midst of sin, to give the noble *rôle* to the outlaw and outcast from society, and to hold up to ridicule the agents of law and order, the magistracy and the police; for the writers of these proletarian works were at one with the aristocrat Vigny in thinking that the *ordre social* is always wrong. A premonitory symptom of 1848 was the sensationally popular melodrama *le Chiffonnier de Paris*, by the agitator Félix Pyat. The rag-pickers were the lowest and most sodden class, and the *chiffonnier*, picking over refuse for a living, was the type of the miserable man, as the little Savoyard chimney-sweep was of the miserable child. In this melodrama Père Jean, the rag-picker, is the upright, honest being contrasted with the infamous and criminal capitalist. In the same

THE RAG-PICKER
From a drawing by Traviès

way the dandy, Eugène Sue, made himself a spokesman for the poor, an *avocat des pauvres*, by *les Mystères de Paris* and *le Juif errant*. The furore which they created compares with that of *Uncle Tom's Cabin* in America. Eugène Sue wrote in a slovenly style, and he was considered immoral through his exaltation of the lower classes and his attacks on the Jesuits and on the social order. But just as George Sand tried to emancipate superior minds, so Sue emancipated the masses. Society, he proclaimed, has brought the working-man to crime and the working-girl to prostitution. In the *Mystères de Paris* Sue gave pictures of life among the wretched before the *Misérables* of Hugo. Before Jean Valjean he created the redeemed convict, *le Chourineur*[1]; before Gavroche, the street arab, *le Tortillard*; before the Thénardier couple, the hag *la Chouette*; before Fantine and Cosette, the *goualeuse*,[2] Fleur-de-Marie, who keeps her chastity amid crime. In the *Juif errant* the tricky agent of the Jesuits, Rodin, embodied the hatred felt for the secret religious orders against which agitators as well as popular novelists were concentrating their efforts.

One type in particular was very convenient as a mouthpiece of criticism and satire, the street arab, or urchin, the *gamin*, or *titi*. Instead of stunting intelligence, as in the London slums, the alcoholism and tuberculosis of the Paris working quarters produced degenerates, indeed, boys precociously old and disenchanted, but redeemed by reckless mischief and amusing impudence. Some of them were criminals, but they had not learned to handle the knife with the boldness of the modern *apache*. Literary crusaders against society could point to them as the result of evil conditions, or portray them as being, even with their vices, better than the offspring of capitalism. Today Hugo's Gavroche casts all the others into the shade, because of the vogue of the *Misérables*, but he was a late comer on the stage. The *enfants terribles* of Gavarni's sketches had popularized youthful impertinence. Balzac and Sue had created

---

[1] *Chourineur* = "donneur de coups de couteau".
[2] *Goualeuse* = "chanteuse".

LES POIRES,

Faites à la cour d'assises de Paris par le directeur de la CARICATURE.
Vendues pour payer les 6,000 fr. d'amende du journal le *Charivari*.

Sur la demande d'un grand nombre d'abonnés des départements, nous donnons aujourd'hui dans le *Charivari* les poires qui servirent à notre défense, dans l'affaire où la *Caricature* fut condamnée à six mois de prison et 2,000 fr. d'amende.

Si, pour reconnaître le monarque dans une caricature, vous n'attendez pas qu'il soit désigné autrement que par la ressemblance, vous tomberez dans l'absurde. Voyez ces croquis informes, auxquels j'aurais peut-être dû borner ma défense :

Ce croquis ressemble à Louis-Philippe, vous condamnerez donc ?

Alors il faudra condamner celui-ci, qui ressemble au premier.

Puis condamner cet autre, qui ressemble au second.

Et enfin, si vous êtes conséquens, vous ne sauriez absoudre cette poire, qui ressemble aux croquis précédens.

Ainsi, pour une poire, pour une brioche, et pour toutes les têtes grotesques dans lesquelles le hasard ou la malice aura placé cette triste ressemblance, vous pourrez infliger à l'auteur cinq ans de prison et cinq mille francs d'amende ! !
Avouez, Messieurs, que c'est là une singulière liberté de la presse ! !

specimens of the type,[1] and in 1836 one of the great successes of the day was *le Gamin de Paris* by Bayard and Vanderburch, of which the young hero, though full of impudence and practical jokes, saves lives and protects his sister's honor.

In spite of the showy uniforms and the fierce bearskins of the *Garde nationale,* the Umbrella replaces the Gun as the synthetic emblem of the Monarchy of July. Romanticists and caricaturists joined forces in heaping ridicule on this article of philistine utilitarianism. An ingenious inventor planned a tricolor umbrella to be placed at the end of a gun as a protection for patriotic militiamen doing sentry duty. Louis-Philippe, the citizen-king himself, was made to embody the spirit of the *bourgeoisie,* with his big cotton umbrella as scepter, his green *redingote,* his tall white beaver hat, and his pear-shaped head, small at the top and broad at the base,[2] always discoursing of the victories of Jemmapes and Valmy, and looking, as Hugo expressed it, half Charlemagne and half notary. Never was man more cruelly lampooned than this well-meaning but stubborn monarch, a king whose motto, said Pétrus Borel in his *Rapsodies,* was: "Dieu soit loué, et mes boutiques aussi!"[3] He had his compeers in the creation of writers and draftsmen, who delighted to represent the worthy *bourgeois* with big stomach, ears stuffed with cotton, spectacles, and projecting collar.[4]

[1] Népomucène of Balzac's *Envers de l'histoire contemporaine.* Another precursor of Gavroche, equally famous in his day, was Fouyou, in a very popular vaudeville, *le Maître d'école,* by Anicet Bourgeois and Lockroy, 1841.

[2] *Une poire* is colloquially used to designate a naïve and credulous person.

[3] "May God be praised and my shops rented!"

[4] M. Maigron (*le Romantisme et la mode*, p. 54) recalls the character in Pétrus Borel's *Champavert,* who, when offered an umbrella as protection against a storm, indignantly spurns it with the words of Hugo's *Hernani*:

> Ah! quand l'amour jaloux bouillonne dans nos têtes,
> Quand notre cœur se gonfle et s'emplit de tempêtes,
> Qu'importe ce que peut un nuage des airs
> Nous jeter en passant de tempêtes et d'éclairs!

The story is familiar of the duel between Sainte-Beuve and Dubois, when the former insisted on keeping his umbrella, declaring that he was willing to be killed but not to get wet.

MONSIEUR PRUDHOMME

As the pacific *parapluie* is the antithesis of the warlike gun, so the prosaic cotton nightcap, or *bonnet de coton*, is in telling contrast to such an accessory of romanticism as the hunter's horn. The *cor de chasse* is one of the important dramatis personæ of Hugo's *Hernani*, and Alfred de Vigny wrote *le Cor*, but Béranger's *roi d'Yvetot* always slept in a nightcap, and so did Marshal Bugeaud![1] The poet Louis Bouilhet wrote *le Bonnet de coton*, an amusing imitation of Béranger, which Maxime du Camp quotes in an appendix to his *Souvenirs*.

Comic papers like the *Caricature* and the *Charivari*[2] were, in part, vehicles for the satire of Daumier and Traviès. These artists, and especially Henry Monnier, are called by Champfleury, in his history of modern caricature, "les démolisseurs de la bourgeoisie". With their names are especially connected those of Monsieur Prudhomme, Robert Macaire, and Mayeux.

Henry Monnier was a writer, a caricaturist, and an actor. His Joseph Prudhomme, who appears in several of his works, is the embodiment of the ponderous, sententious, and self-satisfied *bourgeois*, pompous officer in the *garde nationale*, expressing his sufficiency in grandiloquent but confused metaphors. It was M. Prudhomme who declared: "If you separate man from society, you isolate him." When M. Prudhomme was given a sword of honor as officer in the National Guard, he said: "This sword is the finest day of my life." M. Prudhomme, like Labiche's conceited Perrichon, or Flaubert's sententious druggist,[3] Homais,

---

[1] Cf. supra, p. 101, n. The nightcap, or *casque à mèche*, was to the caricaturists the helmet of the pacific *bourgeoisie*, and "marchand de bonnets de coton" was, like "épicier", an expression of scorn suggesting an ignorant man, incapable of understanding art and engrossed in his petty business.

[2] *La Caricature*, founded in 1830; *le Charivari*, founded in 1832; both by Philipon. *Punch* bears still, as subtitle, the *London Charivari*.

[3] The *pharmacien*, or druggist, in France, because he required certain diplomas, particularly to be *pharmacien de première classe*, became, like the *épicier* or the *marchand de bonnets de coton*, the victim of satire. He was made an example of the semi-educated man, conceited because of his modicum of instruction, by which he thought himself an intellectual, and expressing himself in solemn platitudes. See not only Homais but Floupin of Sardou's *Nos bons villageois*.

THE *GAMIN*
From a drawing by Charlet

is a descendant of Molière's Monsieur Jourdain, who had spoken prose for forty years without knowing it. A "remark worthy of M. Prudhomme" implies to the Frenchman what, just at present, is known in America as a "bromidic saying". Henry Monnier is now considered by many French critics the great ultimate source of the realistic method. Balzac's *bourgeois* have undergone the influence of Monnier, and Champfleury, the forgotten ancestor of realism, followed his example.

Robert Macaire was really the creation of the actor Frédérick Lemaître. Taking a rôle in a wretched melodrama which, at its first appearance,[1] had nearly been hooted off the stage, Frédérick Lemaître transformed it into a character typifying the *chevalier d'industrie* and business charlatan, tricky and unscrupulous, impudently devoting his smartness to every sort of shady transaction. The part was made magnificently comic by the actor's burlesque of the conventional devices of black melodrama, so that it was both a dramatic parody and a heartless caricature of social life in its commercial aspects. Robert Macaire, with his shabby clothes, dilapidated tall hat, and round, squeaking snuffbox, was accompanied by his fellow sharper, Bertrand, both accomplice and butt, and the companion rôles of Robert Macaire and Bertrand became two great types of the humorous stage.[2] Not only did Frédérick Lemaître try to repeat his success by introducing Robert Macaire into later plays, but the artist Daumier, with the aid of Philipon's appended explanatory dialogues, made him, by a series of cartoons, a symbolic figure of the commercial fraud, raising money on worthless inventions, organizing dishonest financial schemes, or of the medical quack, tricky lawyer, etc.[3]

A minor character of Frédérick Lemaître's play, Gogo, the sharper's dupe, has ever since been the type of the easily fleeced

---

[1] *L'Auberge des Adrets*, by Antier, Saint-Armand, and Paulyanthe, 1823.
[2] They reappear, under different names, as recently as in *Erminie*, the great success of the American comic-opera stage during the eighteen-eighties.
[3] Thackeray gives a long account of Robert Macaire in his essay on *Caricature and Lithography* in the *Paris Sketch-Book*.

victim, purchaser of worthless stock, and investor in companies destined to bankruptcy and disaster.

Mayeux first appeared in *le Fossé des Tuileries*, a farce of 1831 by Dumanoir, Mollien, and Lhéris, but it was Traviès who gave him pictorial immortality. A cynical hunchback dwarf, dirty-minded and *égrillard*, grumbling, skeptical, irreverent, vain and conceited in spite of his deformity, Mayeux was a convenient mouthpiece for pasquinades on the *bourgeoisie*.

One of the types of the age still much brought into popular reference is Calino. It is difficult to determine how the character arose, though it is said to be based on a tradesman's clerk who became known for his blunders. In 1856 a one-act play, *Calino*, by Théodore Barrière and Fauchery, was very successful. Calino today is the sort of man who buys two copies of a book in case he may wish to read it twice.[1]

Another character, of a different kind, the popularity of which

---

[1] Other types should be mentioned also. Raton, of Scribe's *Bertrand et Raton* (1833), a political comedy, is presented as a character from Danish history, but he is another descendant of Monsieur Jourdain, whose vanity and conceit led him to reënact La Fontaine's fable of the cat and the monkey (*Bertrand et Raton*), and draw the chestnuts from the fire. Bilboquet, of *les Saltimbanques*, a *comédie-parade* (1838) of Dumersan and Varin, was the traveling showman and "slick" bluffer, living by his wits and always ready with smooth phrases of explanation, but without the cynical dishonesty of Robert Macaire. Many of his sayings became current quotations, such as "Sauvons la caisse", expressive of the aim of financial plungers to make off with the booty; or, to indicate unscrupulous appropriation of property: "Cette malle est-elle à nous?—Elle doit être à nous." M. and Mme Pipelet, of Eugène Sue's *Mystères de Paris*, became types of the *concierge* and his wife. Mme Pochet, who made her advent with M. Prudhomme's first appearance, in Monnier's *le Roman chez la portière* (*Scènes populaires*, 1830) (see above, p. 123), gets a companion figure in Mme Gibou, like Dickens's Mrs. Gamp and Betsey Prig. Dumersan's play, *Madame Gibou et Madame Pochet, ou le thé chez la ravaudeuse* (1832), made "le thé de Madame Gibou", with its horrible experimental mixture of ingredients, a synonym for a mass distasteful to eat. Henry Monnier was the creator, in *la Cour d'assises* (*Scènes populaires*) of Jean Iroux, or Hiroux, the stupid defendant, a sodden and vulgar butt of practical jokes. In the fifties Gavarni created in Thomas Vireloque a shabby and cynical street Diogenes: "L'histoire ancienne c'est mangeux et mangés, blagueux et blagués c'est la nouvelle."

was chiefly due to one man, was Pierrot. Pierrot had always been a minor, clownlike being, or "Gilles", in pantomime and popular comedy; but a pantomime actor and *paillasse*, named Deburau,[1] having assumed this rôle in a proletarian amusement resort, the Théâtre des Funambules, gave extraordinary importance to the part. In all the pantomimes now written, Arlequin, Colombine, Léandre, and Cassandre yielded precedence to this strange figure in white smock and pantaloons and black skullcap, his face smeared with flour, expressing without a spoken word all the emotions of humanity. Pierrot was at will naïve, daring, sly, tricky, or lovable; the acting of Deburau was one of the sensations of the time, and noted authors were glad to supply him with plays. Though he died in 1846, his memory lived, and to the influence of Deburau's impersonations are due the Pierrots of carnival masquerades, the sentimental and romantic Pierrots of Willette, the silhouette plays (*ombres chinoises*) of the *Chat noir* theater, and the vogue of the type in the art and literature of Montmartre.

The true prose mock epic of the *bourgeoisie* under the reign of Louis-Philippe is to be found in Louis Reybaud's *Jérôme Paturot à la recherche d'une position sociale*. The hero of this tale, described as a "Gil Blas without ability", begins and ends, like his father before him, as a maker of *bonnets de coton*. But his *grandeur* and *décadence* carry him through stages as romantic poet, Saint-Simonian, stockbroker, journalist, officer of the National Guard, capitalist, until the smash comes and he finds himself, after arrest for debt, where he started his career.

[1] Cf. Sacha Guitry's *Deburau*.

CHAPTER IX

RESTORATION AND MONARCHY OF JULY. ROMANTIC THEMES AND TYPES

THE Romantic storm burst in 1830: the Battle of *Hernani* of February and the Revolution of July came in the same year, and the merry war was on between *bourgeois* and rebel. The Antony of Dumas and the living model of M. Prudhomme were contemporaries. Moreover, as the romanticists were the innovators and revolutionaries, they made a commotion beyond their actual numbers. It is sometimes difficult for stolid Anglo-Saxons to realize how bitterly the French could fight over books, plays, and ideas. The romanticists undermined in time the conservatism of the *bourgeois* and modified the currents of French thought, but in its extreme forms theirs was, on the whole, the literature of a minority. As the reign of Louis-Philippe progressed, the capitalists and *petits rentiers* became more and more intrenched in material pursuits, and romantic enthusiasms tended to be social and humanitarian rather than individual.

We have already discerned the beginnings of romanticism before the Restoration, and during the reigns of Louis XVIII and Charles X it gathered momentum. Many things contributed to obliterate the old grooves of thought and to prepare a literary and artistic revolution following the political one. Victor Hugo called romanticism "un fait de civilisation, un fait d'âme" and "liberalism in art"; by these phrases he suggested the upheaval which took place in men's souls as a result not only of 1789 or 1793 but of the wars of Napoleon, and the necessity for new means of expression. The physical and nervous exhaustion of a country which had gone through the slaughter of Napoleonic warfare and the catastrophe of his mushroom empire could no longer brook convention and tradition. In literature Musset's *Confession d'un enfant du siècle*, and the pessimism of Jouffroy's philosophy testify to the disillusion which so many experienced. In politics the old régime had cracked and split; the semi-apostolic continuity of the monarchy had been interrupted, and in spite of efforts to reestablish it, it went for good in 1830. The career of Napoleon had impressed people's minds, and its brevity and tragic outcome had a much greater spectacular impressiveness than had the threadbare epics or tragedies of the old school. The blow to conventional pseudo-classical culture by the reorganization of education, and the interruption of studies for military service, made abrupt changes less horrifying. The failure of eighteenth-century science to bring about the millennium, and its ineffectual optimism, caused people to distrust the whole past. Deities like Condillac, La Harpe, and Batteux were massed together for general reprobation. Shakespeare was set up against Racine and Voltaire. The religion of the Middle Ages, the days of Gothic cathedrals, were opposed to the modern neopaganism. The greater freedom of political expression under the Restoration made boldness of all kinds attractive. Rejection of old standards of judgment and taste encouraged emotionalism, egoism, and the search for new sensations and reactions. The tendency was increased by the literary cosmopolitanism which, even before the Revolution, had brought new themes to France. The early romanticists were comparatively mild, usually royalists and political reactionaries, and were satisfied with timid experiments in style or a poetic medievalism which they did not invent. But conditions changed, romanticism was stimulated by opposition, and before long the romanticists became full-fledged revolutionaries, possessed of a creed difficult to express concisely because it was one largely of revolt, and determined to destroy the citadel of conservatism.

The greatest literary figures who paved the way for romanticism are acknowledged to have been Mme de Staël and Chateaubriand. The former gave breadth to intellectual understanding by her cosmopolitanism and by her interpretation of German thought. Though a descendant of an age of rationalism, as a disciple of Rousseau she stimulated people's emotions and helped to turn them to spiritualism. Chateaubriand's sensuous religiosity and æsthetic Catholicism clothed emotionalism more concretely than Mme de Staël did, in the trappings of a supposedly purer belief of olden times. He turned people from irony to faith. His poetical temperament continued the influence of Bernardin de Saint-Pierre in making nature visible in words and in developing local color. At the same time his physical temperament made him the interpreter of the melancholy and *ennui* that were to settle over literature, when it did not become rebellion against fate and circumstances.

The stages of romanticism are various and the ideals change. After the inarticulate sentimentality of the Revolution and the Empire come the conservative royalists of the early twenties reacting against pseudo-classicism and moribund æsthetics, and turning to reverie and sentiment that found more successful poetical expression. Rapidly the young romanticists grew venturesome, and violent against the classicists. In the *cénacle* of 1824, at the *salon* of the worthy Nodier, an omnivorous reader and clever literary dabbler, romanticism was to a noteworthy degree connected with the Foreign and the Fantastic. Instead of being half-academically sentimental it cultivated local coloring and the eccentric. It deified the vague and mysterious rather than the definite and rational, the primitive ballad and popular poesy rather than traditional Latin culture, and declined all literary dogma. Self-conscious and often conceited, posing for stage effect, the romanticists respected nothing. At Hugo's *cénacle* of 1827 the young warriors considered the *bourgeois* liberals more stodgy than the old monarchists. Not only were new utopias conceived, but the theories of literature and art were to be entirely renewed. By a supreme contradiction, though the romanticists found in Hugo's preface to *Cromwell*, the "Tables of the Law of Romanticism", a declaration of their theory, yet every writer or artist (for art and letters were closely interwoven) was a law to himself in interpreting the theory.

By 1830 most romanticists saw in life mere disorder, but Hugo found there systematic contrast. An important element of the *Préface de Cromwell* is the admittance of the Grotesque and the Fantastic into the conception of life. Hugo saw in life and nature the antithesis of the beautiful and the ugly, of the sublime and the grotesque; but he viewed them in forced juxtaposition and not merged, as in life. He emphasized the grotesque because classicism avoided it, and it is found throughout his writings and in the whimsical sketches at the Musée Victor-Hugo. The result in his own works and in those of his disciples was exaggerated license. The *brigands de la pensée*[1] wanted freedom instead of the rules, "truth" and "naturalness" instead of conventions. They demanded a literature of the emotions instead of one of reason; they lauded the *mot propre* instead of pseudo-classical periphrasis and circumlocution. Hugo boasted of calling "le cochon par son nom". Above all, the young romanticists were a mutual admiration society. They encouraged each others' eccentricities with the indiscipline of youth or tried to flabbergast, to *épater le bourgeois*, for we distinguish between the cultivated people of the *cénacles* and the riotous *Jeunes-France*, "ancêtres de la bohème". Romanticism was, among its minor representatives, a riotous orgy of lawless types in literature and life. Many of them were young bohemian art students (*rapins*), claiming the right to paint, as Ingres said of Delacroix, with a drunken broom (*balai ivre*), and affecting to turn up their coat collars when passing a classicist painting, lest the chill grays and subdued colors give one a cold. They divided the world into *flamboyants*, whom they admired, and *grisâtres*, whom they despised. The *bourgeois* were, in the eyes of the romanticists, "mummies", "barbarians", "Hottentots", "*épiciers*". The romanticists were to the *bourgeois* "savages", creators of a "Cossack literature",[2] "slaughterhouse

---

[1] The term "brigands de la pensée" was perhaps suggested by the "brigands de la Loire". This was the army which, after Waterloo, withdrew beyond the Loire. The royalists accused it of atrocities of every sort.

[2] The rough Cossacks had entered France with the invaders of 1815.

singers" (*chantres d'abattoirs*), and "charnel-house troubadours" (*troubadours de charniers*). Because the *bourgeois* affected smooth faces and neat clothes, the young romanticists banned starched collars and were unkempt, with "Merovingian" or "leonine" hair ("On ne peut naître avec des perruques!") and "Assyrian" beards. Beards and hats got a political meaning. By the side of the *Jeunes-France*, who at first posed as religious idealists, were the republican materialistic *bousingots*. These were boisterous young students of law, medicine, or science, dabblers in politics, organizers of irresponsible riots and disturbances. They dressed much alike, with round, shiny leather hats, and wore beards; so that under the Second Empire the republicans of "forty-eight", *bousingots* grown old, were called *vieilles barbes*.[1] As to the *Jeunes-France*, they were numerous and varied. Mrs. Trollope, writing her notes on Paris, records that "Young France" seemed a cabalistic term by which people implied something great, terrible, volcanic, and sublime. She found the two cant epithets most in vogue, expressing the two tendencies of literature and thought, to be *rococo* and *décousu*. Says Gautier in *Elias Wildmanstadius*, there are innumerable types of Young France, the Byronic, the artistic, the passionate, the dissipated, and especially the medieval. Gautier gives amusing comic sketches of the wild young romantic. When

---

[1] Maxime du Camp wrote in his *Souvenirs* (Vol. I, p. 45): "The partisans of the régime inaugurated after the Revolution of July, and they were the majority, wore only side-whiskers; the Bonapartists had the moustache and goatee (*impériale*); the Republicans, who were then called the *bousingots*, grew full beards, and could be confused with the artists, the writers, the young men who, designated by the generic name of *Jeunes-France*, let their beards and hair grow long. The Legitimists, united at that time under the two designations of Carlists [that is, followers of Charles X] and of Henriquinquists [the Pretender, the comte de Chambord, was called Henry V], grew a necklet around their faces. These were, in a way, rallying emblems by which people knew each other." Mrs. Trollope (*Paris and the Parisians*) tells the anecdote of a young provincial who, coming to Paris, made the mistake of buying a hat of the style affected by the romanticists. He was stoned by the conservatives, but was equally maltreated by the other side when he purchased a conservative hat. His final salvation was reached only when he bought for himself a *chapeau juste-milieu*.

Daniel Jovard suddenly became one, he went home, smashed in his tall hat, threw away his tail coat, cut the collars from his shirts, burned the works of Boileau, Voltaire, and Racine, and called his father *garde national*. Then he sought a friend, a fashionable, romantic dandy, who taught him to say "phosphorescent, transcendental, pyramidal, stupéfiant, foudroyant, annihilant".[1] He outlined to Jovard the course of life: at twenty, one was *Jeune-France*; up to twenty-five, *beau jeune mélancolique*; from twenty-five to thirty, Childe Harold; then gradually one became *ci-devant, faux toupet, aile de pigeon, perruque, étrusque, mâchoire, ganache*, until at last, by forty, one reached the last stage of decrepitude and the worst epithets of infamy as Academician and Member of the Institute! He taught Daniel to act the *rêveur*, the *intime*, the *artiste*, the *dantesque*, the *fatal*, and above all to "talk corpse" (*parler cadavre*).[2]

For the bold and bad young rebel two great topics were Adultery and Orgy. Adultery was made more than ever fashionable in literature by Dumas's *Antony*. Says Pétrus Borel at the end of a tirade against the *bourgeois* age in the preface of his *Rapsodies*: "Fortunately as consolation for all this we have left to us adultery and cigarettes!" As for the Orgy, Champfleury wrote in his *Vignettes romantiques*: "Orgy was, along with

[1] The romantic exuberance of style is what Berlioz had in mind when he spoke of his accounts of his own concerts as a "style de bulletin de la Grande Armée". These glorifications of military victories and Napoleon's addresses to his troops (*Soldats!*) are successors of the pseudo-classical harangues of the Revolution (*Citoyens!*), and traces of the style are still seen in the electoral posters of candidates for office (*Electeurs!*). Contrast, by the way, the exuberance of the "style de bulletin de la Grande Armée" with the laconism of the official *communiqués* during the World War.

[2] In 1840 Mme de Girardin wrote: "We had for fifteen years a literature of sugar and water, until the day which suddenly brought forth a literature of blood." She says also that in 1812 a pretty woman read Mme de Genlis and fell asleep "gently lulled by tender memories of a graceful romance where even the purest emotions are veiled, where love is lost in a maze of infinite delicacies." Today, what books have we with which to soothe a pretty woman? *Mauprat*, by George Sand; the *Mémoires du diable*, by M. Frédéric Soulié; the *Auberge rouge* of M. de Balzac; and the sea stories of M. Sue.

beauty and wealth, sensuality, oblivion to life, the joys of hell, revolt against society, delirium of the senses, man become male, woman female. What fair orgies on the stage and in books!"

Orgies had the literary indorsement even of Balzac, in the *Peau de chagrin*; of Hugo, in *Lucrèce Borgia*, where Gennaro transforms the name of "Borgia" on the façade of the palace into "Orgia"; of Dumas, in *la Tour de Nesle*, where the tavern-keeper Orsini says:

> What a fair night for an orgy at the Tower! The sky is black, the rain falls, the city sleeps! The river increases in volume as though to go to meet corpses . . . It is a fair time for love: without, the noise of thunder; within, the sound of glasses and of words of love . . . Strange concert where God and Satan each one plays his part.

So, with cheerful disregard for future headaches and dyspepsia, the young romanticists tried to be bold and bad. The dashing cigarette, the bowl of *ponche*, or punch, were the accessories of such revels, and it was well to hint darkly at having drunk punch from the skull of one's rival in love, as Byron was reported to have done at orgies in Newstead Abbey. Théophile Gautier tells of drinking sea water in a skull in imitation of Hugo's *Han d'Islande*. But, as Champfleury sagely remarks, many a "Young France" who boasted of drinking punch from a skull really sipped camomile tea from a china cup. Many a dabbler in hyperbolical rhetoric who talked of gripping women as with a gauntlet of steel, of dragging them across the room by the hair, or of holding them tightly clasped through the rhythmic sway of a rapturous waltz, really behaved perfectly properly at a fashionable *raout*, when he faced his blushing partner in the figures of a quadrille. The word "orgy" often meant nothing more than a spree. Yet some young men did yield to evil—and Alfred de Musset is an example of one broken by debauchery— if all did not, as did Gérard de Nerval, end by suicide.

Fortunately for the good name of romanticism its greater representatives were less eccentric. Victor Hugo dressed conventionally and kept his footing in good society. The major lyric poets, Lamartine and often Hugo, moved in a sphere of meditations, harmonies, and contemplations, not of pure bliss, but as if gently borne on the wings of brooding melancholy. To such poets Nature spoke a various language. Some of the themes of the previous age had lingered: autumn and the dying year, the drooping willow,[1] the bells of eventide, dusk, moonlight. To these were added the loneliness not only of Ossian but of René and of Childe Harold and Manfred, so that nature reëchoed by its poetic concordances in forest or running stream the passions of the lonely poet, who sometimes seems consciously to seek a picturesque pose. The ocean sounds in the poetry of Hugo and of Vigny. Nature becomes to some a part of the vast pantheism into which God and men are merged. To Lamartine nature is a hymn to the glory of God, and God is "au fond de la nature". To Alfred de Vigny, on the contrary, nature is harsh and cruel in its eternal and impassive contrast to the fleeting life of man. Yet this vague and indefinite concept of nature and poetry was no less mystifying to the prosaic *bourgeois*, and we can understand the bewilderment of the worthy Dupuis and Cotonet of Alfred de Musset when told by an exalted friend:

> Romanticism is the weeping star, the wailing wind, the quivering night, the flitting flower, the fragrance-bearing bird; it is the upleap of the unexpected, the ecstasy of languor, the cistern under the palm grove, and rosy hope with its thousand loves, the angel and the pearl, the white robe of the willows, oh! the beauty of it, sir! It is the infinite and the starry, the warm, the broken, the disenchanted, and yet at the same time the full and the round, the diametral, the pyramidal, the oriental, the stripped bare, the grasped, the embraced, the eddying; what a new science![2]

If we look for the chief underlying theme of romanticism, it seems to be Melancholy. We have seen what political and social conditions had favored its development, and how Chateau-

---

[1] Musset's tomb in the Père-Lachaise Cemetery, with its funereal verses from *Lucie*, is a good example of the Weeping-Willow School, or *genre saule pleureur*.

[2] For an excellent satire of the themes of romanticism see the extract from *Jérôme Paturot* in the Appendix to this volume.

briand gave it striking literary expression. The *mal de René* and the *mal du siècle* became synonymous with the spirit of world weariness and *taedium vitae*, the useless struggle of the oversensitive soul against the cruelty or harsh indifference of Fate, Fortune, Destiny, Necessity. A self-conscious egoism early manifested itself in the morbid inertia of *Obermann*, the analysis of Benjamin Constant's *Adolphe*. The overwrought and restless sensibility was disturbed by the fever of the infinite ("malgré moi l'infini me tourmente"[1]). With undisciplined ardor and insatiable curiosity of imagination it dwelt on the mystery of nature, death, and the hereafter, the insufficiency of life and love. Self-distrust encouraged the fear of contact with life, fostered caprice, produced misanthropy, as expressed in the words of Didier in Hugo's *Marion Delorme*:

> Je voyageai, je vis les hommes et j'en pris
> En haine quelques-uns et le reste en mépris.
> Si bien que me voici, jeune encore, et pourtant
> Vieux et du monde las comme l'on est en sortant,
> Trouvant le monde mal, mais trouvant l'homme pire.

The descendant of René was, therefore, alone in the world. He yearned for solitude if in a crowd, or he suffered from the moral loneliness of the poet (Vigny's *Stello*), whether the acknowledged leader, as Vigny's Moses, "sad and lonely in his glory", or the unappreciated genius, like the same writer's Chatterton. In contrast with the individual, society is wicked and laws absurd, because they thwart individual pride and the right to happiness: "Man is rarely wrong, the social order always is." George Sand applies these ideas to woman and the laws which thwart the right to happiness, that is, passion. The romanticist could reëcho the verses which Maxime du Camp, in his *Souvenirs*, assigns to his friend Ausone de Chancel:

> On entre, on crie,
> Et c'est la vie!
> On bâille, on sort,
> Et c'est la mort!

[1] Musset.

Characteristic of the romantic soul is preoccupation with God, Nature, Woman, and Death. Consequently, when the mystic pantheism of God and nature failed to console, or when woman was false and treacherous, the romantic soul poured forth on them blame for the existing order. Woman is then not always the "angel with a woman's heart" of *Hernani*. Rather, as in Vigny's *Colère de Samson*, or in Musset's *On ne badine pas avec l'amour*, women are "perfidious, crafty, vain, prying and depraved". Woman could be "sibylline" or "seraphic". She is to the romanticists generally an Angel or a Demon, innocent or steeped in corruption, heartless coquette, faithless courtesan. There is no subtlety of character in either type. Edmond de Goncourt says in *la Faustin* that the woman of 1830 was "une âme et des cheveux". The cruelty of God is railed at, as he veils himself behind the indifference of nature, and the way is paved for religious doubt or denial, whether one meets it stoically, like Vigny, or with the alternating tempestuousness and lassitude of Musset:

> Ma raison révoltée
> Essaie en vain de croire, et mon cœur de douter.
> Le chrétien m'épouvante, et ce que dit l'athée,
> En dépit de mes sens je ne puis l'écouter.
> Les vrais religieux me trouveront impie,
> Et les indifférents me croiront insensé.

Moreover, in anger against the dispensation of an unjust order of things the romantic heart opens itself to the grandeur of the outlaws and outcasts of society: adventurers, criminals, bandits, galley slaves, murderers, courtesans. The sympathy of the romanticists with political rebels helps to explain their sympathy for the *déclassés*, the poor and oppressed. In *Notre-Dame de Paris* the gypsy and the monster are noble, the priest and the nobleman foul. The lackey Ruy Blas is grander than the grandees of Spain. To George Sand an artisan is handsomer than an aristocrat. George Sand's Trenmor and Hugo's Jean Valjean are former convicts whose sufferings have raised them above the plane of humanity. The courtesan Marion Delorme is rehabilitated by love, the *courtisane amoureuse* being one of the great romantic characters. Lasserre calls the title of one of the chapters of *les Misérables*, "La boue, mais l'âme", the formula of romantic psychology. Per contra, the representatives of law and order, from king and minister to judge and policeman, are corrupt and perverse. To George Sand a husband, institution ordained by society, is a tyrant and a brute. Thus we can appreciate why the British matron Mrs. Trollope was so shocked by the novels of George Sand: "Alas! her volumes are closed to the young and innocent, and one may not dare to name her among those to whom the memory clings with gratitude as the giver of high mental enjoyment."

The romantic soul *qua* different and egocentric was Superior. Man might be the ineffective noble being, neurasthenic and Wertherian, too sensitive to fight a cruel world. He might be a poet and die young or commit suicide to escape the platitudes of life. "What a beautiful spot for a suicide", said Musset when staying at his friend Guttinguer's villa between Honfleur and Trouville. The adolescent poet Escousse and his friend Lebras committed suicide in 1832 by the fumes of charcoal, and the former left word: "Escousse killed himself because he did not feel in his place here below, because strength was wanting to him."

On the other hand, the romantic superior soul might be the perverse, impetuous spirit, the disciple of Byron, living over the wild legends of profligacy and of war against society told of the great rebel; or he might be the superman, incarnating power, like Napoleon. In the specimens of these types violence of passion often went with a strange inhibition of the will.

The romantic superior soul might be the elect of God, even though unappreciated, or he might be, on the other hand, one of that numerous class of romantic heroes, the *maudits*, like Hernani, living and dying under a blind and mysterious curse, "chargé d'anathème", with "a soul of misfortune built of blackness". The romantic hero, in spite of his superiority and his contempt for mankind, was no intelligent hewer of his destiny, but was, like Hernani, an "agent aveugle et sourd de mystères funèbres". The superior woman too suffered from being different, whether, as with Corinne, from the injustice of caste, or, as with the *femme incomprise* of George Sand, from the tyranny of marriage laws which thwarted her right to happiness.

Love, above all, it was futile to resist. Love was the great experience. Musset wrote: "We are often deceived in love, often wounded and often unhappy; but we love, and when, at the edge of the grave, we turn to look backwards we say: I have often suffered, I have sometimes made a mistake, but I have loved."

Love in its mildest form, *virginibus puerisque*, a concession to the *bourgeois* and the *ingénue* with downcast eyes and wasp-like waist, was still that of "keepsakes" and "albums", or of the silken ladders, masks, and satin cloaks of those *petites oies blanches* of romanticism, the Ninon and Ninette of *A quoi rêvent les jeunes filles*:

> Le père ouvre la porte au matériel époux,
> Mais toujours l'idéal entre par la fenêtre.

Or it might be the innocence of Goethe's Marguerite, that—

> —charme innocent dont rien ne se défend,
> Qui fis hésiter Faust au seuil de Marguerite.

At the theater the operetta entranced the eye with visions of lakes and castles, of brigands in the land of orange and pomegranate blossom; and the maiden dreamed of taking with her lover-husband the conventional journey to Italy, though with George Sand and Musset it could be unconventional enough.[1]

---

[1] From 1800 to 1855 the lure of Italy is omnipresent and the *voyage en Italie* was the dream of those who could afford more than the *voyage à Dieppe* (see the amusing comedy, *le Voyage à Dieppe*, of Wafflard and Fulgence). Chateaubriand, Mme de Staël, Stendhal, Lamartine, and Musset all testify to the vogue of Italy. Italian composers, Rossini and Donizetti, and Italian singers, Pasta and Grisi, were favorites, and the Italian opera was permanently established in Paris through most of the century. Italy was the background of the librettos of French writers, like Scribe, and before the eyes of the theater-goer were spread the Italian lakes, the mountain fastnesses of the Apennines, or the bay of Naples (*la Muette de Portici*).

ROMANTIC THEMES

The ear was lulled by songs of pretty, amorous feeling or humorous sentiment, and the gentle melodies or *flonflons* of composers like Boieldieu (*la Dame blanche*), Adolphe Adam (*le Châlet, le Postillon de Longjumeau*), and Auber (*le Domino noir, Fra Diavolo*).

On the other hand, to the Lamartinian, love was a fleeting moment of chaste happiness, over which hung the shadow of early death with its eternal parting, so that to the lonely wanderer among scenes of the past, in marble halls or lowly cottage, amid the solitude of rocks, forests, and lakes, all that remains is Memory.

Finally, to the more violent romanticists love was the blind yielding to instinct, at times admitted to be *volupté*, at times called "God" or "Fate". Love might be the never-attained, for which life was the constant quest, through its bitter experiences and deceptions. Love purified passion of its grossness and made it a virtuous emotion. The sexual passion, veiled in lyric periphrasis, was sanctified as a mystic communion of mind and heart, to which it was right to yield in spite of conventions and obstacles. Love was violent and tempestuous; love was instantaneous, overwhelming, and unavoidable (*fatal, inéluctable*). Woman is not expected to be strong enough to resist: in Roger de Beauvoir's *Ecolier de Cluny* woman embraces with "an extraordinary mixture of abandonment and of suffering, of lascivious joy and of frenzy". Woman was supposed to want to be brutalized, and not loved, as it is said in *Antony*, "as one loves a stock-broker" (*agent de change*). Love and orgy went together, and virtue was no longer, as with Corneille, the result of a conflict of love and duty, but the conjunction of passion and pride. Poets, novelists, social philosophers deified love. Saint-Simon proclaimed its divine origin; Fourier emphasized the satisfaction of the passions, including fickle love or "butterfly" attraction (*la papillonne*); George Sand popularized the idea in fiction. Love to Hugo sanctifies even the courtesan: "Ton amour m'a refait une virginité." To Musset love itself is the great thing, and he takes a morbid pleasure in the sufferings of desire:

> O muse! Que m'importe ou la mort ou la vie?
> J'aime et je veux pâlir; j'aime et je veux souffrir;
> J'aime et pour un baiser je donne mon génie;
> J'aime et je veux sentir sur ma joue amaigrie
> Ruisseler une source impossible à tarir.

Finally, to Musset, love, though veiled by words of poetry, becomes scarcely distinguishable from lust:

> Aimer est le grand point, qu'importe la maîtresse?
> Qu'importe le flacon, pourvu qu'on ait l'ivresse?

Needless to say, love thus made the sole aim became torture rather than happiness. In literature and in life, reason was banished and love was subject to all the emotional stimuli and reflexes: unsatisfied desire, convulsive jealousy, bitter memories, distrust and suspicion, the nausea of satiety, the horror of old age and decay,—*exaltations, délires, repentirs, désespoirs*. We need not be surprised if all this went counter to the *morale des épiciers*, that Mrs. Trollope was shocked by romantic literature and makes the following prophecy concerning Hugo's plays:

> The startling, bold and stirring incidents of his disgusting dramas must and will excite a certain degree of attention when seen for the first time, and it is evidently the interest of managers to bring forward whatever is most likely to produce this effect; but the doing so cannot but be quoted as a proof of the systematic degradation of the theatre. It is moreover a fact, which the playbills themselves are alone sufficient to attest, that after Victor Hugo's plays have had their first run, they are never brought forward again: not one of them has yet become what we call a stock play.

The most superior romantic spirit was the Poet himself. Lyricism was the greatest literary *genre*, and as Napoleon had been the leader in war, the poet was to be the leader of peace. Hence the poet has the traits of the Prophet, or *vates*, and is the successor of Homer or Ossian. We witness a development which, though independent and of a different origin, seems somewhat like the glorification of the poet and of the rôle of poesy by Ronsard and the Platonists of the sixteenth century. Sometimes, as with Vigny, the poet is lonely, misunderstood by ordinary men, even the victim of heaven which places him outside and above mankind, *puissant et solitaire*, in spite of his love for the *majesté des souffrances humaines*:

> Les animaux lâches vont en troupe.
> Le lion marche seul dans le désert ;
> Qu'ainsi marche toujours le poète.

Like the soldier, stoical servant of duty, he suffers from neglect and lack of appreciation. At times, like Lamartine, the poet abandons poetry and goes into politics to save the world. To the hierophantic Hugo the poet has a *mission sociale*; he has *charge d'âmes*. To Musset, heedless of social reform and centered on his own sufferings, the poet serving humanity at the feast with song is like the pelican dying to feed its young.

CHAPTER X

ROMANTIC THEMES AND TYPES (Continued).
ROMANTIC ART

IF WE try now to review some of the themes of romanticism as seen, not all simultaneously, under the Restoration and the Monarchy of July, we find especially intellectual and moral suffering, the "volupté des larmes", lonely reverie, the unison or dissonance of the soul with nature. The hero is the ardent and aspiring being in rebellion, or the spirit of weary and melancholy renunciation.

The Consumptive School continues for some time. Poets still love ethereal women by moonlight, or die wasted by disease. With Sainte-Beuve's *Joseph Delorme* it even becomes middle-class. The poetry of phthisis and despair connected with this "Werther jacobin et carabin", this "René des faubourgs", no longer shows the elegant *poitrinaire*, but is more akin to the *bourgeois* of 1830 and the world of Béranger.

Sainte-Beuve's *Joseph Delorme* brings to mind incidentally the *genre intime*, the poetry of familiar and domestic life, of realism rather than of the extraordinary. It was to some degree influenced by English writers, Cowper, Crabbe, Wordsworth and the Lake School, and did not have the vogue of the more obstreperous forms.

With Nodier come the types known as the *genre macabre* and *frénétique*, tending to replace the sentimental ballad, or *romance*; and then the *genre fantastique* and supernatural. Nodier condemned "frenzied" literature, but he practiced it, and he was responsible for much of the riotous recklessness (*dévergondage*) of what is sometimes called the *bas romantisme*.

The *genre frénétique* dealt with visions of mystery and horror, and, as the *genre cadavre* and *littérature squelette*, it later reached a climax in Baudelaire's horrid *Charogne*. In earlier days it was sometimes within the realm of the actually possible though improbable, sometimes in that of grotesque and hybrid supernatural creations, of ghosts, specters, and devils. Nodier's *Jean Sbogar* is an example of the mystery tale, in which the fair Antonia discovers the brigand Jean Sbogar led to execution to be her lover Lothario. Nodier helped to develop the literature of Vampires, and of Nightmares, and of Insanity. Lunatics are not always to be pitied, but even sometimes to be envied as elect; for their mad visions may be truer than the cold reasonings of sense, and are in fact Illumination, as in the Middle Ages the idiot was blessed.

The *genre fantastique*, of which a good early specimen is Nodier's *Trilby*, dealt much with the fears and superstitions of night and solitude, with fairies, imps, and hobgoblins, with water sprites and sylphs, and verged on the legends of popular folklore.

These two forms were helped by foreign influences, the mysteries of the English School of Terror, the topsy-turvydom of Jean-Paul Richter and of Hoffmann in Germany. The *Lenore* of Bürger, with its ghostly ride to death, and Byron's *Mazeppa* popularized the theme of the *chevauchée*, or headlong course. So we can understand how the merging of the frenzied and the fantastic help to account for the concrete form taken by the grotesque, opposed to the sublime, as one of the two great elements of life and nature in Hugo's mind, prone to antithesis and dichotomy, and why we find concrete specimens in the *Odes et Ballades*, and why the preface of *Cromwell* speaks of "vampires, ogres, erl-kings, psylles, ghouls, brucolaques, aspioles".[1]

[1] In the first letter of *Dupuis et Cotonet* Musset says: "The Germans have composed ballads and we do the same; 'tis well. They love spectres, gnomes, ghouls, psylles, vampires, skeletons, ogres, nightmares, rats, aspioles, vipers, witches, the sabbath, Satan, Puck, mandragora. After all it pleases them. We imitate them and say the same thing, although it diverts us little, but I am willing."

The *genre personnel*, often a literature of self-exhibition, a term which, indeed, might be applied to a large part of the romantic writings, shows itself in subjective, lyrical, or semi-autobiographical, occasionally psychological fiction, *Raphaël, Graziella, la Confession d'un enfant du siècle*. Sometimes the subjective and lyrical form passes from egoism to sympathy and results in the *roman social*, as in some of the novels of George Sand or in *les Misérables*, on the wrongs of those who suffer from *bourgeois* selfishness. Transferred to poetry, the chief outlet for lyricism, it results in the great works of Lamartine, Vigny, and Hugo, the Spiritual School, or, on the other hand, in the rebellious Satanic School.

The *genre spiritualiste* was apt to be contemplative, religious, or, in the wake of Goethe, philosophical. As the Seraphic or Angelic School it continued the traditions of Chateaubriand, of English poets like Milton or Moore (*Loves of the Angels*), and of the German Klopstock. It touched sometimes on religious consolation, as in Lamartine, to whom even man is "un dieu tombé qui se souvient des cieux"; sometimes on divine cruelty, as in Vigny, that angel, as Sainte-Beuve said, who had drunk gall and vinegar.[1] It dwelt often on the fallen angel who has met evil fate, less by pride than by sympathy or compassion. It occasionally skirted the Satanic School when, as in *Eloa*, the angel falls through pity for Lucifer himself, or when Satan was considered a fallen angel suffering in the moral hell of being able neither to love nor to be loved. Spiritual poetry in its minor keys was the favorite mode of expression for the semi-religious meditations of amiable and tearful minor poetesses or "tenth muses", sometimes local glories (*muses départementales*), sweet singers on the harp or the lyre. Indeed, the Muse of early romanticism, at least, was half woman, half angel.

The Satanic School is one of the most characteristic tendencies, and the one which, as we have already seen, the young romanticists tried to transfer to real life. The gloomy writers

[1] *Nouveaux lundis*, Vol. VI, p. 428. Not so comic and unexpected a comparison as might be supposed. See above, p. 102, for the women who drank vinegar.

were no longer satisfied with Ossian, who reminded them of the Empire literature. Werther, in time Faust, and then Byron took his place, and the old-fashioned *homme sensible* died. The men of the twenties humored their melancholy with the picturesqueness of the gray-bearded Faust, his musty folios and alchemist's retorts, and the satiety of his fruitless endeavors to solve the riddle of the universe. With Faust came Satan, or Mephistopheles, and his sarcasm, or a satanic character, spirit of evil, often presented by the livelier French as a virtuoso of naughtiness. The visit to Paris in 1827 of the Shakespearean actors made the tragic figure of Hamlet again vivid, and the French wept over the sad fate of Ophelia and Juliet. The days of Werther, Faust, and Shakespeare were those of solitude, despair, and suicide.

Meanwhile the influence of Byron grew rapidly, until he overshadowed Shakespeare. Werther and Ossian in particular faded away before the greater violence of Byronism reënforced by Faust. By 1830 and after, the satanism of Mephistopheles was joined by the cynicism of Don Juan. For about fifteen years, roughly from 1820 to 1835, Byron was the supreme influence of the Satanic School. Manfred, Lara, the Corsair, Childe Harold, the Giaour, and Don Juan were the great models:

> Ressembler à Manfred! oh! la joie enivrante!
> Avoir la bouche amère et le front soucieux,
> Ignorer à jamais l'espérance riante,
> Et se sentir maudit! Et blasphémer les cieux![1]

The Byronic Satanist is the brother of Napoleon as the incarnation of the Superior Man. But he is not necessarily the hero of achievement; he may be the protype of the *homme fatal* and the *maudit*, prone to suffer from the English disease, *le spleen*. Like Byron or his heroes he might be a somber pilgrim through an outworn civilization, a fierce pirate on the stormy sea, or a lonely wanderer amid crags and precipices. He was a

---

[1] Quoted by Maigron, *le Romantisme et la mode*, p. 179, from an obscure but typical poet, François Roussel.

man of mystery, proud and scornful, passing with gloomy but flashing eye through the world, yet having no contact with it, brooding in lonely places over some terrible secret, the foe of a mankind which is in some way responsible for his plight and considers him evil because his life runs counter to its vulgar ideas.

The general atmosphere of revolt in literature and life, even in politics and conspiracies, was typified by the name of Byron. Balzac, in the *Peau de chagrin*, speaks of the "little Lord Byrons, who after having rumpled their lives like a napkin after dinner, have nothing left to do but to set their country on fire, blow out their brains, conspire for the republic, or call for war."

The vogue of Byron passed with that of the Romantic School, but Satanism, as a form of mystical religiosity mixed with debauchery, lingered on through Baudelaire to men like Verlaine, Huysmans, and the late nineteenth-century decadents. Barbey d'Aurevilly, in his *Diaboliques*, portrayed the satanism of vampire women.

A lighter form of late romanticism was seen when some writers like Théophile Gautier, not devoid of a sense of humor, realized and expressed the comic side of the romantic extravagance. This is designated as the *genre fantaisiste*, marked by irony, extravagant exuberance, and good-natured caricature, as in Gautier's *Jeunes-France*.

Exoticism and Medievalism are not so much separate *genres* as forms of local coloring which serve as the accompaniment or background of literature. Exoticism had been inherited from Bernardin de Saint-Pierre and Chateaubriand and their descriptions of nature. Chateaubriand's *Itinéraire de Paris à Jérusalem* was an example for Byron, Gérard de Nerval, and Lamartine. Literary exoticism was helped by the writings of Nodier, and the death of Byron drew attention to Greece and the Orient. Fauriel's *Chants populaires de la Grèce moderne*, in 1821, made people think the palikars as brave and as primitive as the Highlanders and heroes of Ossian. Local coloring in poetry replaced the old descriptions in general terms. Hugo's

THE RAFT OF THE SHIPWRECKED *MEDUSA*, BY GÉRICAULT (*LOUVRE*)

early lyrics, the *Odes et Ballades* and the *Orientales*, brought in not only medievalism but bookish Orientalism, an *orient de pacotille*. Poetry and prose became full of geographical names, of brigands, palikars, and bedouins, of Italian lakes and castles on the Rhine, of gondolas, moonlight serenades, mandolins, guitars, stilettos, Toledo rapiers, camels, oranges, lemons, pomegranates, and the miscellaneous accompaniments of adventure and romance.[1]

In romantic fiction and drama, especially the historical novel and play, medievalism was very popular. Two works of great importance for the study of medievalism are the *Génie du christianisme* and *Notre-Dame de Paris*. But between Chateaubriand and Hugo a foreign influence of tremendous importance, Scott, had come into play. Victor Hugo himself wrote in 1819, in the *Conservateur littéraire*, that among a certain class of readers Scott was beginning to share the vogue of Ducray-Duminil! The concreteness of Scott's descriptions, the vividness of his conversations, as contrasted with the ponderous style and indirect discourse then in fashion, had a great effect. The success of *Ivanhoe* and of *Quentin Durward* gave reality to the Middle Ages and to the fifteenth century. Moreover, the sixteenth century was often considered the end of the Middle Ages rather than the beginning of modern times. But it was not long before the fondness for external descriptions and for bric-a-brac made the natural portraiture of manners and of incident drop into the background. Novels, including and after *Notre-Dame*, lack verisimilitude. They are melodramatic, sensational, and overdrawn, and degenerate often into accounts of orgies and of debauchery. Hugo shows some restraint in *Notre-Dame*, yet outdoes himself in endeavors to personify the cathedral and to

[1] "It was all loves, lovers, loved ones, persecuted ladies fainting in lonely pavilions, postilions done to death at every relay, horses broken down on every page, somber forests, heart pangs, vows, sobs, tears and kisses, skiffs in the moonlight, nightingales in the thickets, gentlemen brave as lions, gentle as lambs, virtuous beyond all possibility, always well dressed and weeping pitcherfuls" (*pleurant comme des urnes*).—FLAUBERT, *Madame Bovary*, chap. vi

resuscitate fifteenth-century Paris in architectural and topographical detail. The novels of Dumas bear the stamp of a powerful imagination; but in his melodrama the *Tour de Nesle*, in the stories of Paul Lacroix, or in the *Ecolier de Cluny* of Roger de Beauvoir (source of the *Tour de Nesle*), the characters rarely speak without ejaculating *mort et damnation*, or *enfer et*

VIRGIL AND DANTE, BY DELACROIX (LOUVRE)
Romantic art

malédiction, or *par la carcasse de Satan*, and the ordinary incidents of the day are murder, rape, torture, adultery, and incest. This appealed in particular to the sportive taste of the *Jeunes-France*. The action of romantic novel and drama takes place near gloomy castle walls, among subterranean crypts, secret doors, dark corridors, and hiding-places where lurk mysterious figures in somber array.

Among the favorite types of the romantic period first place must be given to the *homme fatal*. He is a handsome posturing

hero to whom women are drawn, whether they will it or no, as
Doña Sol or Graziella. He is usually high-strung and supersensitive, a *jaloux ténébreux*, swaying rapidly from passionate
adoration to jealous suspicion and back again. He is not necessarily a libertine and profligate, unless it be, like Musset's Rolla,
as one weary of bearing the burden of the *mal du siècle*, and
blasé as a result of having exhausted life's hollow pleasures.
This was the style cultivated by the lions and dandies. He is
apt to be, like Hernani or the Count of Monte-Cristo, a man of
mystery, about whose past there lurks some dread secret, which
has put his life out of joint; or it may be that, as with Vigny's
Chatterton, the fatal gift of poetic genius, or of superiority in
general, brings with it misfortune and unhappiness. For the
romantic hero is usually a *maudit*, the embodiment of Byronic
satanism, suffering from the somber spirit of evil which has
burdened his life and keeps him from ever hoping for happiness.
Sometimes he bears the curse of being a foundling, like Didier
("j'ignore d'où je viens et j'ignore où je vais"); or a bastard,
like Antony; or a lackey, like Ruy Blas ("ver de terre amoureux
d'une étoile"), victim of man's injustice as a social *déshérité*,
and in each case ennobled by the very unrighteousness of fate.

For the romantic hero may be an Outlaw, whether the haughty
rebel against society, the noble brigand influenced by Goethe's
Goetz von Berlichingen or Schiller's Karl Moor,[1] or the wonderful bandit of strange adventure, able to pass from place to place
as though on a magic carpet. People have forgotten today the
effect of the once highly popular romance of *Rinaldo Rinaldini*,
the captain of banditti, by Goethe's brother-in-law Vulpius. It
is one more example of worthless literature contributing to the
development of the most important literary fashions. The composer Berlioz yearned to be a brigand, to live amid scenes of
rape and murder, and sleep upon a bed of lava cradled by
earthquakes: "Et allons donc, voilà la vie!"

Sometimes the outlaw was the Byronic Corsair, like the seduc-

[1] The anticipated history of the Revolutions about to overflow Europe was
entirely in Karl Moor and in Werther.—NODIER, *Des types en littérature*

tive and Don Juanesque Zampa, of the widely popular opera of that name. An important literary, artistic, and society periodical was called *le Corsaire*. Dumas gives to the pirate hero of one of his dramas, a French romantic bastard, the name of the American privateer Paul Jones. Even Balzac wrote in his youth *Argow le pirate*, and introduced into *la Femme de trente ans* the episode of the corsair Victor, "a man whose soul is as vast as this sea is boundless, as abundant in gentleness as the heavens, a god, in short!" On deck "the thunder of his voice often overpowers the raging tempest or the tumult of battle", but to the woman he loves it is "sweet and melodious as the music of Rossini". In the novels of George Sand the hero may be the noble Proletarian, victorious over privilege and caste, who marries the maiden of high lineage. Balzac, Hugo, Sue, Soulié, and others show the romantic Criminal wronged by society. Dumas's Antony is the social outlaw, the satanic rebel, the emblem of revolt typified by bastardy and passion.

Opposite the hero, by the law of contrasts dear to the romanticist, stood the Monster, physical or moral. He might be the freak of nature, such as Han d'Islande, Quasimodo, or Triboulet, or the embodiment of evil, like Don Salluste in *Ruy Blas*, Marguerite de Bourgogne in *la Tour de Nesle*, and Thénardier in *les Misérables*, or the stark incarnation of the harsh rigidity of law, Inspector Javert. He might be a literary descendant of such works as *les Victimes cloîtrées*[1] or of Lewis's *Monk*, the priest faithless to his vows, or the lecherous monk, as Hugo's Claude Frollo, or the priest Magnus in George Sand's *Lélia*. He could then suggest to the political opposition the "infamous" *Congrégation* or the Jesuits, and was in contrast with characters like Chateaubriand's good Father Aubry. Often, in Hugo at least, by a further subdivision of the law of contrasts, physical or moral monstrosity is redeemed by a noble quality. In the melodrama the villain is as essential as the hero.

If, for further detail concerning the types just described, we

---

[1] Cf. supra, p. 45.

seek concrete illustrations, we can find them in the vicomte d'Arlincourt's *le Solitaire,* in Dumas's *Antony,* in the melodrama, and in romantic drama as a whole.

The *Solitaire* was first published in 1821, and therefore precedes *Notre-Dame* by nearly a decade. The book is almost totally forgotten today, but it had an extraordinary vogue and well represents the romantic fiction that made general appeal before Hugo's novel caused all subsequent historical romance to follow in its wake. It is safe, also, to assert that, though the resemblances are of general effect rather than of detail, yet *Hernani* would not be what it is without *le Solitaire.*[1] The spirit is one of medievalism and of Byronism, with a dash of René in the hero, written in a pseudo-poetic style, a sorry reminiscence of *Atala* and the *Martyrs.* The mysterious *solitaire* is the duke of Burgundy, Charles the Bold, who did not really perish in battle, as was supposed, but led a hermit's life on the lonely Mont Sauvage, devoting himself to kindly deeds. He wins the love of the beautiful Elodie,[2] but heavy sin weighs on

[1] "Mon délire t'épouvante, ajoute-t-il, Elodie, ne cherche point à comprendre l'homme de la fatalité; contente-toi de le repousser. Ange de la terre! à l'imitation des esprits du Ciel, ferme-moi l'entrée de ta demeure."—*Le Solitaire,* Vol. I, Bk. vi. Cf. *Hernani,* Act III, Sc. iv:

> Cependant à l'entour de ma course farouche,
> Tout se brise, tout meurt. Malheur à qui me touche!
> Oh! fuis! détourne-toi de mon chemin fatal,
> Hélas! sans le vouloir, je te ferais du mal!

"Adieu, lueur consolatrice du repentir et de la douleur! Fleur virginale dont un instant j'ai respiré le parfum céleste, mais dont mon souffle du moins n'a point souillé la pureté! Douce apparition des régions divines! Espérance, amour, et bonheur . . . adieu!"—*Le Solitaire,* Vol. II, Bk. xi. Cf. *Hernani,* Act II, Sc. iv:

> Ah! ce serait un crime
> Que d'arracher la fleur en tombant dans l'abîme.
> Va, j'en ai respiré le parfum, c'est assez!
> Renoue à d'autres jours tes jours par moi froissés.
> Epouse ce vieillard. C'est moi qui te délie.
> Je rentre dans ma nuit. Toi, sois heureuse, oublie!

There are many passages of this general similarity.

[2] Elodie became a favorite girl's name, with Corinne, Malvina, and Mathilde.

his life. The priest summoned to wed them knows the secret of the past, Elodie dies, crushed by the curse which he calls down upon the marriage, and the *solitaire* expires upon her grave. In appearance this hero is like a tall cedar of Lebanon; his limbs are muscular as those of Hercules; his voice in repose is like that of Orpheus, but as it rises in wrath it seems the blast of a tempest, and his glare is that of a conflagration.

Dumas by his drama *Antony* clothed the romantic hero in ordinary costume. He set a model for the satanic dandy and lion, and made "Antonism" a social as well as a literary phenomenon. Bocage, the Byronic actor, tall, pale, and handsome, gave him an individual appearance. Antony was the bastard, cut off from family and society; but before the vogue of the play had passed he was the hero, and, as Gautier facetiously wrote in the preface of the *Jeunes-France*: "I really only lack being a bastard to be perfect." Antony is the magnificent rebel against a philistine world,—one to whose charm women fatally yield, posturing with panting bosom, sombre looks, sarcastic laugh, and curses against fate.

The form which can, as profitably as any, be taken for the broad interpretation of popular literary appreciation is the melodrama. This *genre* afforded entertainment and delight both to the *bourgeoisie* and to the working classes ("vive le mélodrame où Margot a pleuré", says Musset), and it is one of the important sources of the lyrical romantic drama which we connect with Victor Hugo. Moreover, its vogue, with modifications, has lasted as an entertainment for the multitude to the present. The most popular of melodramas in early days was probably Dumas's *Tour de Nesle*, but Pixerécourt was the most significant creator. Pixerécourt, Ducange, and Caigniez were the deities of the *boulevard du Crime*, as that part of Paris was called where the theaters devoted to melodrama were chiefly situated.

The melodrama catered primarily to the taste of audiences lacking intellectual subtlety, to whom violent emotions and startling climaxes were necessary. Even Berlioz preferred

Ducange's *Trente ans, ou la vie d'un joueur* to *Hernani*. Tears and laughter were juxtaposed as clumsily as Hugo contrasted the tragic and the grotesque. Moreover, the laws of collective plebeian morality demanded the reward of virtue and the chastisement of vice. The hero was absolutely good and the villain absolutely bad. The language of the melodrama was full of stereotyped phrases deemed expressive of dignified and noble "sensibility". The *cloches du soir* and the *voix de la nature* struck responsive chords, and "Virtuous Woman", "Respectable Old Man", "Vile Seducer", "Inhuman Monster", were the recognized vocatives.

Consequently the action of the melodrama had to be gripping in its intensity, full of incident, and startling by unexpected, hence usually improbable, solutions. The play was full of extraordinary coincidences and experiences; victims thrown to death down precipices were miraculously saved by a tree or a shrub, and a character for whose sad fate the audience had wept reappeared, safe and sound, in the last act. If there were no easier way to bring lost kindred together, then spoke the *voix du sang*, as effectively as a strawberry mark, or a treasured article of children's clothing, or "la croix de ma mère"[1]. The memory of the scenes of bloodshed of the Revolution and Empire, and the influence of the turgid School of Terror, popularized scenes of ferocity. The melodrama was full of robbers, brigands, conspirators, corpses, prisons, poisons, counterpoisons, and daggers; mysterious crypts, caves, and forests to hide in; abductions, fires, and thefts of birth certificates, wills, and deeds of bequest. The types of character were four in number: the noble and upright hero, champion of persecuted innocence; the beautiful and virtuous heroine; the villain, tyrant, or traitor; and the comic *rôle* of simpleton or jester. Under the Restoration and the Monarchy of July the seducer or villain was apt, as a recollection of the old régime, to be an aristocrat,—

---

[1] Cf. the "sabre de mon père", the catch song of Offenbach's famous *opéra-bouffe* of the Second Empire, the *Grande duchesse de Gérolstein*, one of the great sensations of the exposition year, 1867.

wicked count or licentious marquis. Says Thackeray, in his *Paris Sketch-Book*, which helps us to understand the times:

The aristocracy is dead now; but the theatre lives on traditions: and don't let us be too scornful at such legends as are handed down by the people from race to race. Vulgar prejudice it may be; but prejudice against the great is only a rude expression of sympathy with the poor; long, therefore, may fat *épiciers* blubber over mimic woes, and honest *prolétaires* shake their fists, shouting—"Gredin, scélérat, monstre de marquis!" and such republican cries.

The hero was perfect bravery and daring. As in the other literary forms of corresponding chronology, he might be the noble bandit in rebellion against society, the proletarian oppressed by injustice, or sometimes the Child of Nature. In this case the innocent, virtuous, generous, and upright negro might be contrasted with the sordid and corrupt white man.[1]

After 1830 the melodrama was used a great deal as a means of democratic propaganda, and the plots were more often than before drawn from city life. At the same time, though Pixerécourt, who disliked the romantic school, and Hugo, who prided himself on his originality, would have denied it, the romantic drama became a glorified melodrama. It used the characters and the devices of the melodrama. Finally, as one looks over the course of years, among countless forgotten melodramas in addition to those mentioned such outstanding titles as the *Closerie des Genêts*, *Marceau, ou les enfants de la république*, with its Revolutionary pageantry, the *Courrier de Lyon*, the *Nuits de la Seine*, the *Deux orphelines*, and the *Deux gosses* all show how the tradition of the melodrama, in spite of modification, has remained popular to this day.

The Restoration and the Monarchy of July were active periods in art and music, both of which would naturally be important in the emotional age of romanticism. In painting, the same rivalry as in literature manifests itself between the

---

[1] Contrast the noble or innocent savage of such works as Florian's *Sélico* (1792), Mme de Duras's *Ourika*, and Lamartine's *Toussaint Louverture* (1850) with the brutality of René Maran's *Batouala* (1921), written by a negro.

THE DEATH OF QUEEN ELIZABETH, BY DELAROCHE (LOUVRE)
Pictorial art of simple anecdote and romantic setting to please the popular taste

classicists and the revolutionaries. The classical group continued the traditions of the Davidian set, and it had the support of conventional and official organizations, like the Institute, which awarded prizes. It emphasized theories of abstract beauty revealed by reason in plastic form with finished outline, to the neglect of color and passion. Its technique resolved itself into correctly drawn platitudes, dull and monotonous in rendering. The most-rewarded disciples of this school were the docile mediocrities, and the school of David seemed very anæmic to those who thought of the storms of the Revolution and the Empire.

The consequence was that the revolutionaries were as much free lances as the young literary romanticists. They appeared no less daring to the conservatives than the others, and they were in some ways even more unconventional in language and behaviour. The writers were often men of good families, whereas the painters were frequently of humble origin, scorned by the prosperous *bourgeois*. The *rapin* repaid the scorn and took supreme delight in shocking his enemy, with the more gusto that he had so little social prestige of his own to injure. To many *bourgeois* romanticism in art was even worse than in literature, being connected with studio pranks and practical jokes.

Therefore the romanticists were united at least in their common assault on the enemy. Individually they proclaimed the right to absolute freedom in art, and the blessings of unconventionality. They demanded, as opposed to the official creed, life, color, character, action, and passion. Thus the battle cries, or rather the war whoops, of the romanticists in art had an analogy with those of the *cénacles*, though the two groups often worked out their ends in different ways.

The object of art became, therefore, an end in itself, art for art's sake, and its field became much broader. The romanticists emphasized color and "expression" as opposed to form and abstract beauty. Any subject was legitimate, even (especially) the terrible and harrowing. The romanticists cultivated the emotional and picturesque by effects of light and movement, complexity of lines and masses, brilliant and noisy coloring, as opposed to the dullness of the Institute. Their art was pictorial instead of statuesque. All this, they said, meant greater truth, fancy, originality.

As to subjects, the romanticists, in order to get as far from the Davidians as possible, avoided antiquity, except mythology. They practiced at first the sentimental groups and figures of the *genre troubadour*; then religious and historical subjects; Italian and exotic scenes, including a factitious Orientalism, where a nude female figure might be surrounded by a few Eastern draperies and called an odalisque; anecdotes; borrowings from literature and authors such as Dante, Shakespeare, Scott, Goethe, or French writers themselves. At the *Salon* of 1831 alone Heine counted over thirty subjects drawn from Scott. As might be expected, the Middle Ages were an abundant source of inspiration. Medievalism was as fashionable in art as in literature and elsewhere. Those were the days of interest in the restoration of ancient monuments, when the founder of the Cluny Museum was making his wonderful collections, when modern architecture was reverting to turrets and moldings, when illustrations and vignettes in books were surrounded by pseudo-medieval fretwork frames with canopies and niches. In consequence local color took the form of emphasis on costume, and on furniture and bric-a-brac, for the setting.

It has been almost hackneyed to call the famous picture of the *Raft of the Medusa*, representing the exhausted and dying survivors of a shipwreck, which Géricault exhibited at the *Salon* of 1819, the first striking example of revolutionary romanticism. But this painting, violent and distressing, should perhaps be regarded only as a step away from academism in the direction of realism. A more genuine incarnation of the feverishness of romantic art is to be found in the works of Delacroix, the great enemy and scornful rival of "Monsieur" Ingres, the latter an artist whose place is the subject of discussion.

Ingres has been called both a romanticist and a classicist. As a matter of fact, he was a revolutionary in that he enlarged the scope of selection for artistic themes and sought greater truth and sincerity of expression. On the other hand, he was so persistently an advocate of the doctrine of perfect form as outline and contour, that in time his critics called him a reactionary classicist and heir to the traditions of David. In the rivalry of *form* versus *color* we find the explanation of the antagonism between Ingres and Delacroix.

Delacroix has been called the incarnation of romanticism in art. He was in technique a colorist and an emotionalist, even at the risk of allowing dislocation or disproportion in the anatomy of his figures, when he thought it necessary for emphasis. Hence he was termed a lyrical painter and the artist of "visions", and was the object of the loathing of Ingres. He had a distaste for doctrines of conventional Beauty, though in life he was as methodical as Hugo, and his theory taught the yielding to originality and personal emotion. His pictures were startling by their portrayal of passionate action and violent gesture. He cultivated the melancholy, the somber, and the terrible; he painted a succession of shocks to the academics, and, as Théophile Gautier said of his *Massacre of Scio* in 1824, made the classical *perruques* stand on end. The *Salon* of 1824 marks a great date in the history of romantic art.

Under the Monarchy of July the condition of art was chaotic, owing to the bitter rivalry between Institute art and the romanticists. Moreover, the growth of socialistic and humanitarian discussion made some people cease to consider art as the expression of a static ideal, or the end in itself of art for art's sake, but to seek through art realism, or at any rate an expression comprehensible to the vast middle classes.

Paul Delaroche was, under these conditions, the popular painter. His "tableaux vivants" or historical anecdotes pleased the *bourgeoisie*, who liked an easy story. At the same time, his subjects were drawn from sources dear to the romanticists and had the restlessness and the rich coloring which pleased them. He liked to present dramatic death scenes, the death of Queen Elizabeth, the children in the Tower, the execution of Lady Jane Grey,—so much so that Heine described him as the "painter-in-ordinary to decapitated majesties". His popularity was helped by the fact that he was an assiduous exhibitor in the annual *Salons*, so that the conventional connoisseurs of the Institute were no longer judges without appeal. Delaroche was really painter-in-ordinary to the *juste milieu*.

The growth of prosperity under Louis-Philippe, and the mediocre ability needed for the appreciation of a pictorial anecdote, encouraged on the one hand abundant portraits of self-satisfied *bourgeois* and their families, and on the other hand scenes of *genre*, neither portrait, scenery, nor commemorative historical painting. These pictorial equivalents to the intellectual standard of vaudevilles and melodramas ranged from what Mme de Girardin described as "lodging-house art" (*gravures d'hôtel garni*), such as *Modestie*, or *Rêverie*, or *Sensibilité*, or *Abandon*, to moral paintings, each telling its own tale to the philistines, or to picturesque fantasies of costume and bric-a-brac for the bold. Finally, Louis-Philippe's gigantic historical picture gallery at restored Versailles catered to the martial ardors of the citizen soldiery, and Horace Vernet recorded the looting of the treasures of an Algerian chieftain as though it were a victory by Napoleon.

The use of art for the presentation of pictorial anecdotes was helped by the vogue of lithography and of wood engraving. The ultraromantic illustrators delighted in fantastic and lugubrious scenes, with witches, devils, skeletons, and gargoyles. Again, an attempt on the part of the artists to portray life resulted in conventionalized types of men with long hair, pointed beards, scowling brows, sharp noses, and high cheek bones. The drawing-room satanists tried to dress this rôle, which merged with that of Antony.

One of the great gains to art from the romantic movement was the development of landscape painting. Hitherto landscape, classified as *paysage historique*, had been treated as background to historical and mythological groups, to classic temples or palaces (heroic "*fabriques*"), or to standardized pastoral cottages. Scenery was painted in a studio, with a north light and without atmosphere, in accordance with set rules which could be traced back to Poussin in the seventeenth century. But now the general breakdown of convention in every sphere,

THE OLD OAK, BY JULES DUPRÉ (LOUVRE)

the widening of artistic scope, the "pantheistic effervescence" of modern art, and the richer reactions between painters and their environment brought about in France a new attitude toward nature. The tendency was favored by Dutch and English influences, especially the latter. The paintings of Constable, exhibited at Paris, and those of the brilliant young Englishman, Richard Bonington, who studied in France, were important factors. There came about a great revolt against studio nature. Artists painted with sincerity and feeling, and with individual variety of expression. The picturesque moods of nature were now interpreted as never before. Even animals, stately cattle, were judged worthy of interest and painted by Troyon. Most of the new nature painters were vilified as daubers, and paintings now worth fortunes went for a song. But Corot (who did not totally abandon the *paysage historique*), Dupré, and Rousseau made possible the supremacy of French landscape art and paved the way for the Barbizon School after 1848. Landscape painting helped, too, in the transition to realism in art and to the "democratic art" of Courbet and Millet.

In sculpture there were obviously corresponding developments, though they were not always so successful. The attempts of Rude to represent motion in stone are sometimes more grotesque than inspiring, as in his famous figures on the Arc de Triomphe. The sculptor David d'Angers was more restrained. At any rate, the only attitude for a lion was no longer considered to be couchant and pawing a billiard ball.

The Restoration and the Monarchy of July were musically very important by their novelties. Of course, the *chanson*, such as Béranger wrote, or the sentimental *romances* of people like Frédéric Bérat (*Ma Normandie* and *la Lisette de Béranger*), were preëminently dear to the multitude. The *genre troubadour* survived to the last in songs about paladins going to the wars, troubadours singing to their ladies. Exotic themes came up with Greek peasants struggling for liberty from the Turks, or faithful negroes of San Domingo dying to save the planter's beautiful daughter. Scribe, prolific author of *bourgeois* comedies, abounded no less in romantic librettos for operas, grand and comic, with "hymns, serenades, convent-prayers, witch-scenes and fishermen's songs", instead of Iphigenia, Alcestis, and Orpheus, as in the old operas. Liszt and Chopin enriched music in lyric expression; Rossini and Meyerbeer developed opportunities for the vocal gymnastics of Pasta, Malibran, and Grisi. Meyerbeer, especially, expressed a superficial emotionalism, blatant in its commercial spirit, and a noisy sensationalism which catered to the popular taste. He made a fortune, and when he died, under the reign of Napoleon III, he received, though a foreigner, a public funeral. Very different by its misfortunes was the career of Berlioz, the most genuine romanticist of French music, the "Victor Hugo of music". The eccentricities of Berlioz, his unwillingness to meet popular wishes, have made even his biographer Boschot speak of him as a musician *strepitoso*, a prancing René, a René-Tartarin, a twin brother of Antony. Berlioz was the musician of expressive sound, the foe to the smooth and conventional, pretty melodies of the Italian operatic school. He liked apocalyptic *requiems*, Babylonian *Te Deums*, gigantic orchestras, and developed program music, in which the surge of the composer's emotions is expressed, if need be, by the text of a printed program. Berlioz cultivated the symphonic poem, and his *Damnation de Faust*, earlier than Gounod's opera, is the full expression of romantic music.

CHAPTER XI

SECOND REPUBLIC. SECOND EMPIRE. POLITICAL AND RELIGIOUS DISCUSSIONS. INTELLECTUAL INFLUENCES

THE Revolution of February, 1848, came about so suddenly and so unexpectedly that people were hardly prepared for its consequences. For years every important incident had been used by the opposition as a cause for complaint. Even a nonpolitical murder, like that of the duchesse de Praslin by her husband, as famous in the annals of French crime as the Webster-Parkman case in America, where the populace accused the government of shielding the aristocratic criminal, increased class hatred.[1] The king had lost prestige; politicians were bickering; the upper *bourgeoisie* seemed engrossed in selfish money-making; the proletariat grumbled at the restricted suffrage; Lamartine's *Histoire des Girondins* glorified revolutionaries, and Eugène Sue's novels eulogized the populace. The truth was, as Lamartine had said as early as 1839, that "France was bored" (*la France s'ennuie*).

But when the "lyre of Lamartine had replaced the umbrella of Louis-Philippe" and monarchy had capitulated to a street riot, the provisional government, largely sponsored and appointed through the influence of two opposition newspapers, *le National* and *la Réforme*, did not know what to do. France was not really republican: the landed gentry were legitimists, the *bourgeoisie* Orleanist, the peasantry cherished the Napoleonic tradition and were disposed to favor a Bonapartist pre-

---

[1] The woman for whom the duc de Choiseul-Praslin was said to have committed the murder afterward came to America and married a Congregational clergyman, a brother of Cyrus W. Field.

tender. However, the accomplished fact was placidly accepted. But for years there had been adulation of the proletariat by journalistic agitators and men of letters. As the lines of the song ran:

> Chapeau bas devant ma casquette,
> A genoux devant l'ouvrier!

Even the *bourgeoisie* petted the populace, calling it innocent, pure, and unselfish, and the romantic age had encouraged orators to indulge in a vague and unpractical grandiloquence. So the Revolution of February was partly built out of rhetoric and had to be bolstered up by the lyric exhortations of Lamartine and the phrase-mongering of Ledru-Rollin.

In the first emotional outburst it was confidently expected that all would go well, especially as a great wave of liberalism had swept over Europe. *Bourgeois* and proletarians clasped hands. The Revolution was not hostile to religion. Its leaders were many of them deists, and the clergy blessed the liberty trees, the poplars (*peupliers*) which were planted everywhere. The utopian reformers, representing just so many shades of opinion, now thought that their opportunity was at hand. Louis Blanc, Proudhon, Raspail, Cabet, Considérant, Pierre Leroux, Pecqueur, even Blanqui, were all proclaiming their remedies (incidentally often trying to discredit each other), particularly as the sovereign power of universal suffrage, with which to interpret Liberty, Equality, and Fraternity, had suddenly been bestowed on the bewildered people. The word "Socialism" was now on everybody's lips, and to most people it did not have its present collectivistic connotation, but vaguely implied those *social reforms* which might remedy economic injustice, relieve poverty, crush selfish individualism, and bring about international humanitarian democracy and the end of war. The deists spoke of Christ as a socialist, just as the Jacobins of the first Revolution had made him out a republican *sans-culotte* like themselves. But, of course, as some of the utopians, like Cabet, did advocate communism, the conservatives and reactionaries made out a plausible argument when they called the socialistic tendencies of the age dangerous to liberty and to property. Ignorant peasants thought that "le père Communisme" was an ogre who killed children under three and old men over sixty.[1] Many *bourgeois*, at first condescendingly sympathetic, were now shocked at the presumption of their former allies, and at the attitude typified by the remark of the working-woman whose husband now held office: "C'est nous qui sont les princesses."

The harvest from the dragon's teeth came when the unemployed of Paris demanded a living wage. At the very beginning of the revolution Lamartine had acknowledged the *droit au travail*, and the opportunity to exercise it was now demanded. Hence the establishment of the National Workshops, a disingenuous and false application of the schemes of Louis Blanc. Pay was guaranteed to all, and wages even to those for whom employment could not be found. In consequence a vast city proletariat was formed in a few weeks, and the prospect loomed of endless deficits. The National Constituent Assembly now elected, and containing a majority of Moderates, was determined to put an end to the scheme. There was an insurrection in June, with street barricades and "massacres" by the troops under the firm guidance of General Cavaignac. Once more the *bourgeoisie*, in which we include the *petite bourgeoisie*, or tradesmen, were in control. Utopia had lasted four months.

The danger of "socialism" being averted, the middle classes proceeded to reorganize the government and create a constitution. But bad blood remained, of which the imperialist pretender took advantage. Louis-Napoleon himself had, in the past, been enough of a theoretical humanitarian socialist and advocate of universal suffrage to attract the working classes, and his name aroused at once the latent Bonapartism of the peasants, who nursed the tradition of Napoleon, world conqueror sprung from the people. Moreover, the same name rallied to its support those conservatives and royalists who wanted a

---

[1] George Sand, *Correspondance*, Vol. III, p. 63, quoted by Weill, *le Parti républicain*, p. 312, n. 1.

strong hand to curb or destroy a government which, it was thought, had pandered too long to the proletariat, and who now thought him a bulwark *against* socialism. The new constitution having provided, against the advice of Jules Grévy, for a president, Louis-Napoleon Bonaparte was elected by an enormous majority, and the *coup d'état* of December, 1851, years afterward described by one of its apologists as a "somewhat summary police procedure", followed as a matter of course. The unpractical, dreamy adventurer, the "Badinguet" of burlesque conspiracies to win the throne, was master of France.[1]

Spasmodic resistance in the way of street barricades, and fighting, in the course of which the deputy Baudin was killed, were futile. A national plebiscite indorsed Napoleon's veiled dictatorship by a large majority. By December, 1852, the Second Empire was in operation, and the "Nephew of his Uncle" was on the throne. Into exile went men like Louis Blanc, Ledru-Rollin, Quinet, Emile Deschanel, lecturer and critic and father of the future president of the Third Republic, Paul Deschanel. Victor Hugo wrote of the *coup d'état* in his *Histoire d'un crime*, and from his own place of exile in the Channel Islands excoriated Napoleon III in *les Châtiments*.

The imperial government ruled for a number of years with a high hand, until at last it was obliged to yield grudgingly to the growing opposition and became, just before the Franco-Prussian War, *l'Empire libéral*. Borne into power partly through the influence of such catch phrases as *l'Empire, c'est la paix*, which Napoleon uttered soon after the *coup d'état* in one of his public

---

[1] The usual explanation of the name "Badinguet" derives it from the name of a mason who is supposed to have helped Louis-Napoleon to escape from the fortress of Ham. But Paul Mantoux, in the *Grande Revue* (December, 1911), says that the real source is a comic picture by Gavarni in the *Charivari* in 1840. A *grisette* in a student's room is looking at a skeleton. The student says to her: "Don't you recognize her? It is Eugénie, Badinguet's old sweetheart!" (*l'ancienne à Badinguet!*) Badinguet was a chance, meaningless name like Calino etc. Remembered in 1853 at the time of the marriage of Napoleon and Eugénie, the picture suggested the joke of Eugénie and her lover Badinguet.

addresses, thus repeating the plea of Napoleon I that he made war under the constraint of enemies, France became before long the country of Europe most given to rattling the sword. Napoleon III was in many ways an attractive man. He was gentle and kind-hearted, and his emotional traits had led him earlier into socialism and sympathy for the liberation of oppressed nations of Europe. But his intellect was confused and his will power weak, so that his policy as ruler became contradictory and ineffective. It is described as a *politique de bascule*, an attempt to balance the Church against the liberals and the Church against free Italy. As a result it gave to everybody an appearance of duplicity, and nobody was grateful for concessions. The *Empire libéral* seemed a victory over enemies, especially the bigoted *esprit cagot*, and not an act of conciliation. Napoleon was led into war with Russia, into the Italian campaigns, into the unfortunate Mexican venture, as well as into the numerous diplomatic machinations which ended in the catastrophe of 1870.[1]

The Second Empire, inheriting the traditions of Napoleon I, inevitably stressed the pageantry of militarism. Under Louis-Philippe the regular army, as contrasted with the National Guard, had, through long absence in Africa, become a separate caste. Napoleon sought popularity with the soldiers. Military ceremonies—reviews and parades—were the accompaniment of the new order, and brilliant uniforms thronged the streets of the capital. There were officers in red pegtops and skirted tunics with tight belts, producing wasplike waists. They had waxed mustaches and goatees (*impériales*) like the monarch, and wore their shakos, and in time their caps, or *képis*, rakishly cocked on one side. There were dragoons and cuirassiers with helmets and shining steel breastplates, the dashing *Cent gardes* with reckless aristocratic officers, *chasseurs d'Afrique, turcos*, and zouaves with great baggy trousers. Smart canteen women (*cantinières* and *vivandières*) strutted by with the soldiers, carrying drink. The military man was a privileged being, and

[1] The *Débâcle* of Zola; the *Désastre* of the Margueritte brothers.

NAPOLEON III AND HIS GENERALS.

France reëchoed Hortense Schneider's song in Offenbach's *Grande duchesse de Gérolstein*:

> Ah! que j'aime les militaires,
> Leur uniforme coquet,
> Leur moustache et leur plumet!
> Ah! que j'aime les militaires,
> Leur air vainqueur, leurs manières,
> En eux tout me plaît!

At the head of each regiment marched a gigantic drum major twirling his stick like an acrobat. There were files of sappers, huge, ogrelike men with bearskin caps, flowing beards, white leather aprons reaching from shoulder to knee, carrying enormous axes. These seemed to symbolize the ferocity of Mars, the immense beard betokened virility, and the *barbe de sapeur*, as a mark of size, replaced in allusion the beard of the *bousingot* of an earlier generation. Thérésa, goddess of song at *cafés-chantants* such as the Eldorado and the Alcazar, popularized the ditty, *Rien n'est sacré pour un sapeur*, so that the Swedish baroness in *la Vie Parisienne* says, with a rich blending of values:

> Je veux, moi, dans la capitale
> Voir les divas qui font fureur,
> Voir la Patti dans *don Pasquale*,
> Et Thérésa dans *le Sapeur*!

France was the leading military power of Europe, and her army was considered invincible. Unfortunately, behind the pomp and circumstance there were weaknesses. Attention was given more to drill and to parade than to strategy; officers, inheriting traditions of guerrilla fighting in Africa, were sure that in war they would readily manage (*se débrouiller*), and there were too many drawing-room generals, like the General Boum of *la Grande duchesse* ("mais je sais d'où ça vient . . . des histoires de femmes"). But the Bonapartist fire-eater, Ratapoil, was sure of the invincibility of France, and his fancy was tickled by new exotic titles betokening victory abroad, such as Duke of

Malakoff, Count of Palikao. The caricaturist Daumier created Ratapoil under the Second Republic. At that time many old officers and soldiers of the Empire were still hale and hearty. Ratapoil travestied this type, with his battered tall hat, shabby

COSTUMES OF *CANTINIÈRES*

frock coat, bristling mustache, enormous stick, and fierce talk. Ratapoil lived on to the Third Republic in the sketches of Gill, now adorned with a big bunch of Bonapartist violets. It was the men of whom Ratapoil was the caricature, and the jingoistic cartoonists of the comic press, who paved the way for the surrender of Sedan and of Metz. But the song by Napoleon's mother, Queen Hortense, *Partant pour la Syrie,* revived from the days of the *genre troubadour,* was a pale substitute, as national anthem, for the stirring *Marseillaise,* forbidden under the Empire.

The religious question is inseparably connected with the history of the Second Empire, and the external policy of the reign

GUIGNOL REPRESENTING TYPES OF POLITICAL CARICATURE
The central figure is Ratapoil

cannot be understood without a consideration of the relations with Rome. Moreover, in the clash with the proletarians of 1848 many *bourgeois* felt it wise, in view of the rising tide of socialism, to become allied with the Church. Napoleon wanted to crush anticlerical republicanism; the well-to-do wanted to keep the socialists and communists (the *partageux*) under. The "Liberal Catholics" took advantage of the situation, and the Falloux Law, dealing chiefly with secondary education, was enacted even before the *coup d'état* in 1850. M. de Falloux, the comte de Montalembert, and Mgr Dupanloup were, in this matter, the leaders of the "liberal" Catholics, a term to be interpreted, it will be remembered, entirely as a political one and not with regard to faith. They carried through what was called the *expédition de Rome à l'intérieur* (see infra, p. 184), a campaign to promote Catholicism at home. In the name of liberty they succeeded in winning the important concession that the state should no longer have a monopoly of secondary education, but that any qualified person might open a private school. In this way, their opponents claimed, education was thrown into the hands of the Jesuits and clericals. At any rate, the measure permitted the development of "free", or unsupervised, education on a tremendous scale under the shadow of the Church. It was one of the greatest victories won by French Catholicism in the nineteenth century; but as it was the result of concessions it of course encountered the opposition of the uncompromising theocrats, under the leadership of the vituperative journalist the absolutist Louis Veuillot, disciple of Joseph de Maistre, and his paper, the *Univers*. Veuillot, the Déodat referred to in Augier's *Fils de Giboyer*, was angry at the compromise between the "sons of Voltaire" and those whom Montalembert considered the "sons of the crusaders". He lumped together the Protestants, the liberal Catholics, and the Gallicans, who emphasized the significance of the State in its relations with the Church, but were by their enemies charged with servility to the civil power. Veuillot's invectives, which spared neither liberal Catholic nor free-thinker, testified to the rupture between the two branches of the Church party. He had a certain power through his recklessness, and noticeably increased the difficulties of Napoleon when the latter tried to conciliate both factions. The liberal Catholics sought alliance with the political liberals and turned against Cæsarism. Their recent victory with the *loi Falloux* did not make them any more grateful to Napoleon. Compared with the theocrats they remained numerically few, but they were influential in the aristocratic Faubourg Saint-Germain, the Institute, and the French Academy, where a fairly strong anti-imperialistic Catholic group could make its voice heard with authority by academic *discours de réception* and similar opportunities for the expression of opinion.

The Emperor did his best to win favor with the Church. The Empress Eugénie, a Spaniard, was a devout Catholic. The dignity of religious ceremonials blended well with the majesty of imperial functions. Priests in their robes took an important part in public ceremonies, religious processions passed through the streets, and the ruler was lauded as the fitting successor of Charlemagne and of St. Louis. The Crimean War was praised as a crusade for the Church, and cannon taken at Sebastopol were melted over into statues of the Virgin at Le Puy. A first disappointment for Napoleon arose when he wanted the Pope to come to Paris for his coronation. But the Pope asked too much as a bargain in return, and refused on the ground that it would be a bad precedent, obliging him to travel about Europe crowning Catholic heads. Matters became more troublesome as Napoleon found himself involved in the contradictions of his foreign policy. The foreign *expédition de Rome* of 1849 to protect the Pope against an insurrectional republic at Rome, had become the Nemesis of his reign.

During the first years of his rule Napoleon was in high favor with the priesthood and had the vigorous support of Veuillot. He allowed religious spirit to influence state education as well as the *enseignement libre*. But his own political feelings had led him since youth to sympathize with the Italians, who wished to free the provinces held by the Austrians and bring about the unification of the country. The principle of nationality was a fruit of the Revolution, though violated by Napoleon I, who assigned territory after the old style. The policy of Napoleon III consistently carried out would ultimately involve the occupation of Rome as capital, and an end to the temporal power of the Pope. In addition to the Pope's own aversion to the loss of prestige, many French Catholics thought that decreased temporal power would diminish spiritual influence, and that the Pope would become an Italian bishop, the tool of Italian nationalistic policy. On the other hand, there was a strong pro-Italian party at court, headed by Prince Jerome Bonaparte, cousin of the Emperor and heir to the throne in case the latter left no surviving male issue, as well as son-in-law of Victor Emmanuel. Consequently Napoleon offended the Pope by supporting the movement of Italian liberation, and he offended the Italians when he maintained French troops at Rome. He also displeased the Italians by his tendency to withdraw without carrying his assistance through, as at Villafranca, and by exacting, in spite of altruistic declarations, the cession of Savoy and of Nice to France in compensation for his help. Both districts were on the French side of the Alps, and the language of Savoy was French, but the action of Napoleon seemed to belie his principles.

Pius IX had given hopes, at his accession to the papacy, of being a liberal pontiff in sympathy with the aspirations of democracy. But each step toward the unification of Italy pointed more openly to his own loss of temporal power, and he was driven by the force of circumstances into a reactionary policy, not only in Italy but, through consistency, in his relations with France as well. The consequence was that he created obstacles for the imperial government, besides giving weapons to those hostile to religion. Napoleon was no longer the "successor of St. Louis" but "Pontius Pilate". The mass of the French clergy became disaffected toward the government and its policies. Veuillot and Montalembert, advocate of a "free church in a free state" in France, joined to defend the Pope in Italy. The ultramontanes triumphed and preached a policy of sectarian exclusivism. An unwise antithesis was formulated between the Church and modern progress, and the use of the expression "counter-revolution" aroused the hatred of those who were afraid lest the gains of democracy in the great political revolution of '89 be imperiled. An opportunity was offered for writers like Augier to attack religious orders, such as the Jesuits, in *Lions et renards*. People were the more suspicious when they saw the "clericals" and the legitimist-royalists gradually coalesce and turn a cold shoulder toward their own political liberals and toward the Gallicans.¹ They felt convinced of the reactionary tendencies of the Church when, in 1864, Pius IX issued an important Encyclical, or letter to the faithful, accompanied by the noted Syllabus, a catalogue of errors, eighty in number, which the anticlericals took as an object lesson in obscurantism. The Pope was partly aiming against the policy of the Italian nationalists, but again his actions touched many Frenchmen to the quick as an attack on their own post-Revolutionary civilization. The Encyclical and the Syllabus called down anathema on those who advocated reconciliation between the pontificate and the new order. The independence of the Catholic Church was declared unlimited; the supreme pontiff was the arbiter between rulers and peoples; all authority was inferior to that of the Church; the direction of education belonged to it; the Church was superior to the State; civil marriage without religious rites was null and void. The French rationalists also viewed with utter lack of sympathy the development, during the Second Empire, of a strong tendency toward religious mysticism and miracle worship, perhaps an after result of romantic emotional exaltation, such as the rapid spread of the cult of the Sacred Heart and the apparitions of Lourdes in 1858.

To sum up, then, the history of the relations of State and Church during the Second Empire: The imperial government, in spite of the influence of the Empress, lost somewhat, as a result of political contingencies, the favor with the Church with which Napoleon had begun his reign. The French episcopate took counsel from Rome, rather than from the government, even in secular matters. The clergy and the royalists, especially the legitimists, drew closer together. Voltairianism lost caste with the *bourgeoisie*, and it became good form to show one's self

---

[1] Historians point out that the word "clericalism" was not used at first. "Ultramontanism" was the general term vaguely used by opponents to characterize the Catholic party. Down to the second part of the Second Empire the word "clerical" was used in a regular sense as an adjective relating to the clergy. Then it acquired an unfavorable meaning.

a devout Catholic to gain power and from fear of losing property through socialism, like Augier's Maréchal in *le Fils de Giboyer*. God was needed to protect one's money bags. The liberal Catholics, in spite of their services to the Church by the victory of the *loi Falloux*, and in spite of considerable intellectual and social prestige, had lost the favor of Rome. They were charged with going too far in the way of compromise. Some of their clerical leaders, like Mgr Dupanloup, the bishop of Orleans, injured their standing still more by venturing to oppose beforehand the doctrine of the infallibility of the Pope speaking *ex cathedra* in matters of faith and morals, which was proclaimed at the ecumenical council of the Church in 1870. This step Dupanloup had opposed, not as a disbeliever in the doctrine but because he considered it *inopportune*. It is interesting to note that the term "Opportunism" used by Gambetta in political phraseology under the Third Republic had thus a clerical origin.

The critics of the religious policy were not to be found among the ultra-Catholics alone. For them a *modus vivendi* was even worse, and they were but taking advantage of the reaction against romantic subjectivism and sentimentalism in returning to authority and tradition. The real hostility to Napoleon came from those who found his policy not insufficiently religious but too much so. The Gallicans thought that the government catered too much to Rome on the occasion of national celebrations and festivities. The free-thinkers, heirs to the traditions of Voltaire, continued to scoff at clericalism, but their sneer, idiotic in the fools pilloried in Flaubert's M. Homais, supremely clever in Edmond About, became a little tiresome. Only the exceptionally militant anticlericals in the *bourgeoisie* flaunted their convictions after death by a lay funeral, or *enterrement laïque*. It took established literary reputation or the independence of high rank to attack the religious party openly, as did the Emperor's own cousin, Prince Jerome, or to scandalize convention, as he did by being present at a dinner at Sainte-Beuve's on a Good Friday, where meat was served. Anonymity was deemed a safer method of attack, as in the sensational story attributed to an abbé Michon,[1] *le Maudit*, now forgotten, but which had in its day a *succès de scandale*. The Protestants were few in number and ineffective because of their exclusiveness. American Unitarianism was the dream of a few who had heard of such exotic movements, but there were no adherents, and the wish of Quinet to see France converted to Protestantism was fanciful. At most, men broke with Catholicism enough to ask for a Protestant funeral instead of a purely secular one. However, through political aversion to the Empire the growing republican party became more and more hostile to the Church, accusing it of being a reactionary force in the government, until the liberal journalist Peyrat devised the phrase which Gambetta adopted and popularized under the early Third Republic: "Le cléricalisme, voilà l'ennemi." The literary leaders were in great numbers anticlerical: Hugo, Michelet, Quinet, Mérimée, Sainte-Beuve, Leconte de Lisle, George Sand, Augier. The republican party was to a considerable degree recruited among lawyers, doctors, and teachers. The physicians especially, as scientific materialists, set a precedent for the radical doctors in modern French politics. The student opposition was antireligious. This feeling was reënforced by the materialism of the increasing number of radical proletarians, as the social problem became more acute with the approaching end of the Empire.

The prevailing attitude among average intelligent people, neither clericals nor anticlericals, was a vague deism and faith in God, accepting, at least outwardly, the official doctrines of a State anxious to stand well with the Church. Some of the more reflecting tried to minimize dogma in their discussions in the interest of individual or collective morals. It was this indeterminate aspiration toward the good that Victor Cousin sought to control by his philosophy of eclecticism, and that he succeeded in influencing so much by his official power in the University; an influence which lasted long after his death, to the annoyance of both extremes, religious and antireligious.

[1] See Charles-Brun, *le Roman social*, p. 206.

The eclecticism of Cousin was a system built up by a process of spiritualized common sense applied to convenient elements selected from different philosophies. It was taught in the state *lycées* and superior Faculties, but it seemed to the rigid church party to concede too much to rationalism, and to the unorthodox it was sanctimonious and vapid. To keep on good terms with the Church, Cousin tended more and more to make concessions. Coincidently, the governmental policy controlling education was to frown on any form of intellectual liberalism. Readers of the life of Taine or of Francisque Sarcey's *Souvenirs de jeunesse* will recall how nagging and persecution drove them, with others, from the careers in education for which they had fitted themselves. It was not until the advent of Victor Duruy as Minister of Public Instruction that an advance was made toward liberalizing the courses of study and broadening the approaches to education, to the great indignation of even such "liberal" Catholics as Dupanloup. To the very end of the Empire and after, the spirit of surveillance and of hierarchal docility in the teaching profession bred throughout secondary education timidity and conventionalism. During the early years of the Empire professors were forbidden to wear mustaches, as suggestive of hirsute republicanism. Nothing could have been more narrow-minded, in spite of genuine intellectual ability, than the teachers in *lycées* and *collèges communaux*, the result of subservience to scholastic superiors and of timidity lest unfavorable reports, transmitted to headquarters, blight a career. The teachers retaliated on the pupils. French fiction dealing with the period abounds in pictures of the tyranny of fossilized professors and of school ushers (*maîtres d'études*, or *pions*) persecuted by superiors and pupils alike, as in Daudet's *le Petit Chose*. Looming behind immediate academic authority were the fear of possible disfavor with orthodox opinion, local or general, and imponderables, the effects of which could be so important. Thus it may be seen that throughout the Empire and far into the Third Republic the power of the representatives of the Church, bespeaking a vague social sanction, though impalpable, was very great.[1] Education was less independent under the Empire than under Louis-Philippe, and in the higher Faculties Renan and Sainte-Beuve found it unsafe to try to lead opinion.

Thus it is not to be wondered at if, under the Second Empire, education perpetuated the numerous class of people whom Flaubert and so many others detested and branded as *bourgeois*. Satirical emphasis was now not so much on the possession of property as a symbol of conventionalism, but on the mediocre mind running in narrow ruts. To Flaubert the *bourgeois* was a person banal, selfish, utilitarian, and inartistic. He planned and partly drew up a *Dictionnaire des idées reçues*, an amusing collection of platitudes and psittacisms. The assaults on the *bourgeois* in the *Education sentimentale* and in *Bouvard et Pécuchet* apply equally well in spirit to the Monarchy of July, the Second Empire, and the Third Republic.

If the relations of Church and State were not free from friction during the Second Empire, these two establishments were united against opposition, whether it came from political and social reformers or from philosophical and scientific realists and materialists. Moreover, the reaction against romantic subjectivism was weakening, in the intellectual world, the conventional spiritualism of Cousin's semiofficial philosophy. The development of positive science, theories of evolution, and the application of historical and philological methods to Biblical criticism diminished in certain places the prestige of the supernatural. So the rising generation was not always satisfied with the ultramontanism of the clergy, or even with the deism of 1848 and the compromises of Cousin, and grew impatient when the government was seen to be irresolute and to waver between the Church and democracy, Catholicism and socialism. Thousands of impetuous youths became disciples in science of Comte and, at the end of the Empire, of Littré; in history and philosophy, of Taine; in Biblical criticism, of Renan. The liberals began to call for the separation of Church and State, and pointed to the

[1] Ferdinand Fabre's *Abbé Tigrane*, Anatole France's *Histoire contemporaine*, Abel Hermant's *Grands bourgeois*, etc.

example of the United States, until in time, with Gambetta's "Programme of Belleville" in 1869, disestablishment became a doctrine of radical republican politics. Philosophers devised the elements of a *morale laïque,* based on justice, to take the place of religion. Littré's popularization of Comte's Positive philosophy condemning theology and metaphysics had great vogue. Finally ardent radicals under the influence of Quinet were not satisfied with demanding the laicization of the schools and the teaching of morals disconnected from religion. Some now proclaimed themselves atheists and, getting control of French Freemasonry, turned it into a political, antireligious organization. A few even became advocates of governmental nihilism and supporters of revolutionaries, such as Blanqui, who wished *ni Dieu, ni maître.* The leaders of the proletarians seized the opportunity to intensify social discontent, and, in the wake of Karl Marx, preached class war for the advancement of the rights of the populace.

In the cult, then, of materialistic science we find the key to the new order. The bankruptcy of humanitarianism and of idealism in 1848 had produced the sort of reaction to be expected. The anæmic idealism of Cousin did not satisfy venturesome minds. Many people turned their thoughts outward and became engrossed in the immediate phenomena. This was the reign of positivism and of scientific studies. It is true that in time a doctrine of "Kantian" neo-Criticism was preached by Renouvier, who wrote during the Second Empire and an important part of the Third Republic. But as he was outside the University, and very technical as well, his importance was more as a solitary philosopher, a thinker for thinkers, than as leader of a numerous school. In time, also, a new idealism, based on firmer foundations than Cousinism, arose, represented by distinguished names under the Third Republic, of which Ravaisson's *Rapport sur la philosophie du XIXe siècle* of 1867 was an important early manifestation. But the chief reaction against Eclecticism was Positivism.

Since it had then become fashionable, with Comte, to consider idealistic metaphysics a creed outworn, and to be occupied with business, or with those deeper sciences, at most, which have to do with man's practical experience, interest centered on the study of man approached from the outside, with methods of cold-blooded analysis and the dissection of mental phenomena. Villiers de l'Isle-Adam satirized this kind of intellectualism in Tribulat Bonhomet, the scientific philistine, "archetype of his century", who kills swans to hear their dying song, whose literary favorite is Ponson du Terrail's *Rocambole*,[1] and who describes Chateaubriand as a "former minister of Charles X, some of whose ethnological studies of savages have, it appears, attracted attention". It is the smattering of scientific phraseology which later creeps into the comedies of the younger Dumas when he writes of "social vibrions". It became fashionable, by the close of the Second Empire, to challenge the miraculous and the supernatural with medical explanations of hysteria and mental pathology. The growth of the doctrine of evolution emphasized theories of determinism and caused a sense of pessimism, resulting from the apparently fatalistic working of the cosmic factors. The new spirit prided itself on its impartiality but was devoid of joy and hope. In adapting scientific evolution to the Hegelian historical method it divested it of its messianic spirit and made history the record of blind cause and effect. A fatalistic psychology is of prime significance in the philosophy of Taine, who shares with Renan the prestige of being the French thinker of greatest influence on ideas during the second half of the nineteenth century. Taine's *Philosophes français du XIXe siècle* was a declaration of war against Eclecticism. The reaction had already begun, and Taine was not its cause, but he was the philosophical leader of the new generation, even reacting on older men like Sainte-Beuve, whose characterization of his own method of universal curiosity in literary criticism as an *histoire naturelle des esprits* repeats the scientific terminology of Taine.

Taine was not a pure empiricist in his positivism. He had a metaphysic, but he had simplified Substance into laws, and the

[1] The stock example in modern French of slovenly plot and style.

sciences were to him catalogues of such laws, based on the analysis of facts and dogmatically enunciated. Applying his method to the study of literature, of history, and especially of psychology, he turned man into a "walking theorem" and made him the fatal result of the three famous factors of time, race, and environment. Psychology is the analysis of the evolution of rigid laws, alike for men and animals. Similarly, ethics registers, the sequence of factors in the same impartial way, and declares that virtue and vice are moral products, just as sugar and vitriol are the result of chemical elements.

The mechanical simplicity of Taine's method, and the ease with which, rigid as it was, he applied it in so many spheres, made him an intellectual force of the greatest significance. The method of *petits faits significatifs* was especially applicable to history and literary criticism, and the success of his studies of the origins of contemporary France and of the history of English literature encouraged hosts of imitators. It was of more dubious value in art criticism and was unable to account for the thrill, or *frisson*, that beauty causes; but Taine was professor of æsthetics at the School of Fine Arts and spoke with corresponding official authority. In philosophy he was important in turning the attention of French thinkers to psychological problems. But it was in fiction that for the nonprofessional reader his influence is most far-reaching. The method of observation was adopted by the new realistic school of novelists, with intensification of the scientific indifferentism of Taine, and its transformation into the records of sordid fatalism. Taine's famous formula was misapplied, and virtue and vice, instead of being considered products parallel in their origin to sugar and vitriol, were spoken of as secretions like or identical with sugar and vitriol. Thus we have the rise of what has been variously designated as "brutal literature" and "putrid literature", the exaggerations of which Taine would have been the first to disavow.

If Taine represents the dogmatic rationalism of later nineteenth-century thought and the positivistic psychology which appealed to an age of materialism, Renan was to exert an influence hardly less considerable upon minds of a less incisive kind, —upon those who liked to play with the passing fancies of their imagination instead of formulating rigid categories. His influence was destined to be especially dangerous upon superficial know-alls, who were lured by the grace and charm of his literary manner, but who had not his scholarship and therefore became dilettantes and cultivators of paradox.

Renan, as much as Taine, professed the cult of positive science, but his versatility and his sympathy with the topic immediately under consideration by him not only kept him from dogmatism but made him delight in the brilliant matching of contradictory views and the semi-serious, semi-ironical espousal of each for the time being. Hence his fondness for the philosophical dialogue. This attitude was likely to engender in others skepticism and verbal paradox. In them, also, Renan's sympathetic irony changed to the Voltairian sneer.

Underlying Renan's positivism was a current of imaginative idealism which led to the poetic interpretation of science, history, and religion. He was a former seminarist who had broken away from dogma as a result of applying the methods of modern scholarship to the history of religion. His faith in revelation had disappeared, leaving only the æsthetic power of its ceremonials and the fragrance of its spiritual values. He replaced it by the cult of science, especially history and philology glorified into religion. Science became God in the making, and the soul of man, in so far as it is a separate entity and not part of divine truth in process, is left as an exquisite sensibility played upon in turn like a melodious instrument by the flow of passing phenomena.

In this position of Renan there is much to recall the romantic temper. This is brought out by the remarks on Renan's *Life of Jesus* by the well-known journalist Benoît Jouvin, as recorded by his father-in-law Villemessant in the memoirs of the latter. The comparisons would be lost on many readers today, but they will be plain enough to those who have read earlier chapters of the present study. Renan's Jesus, wrote Jouvin, is blond like

Mme de Staël's Oswald, dreamy like Goethe's Werther, and *joli garçon* like Byron's Don Juan. This young philosopher speaks the language of René, and the blond youth forgiving the repentant Magdalene is Didier opening his arms to Marion Delorme *et lui refaisant une virginité*. Even the maidens of Galilee portrayed in the pages of Renan's book are of today, and seem like Parisiennes sallying from Mabille and the Closerie des Lilas to pick cherries and ride donkeys at Montmorency!

Taine and Renan are the two greatest writers who exemplify the development of historical studies; but they were under the spell of their intellectual theories. Fustel de Coulanges and his *Cité antique* (1864) are important for the rise of the impartial historical method employed by modern scholars, in which history is freed from preconceived theories either of theocrats or of scientific skeptics. In time the French schools ceased to use the manuals, familiar to those who have rummaged among discarded textbooks, in which, under the influence of the idea that history is the record of personal rulers, separate sections were accorded to every petty Merovingian *roi fainéant*, with a medallion portrait for each king.

CHAPTER XII

SECOND EMPIRE. SOCIAL AGITATION. THE AGE OF MATERIALISM

SINCE the Great Revolution violence had seemed a natural recourse to the proletariat of Paris when driven to exasperation. In 1830, in his *Iambes*, Barbier had deified the *sainte canaille*, just as the "Mountain" had been *sainte*, and had written bloodthirsty verses on Liberty. His poetry and the fierce seminude Liberty in Delacroix's picture of the Barricades help us to understand why movements for popular freedom took their rise amid slaughter in the streets, and why "Marianne", the socialistic republic, is bathed in blood and waves a flag of red.[1]

At the beginning of the Second Empire, however, the working classes seemed for a time thoroughly cowed. Though Cabet and Considérant were still busy with the schemes described in a previous chapter, and Icarian communists were sent to America, still in France utopian optimism had proved a failure. Capitalism held sway and reveled in luxury. Material prosperity apparently prevailed, but the accompanying inflation of values more than offset the advantages of steady employment for the lower classes. The industrial leaders tried to grind more work than ever out of their subordinates, and, with the help of the courts, protests were recklessly met with fines and imprisonment. Consequently the working classes became disaffected, and their leaders, seeing State and Church so often hand-and-glove, and jealous of the favor shown to the clergy, grew antireligious and often atheistical.

[1] The name "Marianne", as a designation for the proletarian republic, came from the name of a secret society soon after the *coup d'état*, or from its password.

THE AGE OF MATERIALISM 197

But the early theorists of the Empire, even republican radicals, were, as a rule, not yet socialists in the modern sense. They were chiefly desirous of opposing to the capitalistic feudalism an economic liberalism. Reform was still desired, on the whole, by peaceful means. Even the "Anarchy" of Proudhon,

LIBERTY ON THE BARRICADES, BY DELACROIX (LOUVRE), GLORIFYING THE REVOLUTION OF 1830

the name of which, owing to the abuse of its principles by later militants, has become a bugbear, was pacific in its aims, and beneath his pessimism at the state of civilization he had a vision of a better future.

Proudhon, except in occasional declamatory excitement, did not preach violence. He wanted the downfall of *bourgeois* government and the abolition of capitalistic property through the refusal of the proletariat to pay the money by which it was supported. Yet he did not want mob rule, but rather the guidance of the intelligent *élite*. Proudhon, a vigorous specimen of French peasantry, was, like most of his race, a sturdy individualist, and his economic theories were based, not on Collectivism, but on Mutualism. He advocated, as we have already seen, a gradual abolition of the complicated mechanism of political government, with its host of petty henchmen, and maintained that the best social order was to be found in an-archy and the substitution for the vast industrial state of a loose federalism of the tiny *communes* which form the smallest administrative unit in the French nation. Each family was to own its small plot of land; the worth of produce was to be regulated by reason and justice instead of by artificial legislation and false monetary standards. The public treasury would be reduced practically to the level of a bureau of statistics, and politics would be replaced by economics.

Mutualism is, then, the chief aspect of proletarian agitation in France under the Empire, as utopianism had been under the Monarchy of July. Even abroad the First Workingmen's International at London, in 1864, though under the influence of Marx, at first centered its efforts on increased wages and shorter hours of labor, and the French representatives were Proudhonian luxury workers and ex-workers. The general desire was for a peaceful solution to troubles.

But there were advocates of violence also among the proletariat: in France the Blanquists; abroad the followers of Karl Marx, who was destined to be the most potent force in modern labor agitation.

Blanqui, the Frenchman of Italian origin, and Marx, the German Jew, were hostile to Proudhon and at odds with each other. Blanqui and Marx both believed in the dictatorship of the proletariat, but Marx was the advocate of immediate communism, for which Blanqui was in less haste. Marx preached class war and invented the battle cry: "Workers of the World, unite!" Blanqui was the leader of the militant minority and wanted the rule of the intelligent fraction of the proletariat, a band of disciplined workers, foreguard of the revolution. The

FRONTISPIECE OF GEFFROY'S *L'ENFERMÉ*

Paris Commune, which followed the downfall of the Empire, was chiefly Proudhonian in principle and Blanquist in method, though the Marxists afterward wrongly identified the "Commune" with "Communism".

Marx abused Proudhon as a phrase-monger and narrow-minded *bourgeois* himself, and considered that he, Marx, had broadened Proudhon's education by introducing him to Hegelianism.

At any rate, the Marxian socialists reacted against all French methods as utopian and ineffective, and introduced the principle of "scientific" fatalism, dubbed "realistic", in truth materialistic. They justified class war, the arrayal of the proletariat in vindictive and destructive opposition to the old order. People were no longer to help humanity. The proletarian was to down the capitalist, and much of the history of the early International was a contest between the anticommunistic libertarianism of Proudhon's followers and the authoritarian communism of the Marxists.

But the French militants, under the Empire, did not need to seek the leadership of a foreigner like Karl Marx. The lifelong agitator Blanqui,[1] who spent more than half his life in prison, called "le Vieux" by the youth who followed his inspiration, was the leader of the atheistic, positivistic republicans as contrasted with the deist republicans of 1848. He was the chief among proletarian workers, poverty-stricken journalists, and impecunious scientific and medical students of Paris, whose reading had led them to materialistic ideas and hostility to Catholicism. Blanqui formulated and acted on the principle of proletarian dictatorship. He was the inspirer of small bands of secret conspirators against the Empire, and his influence encouraged a spirit of military discipline, of diplomatic secrecy, and of sacerdotal consecration. He made possible the Commune, though it was foredoomed to failure, because, at the time, he was himself in prison. This Commune was one of the most important forerunners of the Russian Revolution. Indeed, "Blan-

[1] Read *l'Enfermé*, by Gustave Geffroy.

qui can claim to have originated the two most deadly weapons of the modern Bolsheviks—'the arming of the proletariat and disarming of the *bourgeoisie*' and the 'dictatorship of the proletariat'."[1] Lenin, a follower of Marx's theories of Class War and Internationalism, was avowedly a disciple of Blanqui in his antidemocracy,—his faith in the dictatorship of the enlightened, militant minority, and in revolution for, not by, the people.

The leadership of the malcontents was especially to be found in the *déclassés*,[2] the political bohemians and intellectual proletariat that held their sessions in the *cafés*, where, beneath smoky ceilings, on red plush sofa-couches, discontent was aired over *mazagrans*,—tall tumblers of heady coffee. The Café de Madrid was, during the last seven years of the Empire, the meeting-place of journalists, adversaries of the government. Such was Augier's journalist Giboyer of *les Effrontés*, "son of a door-keeper, doctor *in omni re scibili*, and especially apostle of the social revolution". Such in real life were the journalist Jules Vallès, the great *réfractaire*, who afterwards poured out his bitterness in the largely autobiographical *Jacques Vingtras*, and the young lawyer Léon Gambetta, passionate reader of Proudhon's writings on Justice, and the young doctor, Georges Clemenceau, the friend of Blanqui.[3] Sardou's *Rabagas*, which is interpreted as in part a satire of Gambetta, enumerates the conspirators of the play:

---

[1] R. W. Postgate, *Out of the Past*, p. 8.

[2] Faguet, writing his *Anticléricalisme* many years later, said (p. 26) that nowhere except among the Greeks have there been so many *déclassés* as in France: "The *déclassé* is a man who to such a degree feels himself born for great things that he cannot take upon himself to do small or average ones. So he does nothing, and drifts from expedient to expedient, always dreaming of the great rôles for which he was intended and which circumstances have prevented him from enjoying. France contains many of these men who have gone astray and whom a little knowledge of themselves would have preserved."

[3] Names such as Gambetta and Clemenceau may seem startling in a list of *déclassés*, but the one began his career as a tempestuous *café* orator, the other as a struggling physician of advanced radicalism. President Millerand and Aristide Briand are also examples of the way in which success tempers advanced social and political theories.

The lawyer without a case and the physician without a patient, the author who has been hissed, the discharged clerk, the revoked office-holder and the cashiered officer, a bankrupt, three insolvents, two sharpers, an utopian, seven imbeciles and three drunkards.[1]

These malcontents of the Second Empire were like those who organized the mob in the various social upheavals in different countries after the World War,—men whose education or ambitions were greater than their success in life, and who took revenge in plotting the downfall of the social order. Those intellectuals, brooding over ills amid the confinement of cities until some of them, especially women like the "red virgin" Louise Michel, precursor of Rosa Luxemburg, and Germaine Berton, were victims of hysterical neurotic obsession, became the organizers of the workmen.[2] The Goncourt brothers wrote in their diary as early as 1855: "Now that there are no longer any savages in Europe, it will be the workingmen who will do that job in about fifty years. It will be called the Social Revolution."

Napoleon was determined, though he was unsuccessful, to prevent economic discontent by keeping working-men busy. This also harmonized with his desire for display by embellishing Paris. He wanted to choke off utopian sophists, radical orators, and innovators. Moreover, Paris was bound, in the course of events, to lose some of its piquant individuality and to become heterogeneous and garish by industrial progress. The development of railways made it easy to get to Paris from the provinces, and the position taken by France as the first military power of Europe fostered the cosmopolitanism that international expositions encouraged. Before Napoleon III Paris had been uniformly picturesque instead of picturesque only in special quarters. Napoleon gave over to Baron Haussmann the

[1] Act I, Sc. x. The General Petrowlski of the same play is a take-off of the foreign adventurers and soldiers of fortune of the Commune, like Dombrowski. The name alludes to the petrol which the Communards used for their incendiarism.

[2] After the Commune they were called *pétroleuses*. Compare the *tricoteuses* of the Revolution.

task of making the capital more splendid, though at the risk of frequent architectural monotony and mediocrity in the place of variety, and at the cost of huge sums squandered in contractors' jobs and real-estate speculations. This was, however, not without enormous improvement in sanitation and comfort through markets, sewers, and bridges. The extravagance of reconstructed Paris was by Jules Ferry, parodying the French title of the *Tales of Hoffmann*, called the *Comptes fantastiques d'Haussmann*. Moreover, the Haussmannization of Paris was imitated in many provincial cities, which destroyed to rebuild. Haussmann saddled French municipal architecture with the superstition for straight lines, which had a reason quite as much in a desire to avoid street barricades as in that of interpreting the rigid orderliness of the Cartesian logical temperament. This last showed itself in the uniformity of the exteriors of buildings, with their conventional balconies and arabesques. The opera house, though not finished until the Third Republic, displays the lavish ornateness of the imperial régime, its deification of music amid the sumptuous magnificence of marble, porphyry, and gilt, its glorification of the dance in the statuary of Carpeaux, for the Second Empire was as fond of dancing as was the Monarchy of July.

In 1860 a large number of peripheral suburbs were incorporated into Paris, which now occupied the whole space included in the fortifications erected, through the efforts of Thiers, under the Monarchy of July. These, in turn, lost their individual traits to become the *quartiers excentriques* whither went, especially to the north, the east, and the south, the poorer classes driven from the center by the rich *bourgeoisie* and by the upheavals of reconstruction. One effect of the reconstruction of Paris was a greater separation of classes. Formerly the *rentier* had often lived on a lower floor and a working family in the attic of the same building. Now Belleville, which in the stories of Paul de Kock was still a quiet, rustic locality of homes and gardens, became in a few years a breeding-place of proletarian discontent; at La Villette the slaughterhouses, with the constant flow of red blood, bred the contempt for life and familiarity with the knife that characterize the *apache* of the Third Republic; the hill of Montmartre was in time the home of impecunious bohemia; the cheaper *bourgeoisie* of clerks and salaried officeholders settled in the Batignolles, which acquired what the English call a "lower middle-class" atmosphere. On the other hand, to the west and beyond the Champs-Elysées the lavish private residences, or *hôtels,* of Auteuil, Passy, the *quartier de l'Etoile,* and the Parc Monceau typified the new prosperity and display of the well-to-do and the *parvenus.* The number of municipal wards, or *arrondissements,* sprang from twelve to twenty, and there was now a genuine thirteenth *arrondissement.* Hitherto the designation had been attributed to the mythical land of *galanterie,* so that when in Balzac's *Cousine Bette* a character says, "tu te marieras au treizième", and when the thirteenth *arrondissement* is mentioned in Augier's *Mariage d'Olympe* and *les Lionnes pauvres,* the phrase implies left-handed matrimony. Louis Lurine's *Histoire du treizième arrondissement* was a disquisition on the realm often designated as the *pays de Cythère.*

Such was the shrine surrounding the glory of Napoleon III. The true prestige of the Empire was probably at its height soon after it began, before it had become weakened by diplomatic hedgings, at the time of the exposition of 1856, during the Congress of Paris, and when the baptism of the Prince Imperial seemed the symbol of a continued dynasty. The Empire, in spite of unperceived disintegration, had its spectacular culmination in the exposition of 1867. Paris was the *Ville lumière* of Victor Hugo, the *cabaret de l'Europe* of the Austrian ambassadress, Mme de Metternich. In its gay thoroughfares everyone was welcome who wanted a good time and had money to spend. Says Anatole France in *la Vie en fleur*:

> Paris was, under Napoleon III, the world tavern. Guests from all countries of the globe were welcomed there with cordial magnificence. Nothing foreshadowed the dislike of foreigners (*xénophobie*) which later darkened the Third Republic, those hatreds, those suspicions,

NEW YEAR ON THE BOULEVARDS

poisoned fruits of defeat, which victory increased, fifty years later, and which now will never disappear.

Consequently foreigners thronged the boulevards and the Champs-Elysées, though not in the hordes of today, seeking pleasure. There were superciliously critical "sons of Albion"; Piedmontese plotting for Italian unity; Russian princes on the alert for ballet dancers, for, as Victor Hugo says to Napoleon in *les Châtiments*:

> Victoire! il était temps, prince, que tu parusses:
> Les filles d'opéra manquaient de princes russes.

The Swedish Baron de Gondremarck of Meilhac and Halévy's *Vie parisienne*, whose desire is to see the *petites femmes* of Paris, is a precursor of the uxorious satyr of modern musical comedy. There were American Civil War contractors squandering on champagne and clothes the money got by cheating the Union government. There were dapper South Americans, of the type known later as *rastaquouères*, of whom Balzac gave one of the earliest specimens in the Brazilian Montéjanos of *la Cousine Bette*. There were Levantine nabobs scheming shady financial transactions; indeed, *Grec* in French slang, with memories perhaps also of Virgil's *timeo Danaos*, has long meant a trickster and card sharper. Last, but not least, there were Prussians taking notes.

Under the reign of Louis-Philippe the French had been taught by Guizot to "get rich"; but, though selfish, they had been, on the whole, honest and thrifty. Under the Empire they proceeded to enjoy themselves. Never was there in France a more reckless devotion to pleasure, to good eating and good drinking, than was to be found on the boulevards. The Second of December brought reckless standards which increased the world of corruption. To the genuine *boulevardier*, under the prolonged *fête impériale* from 1852 to 1870, the country, as opposed to the town, was merely a place "full of trees and uncooked birds". His vista was limited by the restaurants of the capital—the

Maison d'or, the *Café Riche*, the *Café de Paris*—and by neighboring theaters—the *Gymnase*, the *Vaudeville*, and the *Bouffes parisiens*. At most he took a brief trip to the seashore at Dieppe, or later at Trouville and in the wake of the duc de Morny at Deauville. Or he followed the court to Biarritz, or the Emperor to a water cure at a *station thermale*, such as Vichy. When he crossed the frontier to Baden-Baden he felt far from home.

The frequenter of the boulevards was now not so much a *lion* as a *faiseur* and a *jouisseur*, a *cocodès*, or futile social parasite, or, when exhausted by dissipation, a *petit crevé*, as he was called toward the end of the Empire. His intellect did not rise above *la blague*, now more in vogue than ever because of the daring cynicism of French journalists, so destructive of enthusiasms. *La blague* was the spirit of universal mockery, the taking of nothing seriously, what in the Goncourt brothers' *Charles Demailly* is called the "caresse de la bête fauve qui lèche jusqu'au sang". In *Manette Salomon* of the same authors it is written:

> *La Blague*, that terrible, frenzied, feverish, evil, almost diabolical laughter of spoiled children, of children decayed by the old age of a civilization, that laughter which jeers at the grandeur, the holiness, the majesty, the poetry of all things, that laughter which would seem to enjoy the vile pleasure of the men in working clothes who, at the Zoölogical Gardens, amuse themselves by spitting on the beauty of animals and the majesty of lions,—*la Blague*, such was indeed this young fellow's name.

Even in moralizing comedy the successor of Molière's *raisonneur*, the man of good counsel, was touched up with *blague*. Desgenais, the modern Diogenes of *les Filles de marbre*, has the *esprit boulevardier*, and Olivier de Jalin in *le Demi-monde* is the worldly cynic even when serving a good cause.

Journalism was the great outlet for the spirit of *blague*. Those were the days of journalists such as the brilliant and unprincipled self-seeker Emile de Girardin, of Arsène Houssaye, and of *chroniqueurs* like Nestor Roqueplan, inventor of the term *la Parisine* to characterize the delicate essence of Parisian atticism;[1] like Aurélien Scholl; like Albert Wolff, a German more Parisian than the Parisians; like Villemessant, original of Montbaillard in *Charles Demailly* and founder of the *Figaro*, which he boasted was intended to be read "when little girls have gone to bed" (*à l'heure où les petites filles sont couchées*), who used to serve walking-papers on an unsatisfactory member of his staff by the gift of a nice walking-stick, meaning: *Allez vous promener*. The journalist and *chroniqueur* was apt to be a scandal-monger and did not disdain to repeat backstairs gossip or to peep through the keyholes of *boudoirs* and bedrooms and record the doings of courtesans, so that *les impures* became as prominent as the ladies of the aristocracy. Weeklies like the *Vie parisienne*, founded by Marcelin in 1863, contributed enormously to the vogue of what was considered abroad "Frenchy" and "naughty but nice". The quintessence of this was to be found in the writings of Gustave Droz, a "modern Crébillon *fils*", or, as Gustave Merlet called him, "confectioner of forbidden fruit", and his *Monsieur, madame et bébé*, of which a characteristic chapter told how the writer helped his young and pretty aunt to make up as Venus for a *tableau vivant*. On the other hand, political journalism, when it evaded the censorship, though intensely parochial, in time contributed enormously, by its own form of *blague*, to the downfall of the Empire, as when the opening number of Henri Rochefort's *Lanterne*, in 1868, declared that France had "thirty-six million subjects, not to mention subjects of dissatisfaction" (*sans compter les sujets de mécontentement*). In addition to the pages of the Goncourt brothers' *Charles Demailly*, Augier's comedies,

---

[1] "Cette essence subtile, délicate et pénétrante que Nestor Roqueplan avait baptisée: la Parisine" (A. Meyer, *Ce que mes yeux ont vu*, p. 174). Madame de Girardin (Delphine Gay) whose delightful *Lettres parisiennes*, written under the pseudonym of the "vicomte de Launay", have been drawn upon so much in the present work for material concerning the reign of Louis-Philippe, was largely responsible for the vogue of the *chronique*, but under the Empire it acquired the smart cynicism remote from her graceful touch. The weekly *chronique*, or review, has remained until today an important feature of French journalism.

POSTER BY CHÉRET, FOR A REVIVAL OF *LA VIE PARISIENNE*

especially *les Effrontés*, give striking satirical pictures of journalists with traits borrowed from the tricky boulevard writers and the vituperative ultramontane Veuillot etc.,—the rich journalist Vernouillet, blackmailer and swindler, and the unscrupulous bohemian Giboyer, whose style is an oratorio on a penny whistle (*le Dies irae sur le mirliton*). "Shameless wealth served by corrupt and corrupting poverty, this is what dominates journalism."

It must not for a moment be imagined that there was no serious journalism under the Empire. There were the *Journal des Débats* and the *Temps*, both political, literary, dramatic, and musical. They were together upholders of dignified traditions, and because, under the press laws of the Empire, articles had to be signed, they helped leading intellectuals of France to gain an audience which these would not otherwise have had. But the circulation of these papers was relatively small, and it was frivolous rather than intellectual journalism which set the pace.[1]

The finest literary flavor of *blague* and Parisian atticism combined is to be found in the *opéra-bouffe* as developed by Meilhac and Halévy, with music by the Gallicized German Jew Jacques Offenbach. The composer Saint-Saëns once remarked that the opera bouffe was a daughter of the opera who had gone wrong, but he added that "a girl *qui a mal tourné* is not necessarily unattractive". The opera bouffe was the great dramatic novelty of the second half of the century. The mythological liberties of *la Belle Hélène* and of *Orphée aux Enfers* were thought dreadfully daring, though they seem mild today. Meilhac and Halévy also found objects of satire nearer home than the divinities of Greece. *La Grande duchesse de Gérolstein* ridiculed the petty German duchy of the species described by Thackeray as Pumpernickel, and memories of conspiracies in melodramas and in romantic dramas like *Hernani*, and of grand opera, such as Meyerbeer's *Huguenots*, for a time made the conspirators' scene an almost obligatory comic device. The gay tunes of Offenbach's "*répertoiriculet*" were heard everywhere, and singers like Hortense Schneider and Zulma Bouffar were world famous. At

---

[1] The cheap newspaper is not an American invention. The *Petit Journal*, established in 1863, catering to the semiliterate (the *feuille de chou* and *journal des concierges*), nonpolitical, with lively items and sensational serials, won an enormous circulation.

the time of the Exposition of 1867 and the vogue of the *Grande duchesse*, visiting potentates engaged boxes at the opera ahead of their arrival, and Hortense Schneider's stage dressing-room was so thronged with Russian grand dukes and other noble foreigners that it was dubbed the *Passage des Princes* in humorous allusion to the commercial, glass-roofed, arcaded thoroughfare of that name.[1]

The development of the *cafés-chantants* and the continued vogue of dance gardens encouraged the reckless spirit of *blague*. Every quarter had its open-air concerts, with flaring gaslights and gaudily painted woodwork, where people sipped their *consommations* at little tables and listened to songs in which the sentimental theme was apt to be replaced by double meaning and lightly veiled *polissonneries*, where the ever-popular Thérésa sang delicate ditties such as "It tickles my nose!" (*C'est dans l'nez qu'ça me chatouille!*) The Bal Mabille and the annual dance at the opera flourished, but they had become commercialized and were partly show places for foreigners. The first act of *Henriette Maréchal* by the Goncourt brothers takes place at the opera ball.

[1] Anecdote relates that a Russian grand duke, on his way to Paris, telegraphed ahead, "I wish to see Schneider", and was disappointed when the Russian embassy sent Eugène Schneider, president of the Corps législatif, to greet him.

CHAPTER XIII

SECOND EMPIRE. SOCIETY. THE CLASSES. LITERARY TENDENCIES AND THEMES

AT THE top of the social order was the imperial court. The Emperor and the pleasure-loving Empress were neither of them discerning judges of literature, and each had at times an unofficial mentor. The historian Victor Duruy helped Napoleon to write his life of Cæsar, and Prosper Mérimée was for years the counselor of Eugénie. Literary merit was rewarded by an invitation to join the court parties at Compiègne. Life was a round of entertainments and of occasions for men to display smart uniforms and women their white shoulders. It was the "règne du costumier et de la couturière". Those were the days of *chignon* and crinoline, when men dressmakers, like Worth, were a daring innovation and were deemed a symptom of the growing depravity of society, when a party of sixty guests at Compiègne took nine hundred trunks and Mme de Metternich and Mme de Pourtalès needed special cars for their clothes. The fashionable court painter Winterhalter has left us the record of all these beautiful but often shallow women.

The Emperor had private theaters in the palaces at Compiègne and Fontainebleau. Besides gorgeous hunting parties of green-clad guests coursing the stag to the sound of St. Hubert's horn and the tune of the *Bon roi Dagobert*, amateur theatricals (the *comédie de salon*), charades, and pastoral or mythological *tableaux vivants* were all the rage and were imitated through all smart society. The Emperor's half brother, the duc de Morny, tempted fortune in original comedy, and the novelist Octave Feuillet was a frequent director of court charades.

History still remembers, and Edmond de Goncourt sought to depict in *Chérie*, the smart life of the Second Empire.[1] We recall the names of gay, aristocratic women, some virtuous, some not, and of their attendant knights: the dapper guardsman, the marquis de Massa, and the daredevil horseman, the marquis de Galliffet. There was Mme de Metternich, wife of the Austrian ambassador, enthusiast of the new Wagnerian music, the heroine of the *chroniqueurs*, impishly plain but possessed of supreme elegance, what in *Chérie* is called *le chic Metternich*. She turned a foreign embassy into a Parisian *salon*, played a preponderating social rôle in the second part of the Empire, and was one of those who predicted a Franco-Prussian war. There was the beautiful Mme de Pourtalès, and the beautiful Italian, the Countess of Castiglione, who, in holding Napoleon under her spell, acted for Victor Emmanuel and Cavour the part which the Duchess of Portsmouth acted for Louis XIV with Charles II. Mme de Castiglione's whole life was centered on her own physical beauty, and when, years later, under the Third Republic, old age came to her, she shut herself up in darkened rooms and crept out only after nightfall, that cruel daylight should not testify to the disappearance of her charm, as she mourned the loss of all that made life to her worth living. There was Napoleon's distant cousin, granddaughter of Lucien Bonaparte, known by the names of her successive husbands, Mme de Solms, Mme Rattazzi, and later, after the Empire, Mme de Rute. She was a lively writer and a political marplot, like a heroine of the *Fronde*, the "Princess Hullabaloo" (*Brouhaha*) of Alphonse Karr's *Guêpes*.. Her *salon* in the early period of the Empire was the resort of novelists, politicians, and bohemians, but she passed beyond the pale of Napoleon's favor and went downhill. A more favored cousin of the Emperor was Princess Mathilde, daughter of the ex-king of Westphalia, brother of Napoleon I, at whose home all clever men of letters were welcome. Her name recurs in biographies, correspondence, and diaries of con-

---

[1] Paul Reboux has tried to picture the life of the Second Empire in his novel, *Arthur et Sophie, ou Paris en 1860*, published in 1924.

temporary writers, like the Goncourt diary, as the cleverest member of the imperial family.

Society aped the court and lived for frivolous enjoyment. Even charity for the relief of suffering had to take the form of subscription dances and galas. Meilhac and Halévy's *Froufrou* portrays the pleasure-lover whose thoughtlessness is her undoing. Octave Feuillet, discussing the Parisienne in *Monsieur de Camors*, tells how the artificial civilization of Paris had taken away all sentiment of duty, leaving only the taste for enjoyment. Intelligent women, he says, were pagans, interested only in the "volupté des sens et de l'esprit". The others moved in a round of childish excitement, busy triflers, "who visit, make appointments, lure each other along, dress, gossip, bustle about day and night in emptiness, and dance with a sort of frenzy in the rays of the Parisian sunlight, without thoughts, without passions, without virtue and even without vices".

In all this there is undoubtedly the exaggeration of the censor. But even in the sentimental and pseudo-moral novels of Feuillet, men are nearly always loving their friends' wives, while the women love other women's husbands. Were it necessary, which it is not, to believe all the scandal of Viel-Castel's memoirs, one might think the whole world of fashion utterly decadent. Yet for real perverseness one turns to the horde of vampire women who swooped down on Paris, the *demi-mondaines* and *femmes entretenues*. The fashionable *cocodette*, with social standing but *blasée*, exaggerated in costume, slangy in speech, fit successor of the *lionne* and companion of the new dandy, or *cocodès*, often aped the style of the venal courtesans, or *cocottes* and *biches*, the "Amandas" and "Coras", the "Tatas" and "Titines" of comedy, the "Mlle Taffetas" of Emile Augier.

Meanwhile, what of the *bourgeoisie*? As might be expected, the solid middle class made the vigor of the country, and even its defects were often its strength. But, in Paris especially, the frivolous, yet alluring, enjoyments of the rich could not be without effect on the weak. There is an interesting description in *Monsieur de Camors* of two *bourgeoises* whose happiness and

THE EMPRESS EUGÉNIE, BY WINTERHALTER (VERSAILLES MUSEUM). SEMI-OFFICIAL PORTRAITURE OF THE SECOND EMPIRE

pride it was to be acquainted with all the petty details of Parisian high life, to follow its *fêtes*, to talk its slang, to copy its toilets, to distinguish the different liveries, and who delighted in knowing all the tittle-tattle of "aventures équivoques".

The fashion for men was to be smart, devoid of ideals, and unwilling to admit their existence in others. The young student no longer felt the literary and artistic enthusiasms of 1830, or the political raptures of 1848. He prepared himself for a money-making career as civil engineer, lawyer, or doctor. He no longer had sentimental affairs with *grisettes*, but illicit love was a commercial transaction. Taine, in *Thomas Graindorge*, emphasizes the difference between the young man of 1820 and the positivist and materialist of 1860, self-seeking to the core. The young man of comedy, he says, is no longer the adorer, but lacking in gallantry, cynical and rude, skilled in contests of sex hostility, playing "froidement et savamment de la mécanique féminine". The whole aim of life among men and women, he says, is *jouir et paraître*, and he describes life in these terms:

> People of society who live for pleasure and catch it once out of ten times, *bourgeois* who pursue it without obtaining it, fast women and a shady low-class population who sell it, or act the swindlers with it, such is Paris.

Théodore de Banville expressed the same general idea in a striking ballade of regret for 1830 contributed to the *Parnasse contemporain*.

At the foot of the ladder was the vast working population, whom it behooved the government to keep busy or to amuse, like children, with pageantry and display. Some workers, we have seen, were sullen and brooding, and schemed a social revolution, but until the rude awakening of the Franco-Prussian War the majority let themselves be lulled into satisfaction with the state of things, and accepted in the prevalent tone of jesting *blague* the contrast between the extravagance of boulevard restaurants and the penny pleasures of the *ouvriers*. As the open barouches full of lavishly dressed women and of *fêtards* swept

AT A FIRST PERFORMANCE UNDER THE SECOND EMPIRE (1860)
Drawings by Marcelin

up the Champs-Elysées and the avenue de l'Impératrice to the Bois de Boulogne the working-men's children romped happily in the streets in their belted black play frocks, or *sarraus*. Their luxury was to buy for one or two sous a glass of licorice-root water from the itinerant *marchand de coco*, carrying on his back a tank adorned with tinsel and bells ("à la fraîche, à la glace, qui veut boire?"), or to listen for the cry of the vender of *plaisir* ("voilà le plaisir!"), a favorite sweetened and brittle wafer. For these children art was the roughly printed and colored *image d'Epinal*; for music and poetry they had *mirlitons*, little hollow reed pipes sealed at each end with waxed paper and pasted round with spiral strips bearing cheap jingles, —whence the name, *vers de mirliton*, given in general in France to cheap doggerel.

Opposed in spirit to the *bourgeoisie* were not only the envious working classes and peasantry but also the supercilious aristocracy and artistic dilettantes, as well as the *bohème*, who joined the scorn of one group with the envy of the other.

Deprived of many of its privileges, the legitimist aristocracy shut itself up more than ever in caste and took pleasure in making *bons mots* about the *parvenus*. The legitimists, believers in the rights of God, were "reactionaries" like the Marquis in *le Fils de Giboyer*. The partisans of the comte de Chambord as pretender even looked down on the Emperor. The aristocrats secluded in the country became of necessity hidebound fogies, as in Sardou's *Ganaches*. The young men were elegant cynics and were copied by the rich sons of the *bourgeoisie*. On the other hand, Octave Feuillet idealizes the high-minded but impoverished young aristocrat in his *Roman d'un jeune homme pauvre*. George Sand, in the two brothers of *le Marquis de Villemer*, opposes the two types, the profligate and the man of honor.

The bohemians were in reality envious of the well-to-do *bourgeois*, not only the capitalist but the small tradesman (*petit commerçant*). Impecunious writers or artists, struggling against the duns of landlord or creditor, and comparing their hardships with prosperous respectability, vented their spleen more

MARCHAND DE COCO
Drawing by Bertall

than ever in caricature of the platitudes of the inept *bourgeois* as contrasted with the brilliance of unrecognized genius. Some, with the exuberance of youth, tried, like the *Jeunes-France*, to mystify and *épater*. The poverty-stricken bohemians consoled themselves for their hardships by idealizing them, and threw a glamour of romance about the experiences of attic life and the sordid women with whom they had to consort. Again, the reaction against a society veiling its materialism in what seemed a hypocritical idealism made them gravitate to descriptions of the vulgar, the low, and the ugly. In these tendencies it is now the custom to seek the origins of modern Realism and, in time, of Naturalism.

The literature of the Second Empire was, on the whole, more prosaic than poetical. Of course some of the important lyrical works of Hugo belong to this period, but the novel and prose comedy are the characteristic products of the age. Poetry itself was often influenced by the forces which made the reign of Napoleon III one of science and of "scientific" realism in literature. In fact some poets tried to develop the poetry of industrialism.

The literature of realism seems to have been to a noteworthy degree the outcome of conditions both intellectual and social: The bankruptcy of romanticism, as an imaginative outpouring, the cult of the concrete fact, the theories of historical transformism, and the pseudo-scientific German Hegelianism, culminating in doctrines of evolution, had emphasized cause and effect. At the same time the new products of applied science, even such apparently remote devices as the daguerreotype, had led people to be interested in the accurate pictorial as well as the artistic representations of life.

But just as important a contributing influence came from a different cause. Socially the sponsors of realism were either those who had themselves suffered from the hardships of economic conditions or those who sympathized with such sufferers. They were the new bohemians, successors in a certain sense of the romantic *Jeunes-France*.

Many of the *Jeunes-France* had been skylarking boys, occasionally even from families in comfortable circumstances. The standards of living were so simple that even poverty could be cheerful, and find poetry in a *grenier à vingt ans*, or throw a glamour over the *vie de bohème* and the cheap stews in which Murger's students found the heads of the "bicephalous rabbit". But even by the end of Louis-Philippe's reign the gradual though slight rise in prices, and the contrast between poverty and wealth, turned Bohemia into an envious intellectual proletariat. It saw life as sordidly "real" in its poverty and disease.

Therefore, under the Second Empire, the noteworthy tendencies, besides the survival of Hugoism and such individual romantic eccentrics as are still found in the Third Republic, in Villiers de l'Isle-Adam and Barbey d'Aurevilly, were the following:

1. The *bourgeois* writers and the *école du bon sens* of Ponsard and Augier, advocates of law, order, and respectability, representatives of the poetry of hearth and home, the *lyrisme du pot-au-feu*, and the *juste-milieu poétique*. They expressed themselves particularly in the comedy of manners and preached through the example of the stage. Yet the virtuous lessons of Dumas's prose comedies sometimes serve their cause but ill, by what was at the time undue prominence given to the portrayal of social evils.

2. The anti-*bourgeois* writers, poets, and prose writers. They set up an absolute antinomy between the practical, and therefore, as they felt, essentially narrow-minded, *bourgeois* and the unpractical artist or man of letters. The poet justified his inability to handle realities by proclaiming the cult of art for art's sake. The prose writers, tired of the exotic, the fantastic, and the self-consciousness of romanticism, began to write novels of contemporary manners in a style of supposedly impersonal, objective, and impartial sincerity. They shared the hatred for the middle class felt by the devotees of art for art's sake. The *bourgeois* now became the equivalent of the Philistine. He was

the upholder of the established order of things. On the other hand, the men of letters were, for the most part, politically in the opposition. Hugo called realism "democratic literature". It was scorned as "socialistic", because it dealt so much with the poor and lowly, and with the scenes most familiar to many of its writers, and because it held up to ridicule the *bourgeois* of Paris and of the small towns.[1] The Goncourt brothers, who finally launched Naturalism, the acute form of realism, were of aristocratic temper in their neurotic aloofness from life, and partisans of art for art's sake, but they too proclaimed the right of the lower classes, in days of universal manhood suffrage, to be admitted to fiction. They, more than anybody else, were responsible with *Germinie Lacerteux* for modern French naturalism and the detailed description of vice and corruption. In the preface of *Chérie* Edmond de Goncourt distinctly claims that *Germinie Lacerteux* was the *livre-type* of realism and naturalism, and of all that has been manufactured since. He calls his brother and himself *apporteurs de neuf* and revolutionaries of book and picture, and they boasted the invention of the term *document humain*. Their love of the morbid seems in part their reaction against the academic and *bourgeois* ideal of the *beau*.

Unfortunately for French literature some of the most important representatives of the anti-*bourgeois* group owed their scorn for ordinary people to constitutional defects. Without being paranoiacs they were temperamentally on the other side. Flaubert had some form of epilepsy; Baudelaire was the victim of drugs and disease; the Goncourt brothers were neurotic degenerates. Flaubert had the sturdiness of the Norman, but Baudelaire and the Goncourts turned their talent to the morbid and unhealthy, and thus exerted a cruelly baneful influence on the poetry and prose of the Third Republic.

Outside the *bourgeois* and anti-*bourgeois* schools we have:

3. The pseudo-idealists of whom Feuillet is the most noteworthy example, painters of high life, of men and women of

[1] Champfleury's *les Bourgeois de Molinchart*; Flaubert's *Madame Bovary*.

wealth and fashion, idlers for the most part, with the opportunities for insidious and veiled immorality to which excessive leisure lends itself.

4. The *fantaisistes*, journalists and writers of fiction, clever but superficial, smart and irreverent as well as unmoral, but favored by authority because they turned people's thoughts from economic grievances. These writers were the characteristic representatives of French wit and *blague*, though they are vastly less esteemed now than in the days of their vogue.

With the Second Empire it becomes more difficult to enumerate literary types. Paris and France were cosmopolitan; novels were numerous and miscellaneous; the characters and *poncifs* became more varied and less accentuated. Moreover, Gavarni and Daumier no longer gave them such vivid pictorial form. It is, therefore, especially in drama, notably the *comédie sociale* of Augier and Dumas, that we find themes and characters.

In poetry the chief writers were the Parnassians. Usually described as a school of unemotional formalists, they were not really such. The *Parnasse* was not impersonal or anti-individual. Théophile Gautier, who serves as transition to the school of art for art's sake, had been an ardent romanticist. Leconte de Lisle began life as an impecunious young radical and socialist, and was never, all his life, in easy circumstances. The young Parnassians were obstreperously bohemian, and the wild escapades over which Nina de Villard presided in her apartments testify to the desire of youth to be unconventional.[1]

Viewed, however, in its more serious aspect, Parnassian romanticism reflects tendencies of its age, in that it is in part a reaction against the ineffectual socialism and humanitarianism which came to grief after 1848. Leconte de Lisle, former Fourierist, became an intellectual aristocrat who replaced democratic mysticism by stoicism and a non-Christian pessimism in harmony with the scientific doctrines of the times. The Parnassians protested against the exaggerations of Hugoesque

[1] Catulle Mendès, in his play *Glatigny*, tried to portray the bohemian life of young poets and students at the famous *Brasserie des Martyrs*.

romanticism and the "blubberings" of the Lamartinians. They proclaimed the independence of art from morals, the cult of beauty and of form, distinct from ethical right and wrong, and banished the overdisplay of personal sentiment in favor of objective art.

During the Empire the Parnassians met their sharpest attacks from the "figarists", boulevard jesters typified by the newspaper, the *Figaro*, who replaced criticism by *blague*, who opposed the "dry lyricists" (*lyriques secs*) to the "moist lyricists" (*lyriques humides*) and "wet hearts" (*cœurs mouillés*), and waxed merry at the expense of the "formistes" and "impassibles".

Comedy and fiction reflect the new conditions either as a picture of reality or as an object lesson for use by the moralist, and the novel becomes more than ever what the Goncourts defined it, hypothetical or constructive history, "de l'histoire qui aurait pu être". The great themes are the general moral anæmia and the corrupting influence of the courtesan and of money.

The Goncourts, in Chapter LVIII of *Charles Demailly*, describe the general weakening, in the nineteenth century, of men whose brains are ever in tension seeking fame and fortune,— bankers, business men, statesmen, artists, writers, those who live on the impressions, enjoyments, satisfactions, deceptions, and moral defeats of each succeeding day:

> And anæmia is taking hold of us, that is the positive fact. The human type is degenerating. Stretching from family to species there is the wasting away which royal races undergo at the end of dynasties . . . You have seen those kings of Spain at the Louvre . . . What exhaustion of an ancestral blood! Perhaps such was the disease of the Roman Empire, certain emperors of which show faces whose features seem to have melted away, even in the bronze . . . But then there was a remedy. When a society was lost, physiologically exhausted, there came to it an invasion of barbarians who transfused into it the young blood of Hercules. Who will save the world from the anæmia of the nineteenth century? Will it be in a few hundreds of years an invasion of workingmen into society?

SOCIAL AND LITERARY TENDENCIES

With the increase of luxury the days of happy-go-lucky *grisettes* were ended. This was to be the age of the courtesan on a great scale, the *demi-mondaine* and *femme entretenue*, or kept woman. *Demi-mondaine, biche,* and *cocotte* became almost synonymous terms. Dumas *fils* had created the term "demi-monde" in his play of that name, where his baronne d'Ange is not beyond the outskirts of society and still struggles for respectability and recognition; but Balzac had already, in Valérie Marneffe, given an example of the unscrupulous woman who subordinates everything to money. It was not long before women of this type, often ignorant adventuresses of peasant origin, became a recognized caste, selling themselves for the gold, jewelry, and finery that the rich *viveurs* were ready to squander upon them. During the last years of the Empire photographs of the famous *demi-mondaines* were sold in the shops with pictures of royalty and statesmen. They welcomed their admirers in their boxes at the fashionable Italian opera in the Théâtre des Italiens, and were the subject of newspaper *chroniques*. Who knows, even, how many times one of these women may have blasted the reputation of a better one? It is not difficult to imagine an unscrupulous journalist like Emile de Girardin influenced for evil by the vindictive jealousy of his spiteful mistress Esther Guimond. Of these women Augier wrote in his *Mariage d'Olympe*: "A man does not bow to them when he is giving his arm to his mother or to his sister; but he takes them to the Bois in an open carriage and to the most conspicuous seats at the theatre . . . and without passing for a cynic." At the races of Satory in 1860 the *demi-mondaines* showed themselves openly in the world of fashion, and Esther Guimond declared: "Though I do not belong to the society of the ladies, I belong to the society of the gentlemen." Zola typifies the courtesan of the Empire in his *Nana*, and in *Au bonheur des dames* he makes the large department store, a new institution, a symptom of the greed of women for luxury, and an opportunity for men to ruin themselves by extravagances for women.

Paris became the haven of international adventuresses. Already, under Louis-Philippe, Lola Montez had appeared, who afterward caused a political revolution in Bavaria, but now sleeps peacefully in Greenwood Cemetery, in Brooklyn. There was the American Jewess, the actress Adah Isaacs Menken, who wrote *soi-disant* poetry and played Mazeppa in tights, strapped to a horse's back, whose name is linked with those of Swinburne and of Dumas *père*,—"ce beau corps qui fut Adah Menken", as the younger Dumas described her in an unpublished letter in the possession of the present writer. There was the Irishwoman Cora Pearl, for whose sake a *petit crevé* named Duval tried to shoot himself toward the end of the Empire, but, surviving, lived for over fifty years to supply in his numerous *Bouillons Duval* inexpensive food for those Parisians who have no money to spend on Cora Pearls. But the quintessence of this flashy world may be found in the career of the marquise de Païva, a German Jewess born in the Frankfort ghetto, married to a Portuguese nobleman to acquire a title, who enriched herself by a life of *galanterie*, whose gorgeous *hôtel* in the Champs-Elysées, with magnificent marble staircase and ceilings frescoed by Baudry, was frequented by scores of prominent people, even respectable professors like Taine. Finally, under the Third Republic, she married Count Henckel von Donnersmarck, one of the richest men in Germany, an agent of Bismarck, and her home was the scene of the political intrigues by which it was hoped to bring about meetings between the German chancellor and Gambetta.

It will be remembered that when romantic literature had portrayed the courtesan, she had often been held up to pity, as when Marion Delorme's love gives her a new virginity. The sentimental attitude has its last noteworthy example in Dumas's *Dame aux camélias* which is based on the amazing experience of the young peasant girl Marie Duplessis, who, after beginning her career in Paris as an illiterate kitchen drudge, soon blossomed into a queen of luxurious harlotry and died of consumption in her early twenties. But it was next in order to crucify the courtesan and the married woman who imitates her and lapses into adultery through love of luxury or the romantic folly of making a religion of love. Théodore Barrière's *Filles de marbre* is the counterblast to the *Dame aux camélias*, picturing the artist ruined and driven to death for having "sought a pearl beneath the dung hill and found the dung hill without the pearl". Augier's *Mariage d'Olympe* shows the evil woman rescued and yet returning to her vice, through the *nostalgie de la boue*. The *Lionnes pauvres* depicts a woman dishonoring herself for money and clothes. Dumas's *Ami des femmes* and *Diane de Lys* show the degradation of adultery. Dumas's flagellation of woman becomes in time an obsession, until in his later plays, with a revival of old romantic mystic frenzy, he brands her as a thing of infamy corrupting man. Couture's famous painting, *les Romains de la décadence* (1847), portraying an orgy, seemed to have a meaning applicable to modern times, and in the *Filles de marbre* courtesans and dissipation are spoken of as characterizing the *Parisiens de la décadence*.

The worship of the golden calf, anticipated in Balzac's *Mercadet*, is also shown in the plays of Ponsard, Augier, and Dumas.

The literature of the Second Empire, then, offers the picture of a selfish society from which the poetry of romanticism is absent and in which the *bourgeois* respectability of the age of Louis-Philippe is giving way before a still more reckless materialism. Plays and novels depict marriages for money, adultery, cynical men about town, flaunting *demi-mondaines* imitated by married women. Middle-class respectability is often ridiculed. The leading men are smart explorers or physicians, or brilliant young civil engineers, skilled in dancing, versed in the ways of a young girl's heart, and successful in making a rich match. They are self-centered and devoid of ideals. The "homme fort" of Balzac still appears, as in Feuillet's play *Montjoye*.[1]

---

[1] What the "homme fort" has become under the Third Republic we find in Alfred Capus's *Scènes de la vie difficile*, chap. v: "Without being conscious of it, merely following the line of ambition traced by circumstances, Gonzague tended towards a certain type of 'homme fort', which is not, in the

Two famous literary types are Dumas's Monsieur Alphonse (belonging chronologically to the Third Republic), and Feuillet's Monsieur de Camors. Monsieur Alphonse is the man, heartless and without conscience, devoid of any feeling of duty or paternal love, who conceives no obligation to the children of his caprice. Nowadays, in accordance with the usual progressive perversion of unfavorable terms, an "Alphonse" has degenerated into the designation of a man who subsists by the vice of women. This is not in real accordance with Dumas.

Feuillet's Monsieur de Camors is the equivalent under the Second Empire of what Molière called his Don Juan, a *grand seigneur méchant homme*. He is the man of the world, of *bonnes fortunes*, or amorous intrigues, enjoying the luxuries of life, music, painting, literature, and horses. But he is unrealistic in the sense that, though his theory of life is purely material, he has a sentiment of honor in his wickedness, and is idealized above the mere *viveur*.

Even the young girl was beginning to seem emancipated. It is true that the *ingénue*, the successor of Molière's Agnès, still appeared on the stage and was impersonated at the Théâtre-Français for many years of the Third Republic by Suzanne Reichenberg of the piping voice; but in comedy and in the worldly society of real life she was far from being a *niaise*. She is sometimes portrayed as clever and audacious, but honest like Molière's Henriette. But again she is materialistic, schemes to catch a prominent official, a prefect or the like, and is frivolous and slangy. Taine, in his *Thomas Graindorge,* has a bitter tirade against woman portrayed in the drama of 1865.

democratic environment, what it appeared under the Second Empire or under the Monarchy of July. It requires much more suppleness and consideration for the interests of others, precisely because society is too mixed and bustling for one to cleave one's way with one's fists. More subtle devices are required, more sinuous methods, a more universal consent. No success to-day can prevail against the combined efforts of all rivals. The art of the 'homme fort' consists, therefore, rather in causing one's ambition to be accepted than in imposing it. This phenomenon is as visible in politics as in literature and in business."

Sardou's *Famille Benoîton* sums up the dramatic satirist's picture of the social corruption of the Empire. The members of the Benoîton family think of nothing but slang, dress, racing, gambling, and business speculations. The mother, Mme Benoîton, never appears on the stage, but is always away from home enjoying herself, and is as elusive as Dickens's Mrs Harris.

A most somber picture of life under the Empire is presented in the Rougon-Macquart series by Zola, in which that novelist endeavored to be the Balzac of the new age. But Zola composed most of his novels under the Third Republic, and his own experience of society under Napoleon came from seeing it through his attic window. He wrote to prove a dubious scientific theory, and he followed as historical authority Taxile Delord, who was a journalist and pamphleteer rather than a scholar. Zola's indictment is therefore even more bitter and exaggerated than that of the moralists that we have enumerated. But the picture of the Second Empire is the familiar one which a hostile republican generation has caused to prevail,—a weak and vicious monarch surrounded by selfish schemers masquerading as defenders of faith and morals, cringing to the Church and governing by sneaks and spies; a society corrupted by evil examples in high places, given over to luxury and immorality; families disunited, religion a form, and patriotism an empty phrase. In all this there was some truth and much fiction.

The literature of the Second Empire gravitates around Paris, because Paris was more than ever the nerve-center of France. It is true that some novelists, especially the realists, depict provincial life, but usually to portray that life as humdrum and a petty imitation of what goes on in the capital. As proof a quotation from the fifth chapter of Feuillet's *Monsieur de Camors* is appropriate:

> Does not Paris undertake to live and think for us? Does it not deign to cast to us every morning, as the Roman senate used to do to the mob, our food for the day, bread and vaudevilles, *panem et circenses!* . . . Yes, Sir, after the past, behold the present, behold France of to-day! . . . A nation of forty million inhabitants awaiting every morning

the word from Paris to know if it is day or night, if it is to laugh or to weep! A great people; once the noblest and the cleverest in the world, repeating together on the same day, at the same hour, in all the drawing rooms and at all the street corners of the empire, the same inane broad jest, hatched the night before in the mire of the boulevard!

The art of the Second Empire, though not necessarily the best of the nineteenth century, was extraordinarily flourishing because of patronage and the prominence given to it at the great expositions, culminating in that of 1867. At the same time the stamp of official approval placed on certain artists and their methods stimulated to rival action the independents. In 1863 the Ecole des Beaux-Arts became a state school and, like the Institute, a stronghold of regularity. On the other hand, that same year the Emperor gave his patronage to an exhibition of works rejected by the Salon, the famous *Salon des refusés*. Much of the "independence" of artists and poets is due to their exclusion from Salons and *cénacles*.

The official influences supposedly continued the traditions of David and Ingres, with emphasis on form. The antique was fashionable in reaction against the medievalism of the days of Louis-Philippe, and "romantic" was as bad form as "Orleanist". The word "Empire" made people think of Rome and Pompeii in decoration, as under Napoleon I, and Prince Jerome built a famous Pompeian villa. But this art was neither Napoleonic martial classicism nor genuine classicism; and, in so far as it was also expressed by the term *néo-grec*, as in pictures by Gérôme, it consisted of decorative anacreontic scenes of ancient life, and was often the pretext for a sensuous and skeptical age to indulge in mythological nudities. Cabanel's *Birth of Venus*, an over-life-sized nude, startled but pleased the *bourgeois*. Gérôme became under the Empire, and remained for many years of the Third Republic, a controlling influence in the teaching of art, because of his studio and his professorship at the Ecole des Beaux-Arts.

Meanwhile the early realists in art were reacting against the *beau idéal* and the heroic. Influenced by the social theorists

BURIAL AT ORNANS, BY COURBET (LOUVRE)
Famous early example of realism in art

and the humanitarians, they painted the lowly, peasants and their cattle, in everyday occupations and attitudes. The Barbizon landscape school, one of the chief artistic glories of the Second Empire, prolonged its prestige into the Third Republic. Realism merges into Impressionism, of which we shall have more to say.

Finally, domestic art, in the shape of furniture, was eclectic but ornate and influenced by the production of furniture, machine-made or constructed after uniform patterns, as a result of industrialism. There was elaborate upholstery, and talkers gathered around the *pouf*,—"des sièges de cette sorte qu'on nomme poufs", as Anatole France's abbé Lantaigne says; that is, heavy, round upholstered ottomans with fringes and tassels.

CHAPTER XIV

THIRD REPUBLIC. INTELLECTUAL EPOCHS

IT IS customary to divide the intellectual history of the Third Republic into three chief periods, the first extending from the downfall of the Empire to about 1885-1890, the second lasting until the beginning of the present century, and the third comprising the decade or so preceding the outbreak of the World War.[1]

The first period was one of disenchantment. The materialism and positivism of the Empire continued, embittered by defeat. There were outbursts of noble patriotism, as in Henri de Bornier's *Fille de Roland*; "Souvenons-nous" was the motto of various *sociétés de gymnastique* which were in time organized in the *lycées* and colleges; but the patriotism was usually one of resignation. To use an expression now current, France was "shell-shocked".

Naturally, therefore, the generation which came of age about 1885 was pessimistic. Its earliest years had been under the shadow of the *année terrible*, and it was even maintained that those born in 1870-1871 were, many of them, physically weaker or more nervous than is normal. Young men reaching manhood read Taine, Renan, the Goncourts, Zola, and Baudelaire. They saw nothing to stimulate them spiritually in the fatalism of Taine, the dilettantism of Renan, the morbid brutality of fiction and poetry. They were skeptics, evolutionary agnostics, ironists. It is the period of the apogee of Naturalism, of the sar-

---

[1] The incoherent Goncourt prize novel *Rabevel*, by L. Fabre, speaks of three generations, *down to the present*; first, the generation of cowardice after the disaster; second, the generation of selfish business and money-making, suffering from what, with a new meaning to an old medieval name, he calls *le mal des ardents*; third, the generation sacrificed in the war.

donic *genre rosse*, of Bourget's *Essais de psychologie contemporaine*, of the early writings of Maurice Barrès. It was a period psychologically characterized by introspection and the literary analysis of the weak and diseased will. Morally it had developed in many people a timorousness in facing life, a *peur de vivre*, a dread of responsibility,[1] in which the easy life of a state officeholder, or *fonctionnaire*, seemed the happiest refuge; in which people practiced a philosophy of *ennui* and *je-m'enfichisme*, the "I-don't-care-a-hang" attitude. Critics have pointed out that Rostand's *Aiglon* is like his own generation of 1870, men incapable of action, but with yearnings for an ideal which they cannot put into being. There developed a spirit of egotism and selfish intellectualism, which, in literature, delighted not only in the brutality of naturalism but in ironic nihilism, morbid and neurotic dilettantism and satanism, as expressed in the novels of Huysmans. The horror of war took the form of internationalism, pacifism, antimilitarism, of novels discrediting the army, such as Charles Leroy's *Colonel Ramollot*, Abel Hermant's *Cavalier Miserey*, and Lucien Descaves's *Sous-offs*. People interpreted life largely through books, and gave unnecessary importance to sensationally somber pictures of existence. Even social theorists began to talk about the "decadence of the Latin races", and wrote books such as Edmond Demolins's *A quoi tient la supériorité des Anglo-Saxons*. The Panama scandals, the Fashoda misadventure with England, the bitterness of anticlerical disputes, and the Dreyfus Case disheartened people. As late as 1905 we find this remarkable passage in Emile Faguet's *Anti-cléricalisme*:

> France feels herself to be a second class nation; she no longer dreams of conquest, no longer feels herself invoked by oppressed peoples, or cannot reasonably imagine herself to be invoked by them; and as for the principle of nationalities, however idealistic it may be, it has been too terribly baneful to her for her not to have banished it somewhat from her heart.[2]

[1] *La Peur de vivre*, title of a novel by Henry Bordeaux; *l'Horreur des responsabilités*, title of a study by Emile Faguet. [2] Page 307.

The chances of chronology also imperceptibly contributed to discouragement. The close of the nineteenth century seemed to emphasize the notion of an *end* to a period not spiritually

A TYPICAL "RAMOLLOT," INCARNATION OF CONCEIT AND RED TAPE
Drawing by Uzès

noble. Some æsthetic writers began to call themselves *décadents*, and the term *fin-de-siècle* came into use as suggesting an art refined to enervation and deliquescence. Max Nordau wrote

Entartung, arguing the decay of French poetry, the translations of which (*Dégénérescence* and *Degeneration*) had considerable vogue in France and in English-speaking countries.

The third period, covering the beginning of the twentieth century, is difficult to explain systematically because of its chaotic lack of unity, because of the conflicting forces at work, and especially because neither politics nor literature really reflected the life of the people. Outwardly the political and social picture was not inspiring. The bitterness between clericals and anticlericals was venomous; there were industrial strikes with *sabotage*, and at least one mutiny in the army; parliament was run by petty cliques and intrigues ("coalitions de couloir") and managed by shifty political give-and-take. The condition was what a clever journalist, R. de Jouvenel, characterized in the title of a book, *la République des camarades*. The climax was reached in the sordid murder trial of Mme Caillaux in 1914, in which the wife of one of the leading French politicians was tried for the murder of the editor of the *Figaro* and acquitted. Paris seemed outwardly more flashily cosmopolitan than ever, and given over to money-making, pleasure, and pornography. At the same time there was little relation between literature and life. There was a great deal of literary commercialism. Writers catered to fleeting moods. Publishers outdid each other in vaunting their wares (a practice even increased since the war), and the most insignificant work of fiction was termed "roman passionné", "évocation saisissante", "œuvre originale et troublante". At the same time, where commercialism was not the issue, there was a vast amount of literary *snobisme*. This rendering of an English word was often changed to mean to the French idlers who pursue the latest fad, intellectual, literary, artistic, or musical. The *littérature de cénacle* had almost no connection with life, and gave itself over to subtle and overrefined mannerisms in thought and style, as well as to fads for foreigners and French æsthetes. The trouble was that foreigners took these faddists more seriously as artistic forces than they did themselves. Hence their evil influence on naïve Anglo-

DIVERSIONS OF THE PEOPLE

Saxons. Romain Rolland, in the volume of *Jean-Christophe* called *la Maison*, criticizes the ineffectiveness of the intellectual leaders of France through overindividualism and the innumerable mutually destructive small groups, the "outside" reviews and "outside" theaters, the distrust in literature and in politics, the super-refined criticism made still less helpful by the dead weight of conventional public opinion in politics, religion, and social convention.

In reality conditions were much less serious. Behind the bickering and bargaining politicians recalling the councilors of state in *Ruy Blas*, behind a façade of unreal and detached literature, France, heedless of politicians, was toiling. The peasants, the artisans, the *petits commerçants* were working for their comfort and adding to the prosperity of the nation. Moreover, the reaction against national discouragement and philosophical pessimism had been going on for some time. The earliest Nationalists had blundered egregiously in the Boulangist and Dreyfusite campaigns, but in the early twentieth century patriotism acquired a more spiritual quality, and was exalted by contrast with the antimilitarism and internationalism of the socialists, which had reached its climax in the *hervéisme* of Gustave Hervé, who wanted to drag the flag through the muck ("le drapeau dans le fumier"). Coincidently Brunetière had long led a campaign against the brutality of the naturalistic novel, based on supposedly scientific premises, and had later dramatically proclaimed the failure, or "bankruptcy", of science itself.

If we now undertake to analyze more fully the intellectual influences and their results, we find that the first period of the Third Republic is dominated by Taine and Renan, whose power was never greater than about 1880. At the same time, in scholarly circles the Kantian neocriticism of Renouvier was respected, but in reality it was critical rather than constructive, and its technical nature precluded it from having much influence except among trained thinkers.

The influence of Taine furthers the scientific materialism of the age, and Taine and Renan together, though in different ways, help to quench the religious spirit. But Taine did not arouse the hostility of the Catholics that Renan did. The influence of Taine was great on Naturalism in literature, that of Renan in undermining moral idealism.

Taine, the philosophical scientist, was confident that science would in time solve everything and that there would be no more mystery. But the banishing of the aspirations of faith and religious belief made his influence lead to pessimistic determinism. In men like Taine himself this could be exalted by a noble stoicism; in less sturdy natures there was facilitated a morbidly brutal and discouraged interpretation of life.

Taine taught the value of exact observation and experimentaion. Among the good results of his influence were the following:

1. He paved the way for the modern French psychologists, who, however, became differentiated from the metaphysicians: Charcot, Ribot, Binet, Pierre Janet.

2. He taught to the historians, such as Lavisse and Sorel, conscientiousness, modesty, the accurate study of documents.

Taine's literary influence, for the exaggerations of which he was not responsible, included the following:

1. The idea of applying to literary criticism the methods of science and of natural history, as with Brunetière, and of psychological analysis and explanation, as in Bourget's essays.

2. The pessimistic and deterministic interpretation of life in fiction. For the concentration by the school of Zola on the brutal and the *bête humaine*, Taine is not to be blamed so much as is the commercialism of the pornographers.

3. Pseudo-scientific psychological fiction and the subtle analysis of character. For circumscribing the analysis of passions to cosmopolitan and "high-life" circles, to cattish and feline emotions, Bourget, in his early novels, rather than Taine, is to be blamed.

The scientific influence of Renan included the following:

1. A sincere devotion to truth, as he saw it, in historical scholarship. Whatever charges may be brought against Renan, that of disloyalty to science is not one.

2. Sympathy and amenity. These were certainly not superfluous in a country where there is still much of the Jacobin spirit.

3. What seems to contradict the preceding,—a human interpretation of the supernatural which was, inevitably, in the highest degree offensive to Catholics and followers of Christian dogma. To Renan, as to psychiatrists and mental alienists like Dr. Charcot, acute religious experiences are forms of hysteria and neurosis. Christianity itself is not dogma or religion but poetry.

The literary influence of Renan, for all of which he is not to be made responsible, included the following:

1. Popularization of religious themes and higher criticism,—a patronizingly friendly treatment of matters held in reverence, which continues Voltairian irony, though it is more subtle and restrained. It finds its flower in some of the short stories of Anatole France and in his *Jeanne Darc*.

2. Dilettantism, granting equal value to all things, superiority to none,—*je-m'en-fichisme*, even, with a few, scoffing at patriotism. To the critic such as Anatole France or Jules Lemaître life is a "charming stroll in the midst of reality".

3. Intellectual egotism, the encouraging of an intellectual *élite*, belief in the superiority of the "artist" and æsthete, on the score that the philosopher is king. This was tremendously fruitful and fateful in the years 1885-1900. The early works of Maurice Barrès represent an effort to apply the method of Taine to the dilettantism of Renan.

4. Even in the Church some clever *abbés* felt that concessions must be made to save it, and that a new apologetic must be devised. Lacordaire and Dupanloup were out of date. Thus were sown the seeds of Modernism.[1]

During the eighties and the nineties the intellectual conditions become very complicated:

The evolutionary positivism of Taine and the critical irony of Renan, though modified, do not cease, and still inspire many

[1] Rawlinson, *Recent French Tendencies*.

French writers. Moreover, there are efforts to develop rationally and critically the fundamental principles of a nonclerical system of ethics, sometimes professedly "republican", a *morale laïque* to be taught in the state schools.

On the other hand, the spiritualistic reaction against positivism is sometimes sentimental and Tolstoyan, sometimes technically philosophical. In the twentieth century the spiritualism culminates in Bergsonism, in various nonintellectualist mystical movements, and in the Catholic revival.

The tendency of nonreligious ethics was toward emphasis upon the duties resulting from the relations in life of human beings, a new humanitarianism. One philosopher who for a time exerted considerable influence upon French nonreligious young intellectuals was Guyau. He wrote on the "nonreligion of the future" and sketched an ethical system "sans obligation ni sanction". Guyau's thought had great appeal to those numerous people who, without interest in ecclesiasticism, have spiritual impulses and desire to interpret life in such terms. Religion was to Guyau, in large part, precisely those ties which bind men together and create, therefore, moral and social obligations. In opposing dogma or fanaticism he had no sympathy with antireligious persecution, but the dogmatists felt toward his system very much as the orthodox feel toward Unitarianism, that it was a vague religious and righteous feeling, without content.

In 1886 the radical parliamentary leader Léon Bourgeois gave political expression to such impulses by his work on *Solidarité*. The idea that the conditions which throw men together in life necessitate reciprocal *duties* was the basis of the morality promulgated in manuals of ethics used in French schools.

Finally, one is led to record the significance of the Sociological School, which in the early twentieth century, under the lead of Emile Durkheim, took a strong hold on university teaching. According to this school society is based not on ideology but on facts. It is wrong to begin with the abstract analysis of ethical principles and ask society to conform to them. Morality is the product of a collective historical growth, proceeding from instinct and custom, regardless of logic, when human beings are in association. We should study, not the *ideas* of social phenomena, but the phenomena themselves. The objective sociological method is applicable to all concepts, including those of religion. The study of man rests on Sociology, and philosophy is not separable from science.

If we turn our attention now to the rival tendency in French thought, opposed to the new positivism and destined to culminate in Bergsonism and the Catholic revival, we must record, as well here as among the spiritualists, the influence of Ravaisson and of men such as Guyau. One great university teacher, Jules Lachelier, was still important, long after he had ceased active instruction, in getting academic philosophy out of the rut of Cousinian eclecticism. This tendency, which had got from the scientific post-Comtian positivists much of the best of their methods, culminates not only in the nonintellectual deliquescence of Bergson but in the intellectual relativism of Boutroux and Henri Poincaré.

To the student of letters the reaction against positivism, translated into terms of pessimistic naturalism and fatalistic philosophical materialism, shows itself in some striking books. In 1883 Brunetière led an attack on the *roman naturaliste*. A few years later the vicomte Melchior de Vogüé made the Russian novelists known in France and inaugurated in fiction a vogue of sympathy for suffering, of mystical, nondogmatic humanitarianism. It encouraged efforts toward organization for ethical reform and "uplift", of social coöperation, although, at the same time, the new "democratic" literature did not banish from fiction the plain discussion of the vices and horrors of modern civilization. These were as elaborately described as before, though relieved by sympathetic emotion and by attacks on individualism and selfishness.

The weakening of scientific positivism correspondingly encouraged the church party. The vicomte de Vogüé held up the Catholic Church as a refuge from egoistic individualism. Paul Bourget, in *le Disciple*, preached lessons of moral responsibility.

Renanism, as applied to religion, seemed a little on the wane, and in many circles of society it was again good form to be careful about one's religious observances. Even writers like Huysmans dabbled in the æsthetic sides of Catholicism. Church people and anticlericals sometimes joined forces, as Christian Democrats, in charitable and ethical organizations. It was the time of the *esprit nouveau* and of the Pope's efforts to rally the Church to the republic. But there could be no real compromise, and, with the Dreyfus Case, the hostility approached that of civil war. This bitterness was translated into politics by the separation of the Church and the State and by the victory, in the first decade of the twentieth century, of the anticlericals, of the pacifists and internationalists, and of the radicals who compromised with socialism.

On the other hand, the conservatives were no less active, and, though politically defeated, in intellectual polemics they often came off better than their opponents. Brunetière's attacks on science and its bankruptcy gave expression, in a popular phrase for the general reader, to the conviction of many that scientific positivism was too dogmatic and was presumptuous in its claims. François de Curel's *Nouvelle idole* contrasted religion and science to the discredit of the latter. Lavedan's *Duel* portrayed the conflict in the persons of two brothers, a priest and a materialistic doctor, both struggling for the soul of the same woman. Not only morally was there rising disgust against the sordid politics of the anticlerical materialists and the futile pornography of fiction with scientific pretensions, but there was a reaction against intellectualism. People began to argue that human science does not and cannot express ultimate truths, that scientific facts themselves are relative, that they are of temporary convenience and under other circumstances are different, that science is not above life but subordinate to its deep sweep and impulses. Of this tendency Bergsonism has been the most noteworthy example.

The philosophy of Bergson is in direct opposition to the forms of intellectual positivism which had enshrined science in the place of theology. It subordinated reason to intuition, and therefore fostered impulse and emotion. It sought to bridge the abyss between the self and the outer world and to make it become one with it. It encouraged philosophies laying stress on the value of shifting experience, and therefore was akin to the more purely utilitarian Anglo-Saxon pragmatism. It gave a helpful explanation to the abortive movement of Modernism in the Catholic Church, of which the chief French spokesman, the abbé Loisy, declared that the Church, without ceasing to be eternal, must constantly restate its creed in changing symbols to suit the times.[1] It did not go counter to the nonevangelical Catholicism in vogue among many people, which was clerical rather than religious, was based on heredity and tradition, and had itself scientific and positivistic pretensions, as with some of the neo-Royalists.

The effect of Bergsonism, whether or not so intended by its creator, was to introduce an element of looseness into intellectual methods. The abundant use of metaphors in its exposition led to vagueness of thought in others; it encouraged the substitution of the indeterminate for the concrete, the use of symbol in place of the idea, the notion that mystical brooding is more profound than clear-cut reasoning, and that the wellsprings of thought are to be found in feeling, the more incoherent the truer. As a metaphysical background it was so plastic as to be applicable to almost every form of human expression,—poetry, art, theology (Modernism), politics (neo-royalism), even sociology (Sorelian syndicalism),—and it helps greatly to account for the chaotic state of intellectual life in France at the opening of the World War, creditable though some of these tendencies may have been to the sincerity of their creators. By putting practically on the same plane of truth and reality the multitudinous outpourings of writers, sincere or affected, it drove literature and life apart, and encouraged more than ever the cliques and *chapelles littéraires*, still more numerous since the war, of petty masters, boomed by disciples and publishers.

[1] For Modernism treated in fiction, see Bourget's *Démon de midi*.

Even when Bergsonism was not a direct cause it may be looked upon as an aspect of the wave of nonintellectualism which was replacing the self-satisfied scientism of the previous age, without furnishing a more satisfactory solution. Literature was full of writers of fiction expressing restless, chaotic impulses. It tried to reach down beneath intellectualism and to bring the vagueness of the unconscious self into conscious portraiture. This it did largely by obscure symbol and metaphor.

One of the most influential and representative writers of the period immediately preceding the war was Romain Rolland, who suffered from the discordant impulses of his generation, yet hoped that the chaos would work itself out through humanitarianism, democracy, and universal brotherhood. But he lacked the practical ability or militancy of the true leader, so that he was an ineffective crusader. *Jean-Christophe* is a good specimen of intellectual cosmopolitanism, indeterminate musical vagueness, and sentimental emotionalism. Other writers, like André Gide, exemplify the restless *inquiétude* of "nostalgic souls", whose inbred intellectualism turns against itself, deprived of guide and direction yet finding no true substitute. Some, like Claudel and Jammes, sought refuge in religion, and to many of these the philosophy of Bergson was a convenient *passerelle*, or gangway. Some, like Péguy, became religious mystics, and as the reaction against anticlericalism and internationalism brought religion and patriotism together, it awakened in some, like Péguy himself, the religion of country and of Jeanne Darc as its symbol; in others, like Ernest Psichari, a revival of militant patriotism and of the war spirit in its chivalrous moods.

Among some conservative men of letters and nationalists, like Barrès or the neoroyalist Maurras, religion was more literature or a political tool than part of life. Charles Maurras, an unbeliever, advocated Catholicism as a cohesive force for the reestablishment of royalty and of tradition. The religion of Paul Bourget (*l'Etape*, and so forth) has an element of aristocratic snobbishness in contrast with proletarian anticlericalism.

CHAPTER XV

THIRD REPUBLIC. THE HISTORICAL AND POLITICAL SETTING

THE downfall of the Empire on the "Fourth of September" was engineered by a Parisian republican minority; yet such had the influence of the capital become that this action was accepted by the rest of the country.[1] France was anti-republican and, because of the disaster to the imperial régime, inclined to take refuge in the rule of a king. Catholicism was fashionable throughout the land, and predominant in the upper classes and in much of the *bourgeoisie*. Thus the first social and political division was between the radicals, on the one hand, who wanted to blot out the Empire and go back to 1848, and the conservatives, on the other hand, who dreaded the leap in the dark of republican agitation. Moreover, Paris was the goal of the Prussians. The Parisians were consequently eager to resist. The conservatives in the provinces were more ready to come to terms. If a monarchist like Thiers was inclined to accept a republic as compromise, it was to be a conservative one (*république conservatrice*), and his aim was peace. Hence the partisans of *la guerre à l'outrance* were to him rash, and Gambetta a *fou furieux* for being an extremist and wanting a "republican republic".

The siege of Paris made things worse. The Parisians glorified the heroism of their own defense and its hardships. After the capitulation, wrought to high nervous tension by what historians have described as siege hysteria (*folie obsidionale*), they were angry at the provinces for yielding to the Prussians, and con-

[1] For a fuller account of the political history of this period see the present writer's *History of the Third French Republic*.

sidered the rest of the country *capitulards*. The national guard of Paris, inactive but not disarmed, and swayed by the harangues of *café* politicians, resented such concrete evidences of surrender as the removal of heavy guns from Montmartre. The mob broke into rebellion on an unhappy day in March, 1871, and the Commune followed, by which Paris wanted to save France.

The *communards* were not by any means necessarily "communists", though the Marxians afterward falsely adopted the Commune. They greeted it as a rebellion against *bourgeois* civilization, though many of the original *communards* had been of the *bourgeois* class.[1] They identified the conservative population of the provinces with the *bourgeois*, and the Parisian working-men had never forgiven Thiers for having, as long ago as 1850, at the time of the campaign for the restriction of the suffrage under the régime of 1848, spoken of the *vile multitude*. They were angry because, in the plebiscite of 1870, Paris and the large industrial cities had pronounced against the Empire but had been swamped by the country vote. This helps to explain Parisian jealousy of the rest of the country and desire for emancipation from it.

The aims of those who established the Commune were, therefore, very mixed, as is always the case in a revolutionary movement. They were united only in opposing the régime which they overthrew. Social reform was vague and indistinct to this incoherent alliance of excited proletarians, penniless middle-class intellectuals, and *déclassés*, goaded to action by Blanquist agitators. Many harked back to the Revolutionary Commune of Paris and wanted the dictatorship of the capital once more. To complete the illusion of a parallel, they readopted the republican calendar and dated their newspapers according to the old system, by which "Year I" had been that of the Revolutionary

---

[1] The French distinguish between "communists", believers in a form of collectivism, and the "communards" of the Commune; in the word "communard" the ending *ard* is used in a derogatory sense. The word "communeux", like "partageux", was originally sometimes used for collectivists.

republic. Those who might actually be called socialists were, on the whole, followers of the Frenchman Proudhon rather than of the German Marx. They were hostile to a powerful centralized state, and wanted a federation of autonomous communes of France, in which the superiority of Paris came only from its size and its moral example. This is why, in the civil war of 1871, the Paris insurgents opposed to the "Versaillais" of Thiers and MacMahon called themselves *fédérés*, a term perhaps influenced by the word "Federal" made familiar by the recent American Civil War.

After the final settlement with Germany, and especially after the resignation of Thiers from the presidency in 1873, the opposition was between the conservatives, represented by MacMahon, and the republicans; for the proletarians of the Commune had been disposed of by shooting or by deportation to convict settlements in New Caledonia. The catchwords of the epoch are the *ordre moral*, recalling the *ordre* of the Monarchy of July, which MacMahon and the conservatives opposed to radicalism, and Gambetta's new phrase on the advent of a *nouvelle couche sociale*. By this was implied the new political generation seeking power since the fall of the Empire, consisting of the *petite bourgeoisie* and the representatives of the workingmen and peasants. These were apt to be journalists and politicians who, with young students, had boisterously aired their views under the Empire and had not received the tardy concession of *l'Empire libéral* with gratitude. Their policy was directed against clericalism, and they demanded lay, free, and obligatory education in the schools, and the separation of Church and State. The scholastic changes were brought about by the end of the first decade; separation did not come until 1905.

The fusion of the monarchist opposition (Legitimists and Orleanists) having failed through the stubbornness of the comte de Chambord in refusing to give up the white flag and accept the red, white, and blue of modern France, the republic became permanent. When the party of Gambetta came into power, he grew moderate instead of remaining an extremist, and formulated the policy of Opportunism to take advantage of each favorable occasion, as contrasted with the Jacobinism of the ultras, to which the name of Rochefort's newspaper, *l'Intransigeant*, helped to attach the name of *intransigeance*. With the advent of Jules Grévy to the presidency in 1879, and of Gambetta and Jules Ferry to real power, the "republican republic" was really established. The death of the Prince Imperial, Bonapartist pretender, in South Africa during the Zulu War, practically destroyed the chances of that line.

During the first decade of the Republic the conservatives still remained influential both administratively and socially. The officials were largely hold-overs from imperial times and possessed large powers of spying and nagging; the magistracy, the army and naval officers, and the diplomatic corps were hostile to the republic and hand-and-glove with the clergy. The smart, or *chic*, education among the well-to-do was to have a private tutor and finish one's studies with the Jesuits or the Dominicans.

During the second and third decades of the republic, the eighties and the nineties, the opposition, though on the downward grade, was still powerful enough to make itself dangerous, and three determined attacks were made to undermine republican institutions. These were Boulangism, the Panama Affair, and the Dreyfus Case. Meanwhile, at the other extreme, socialism was beginning to worry *bourgeois* republicanism. Anger at losses caused to small investors in town and country by sensational bank failures embittered many people and turned them to socialism in revulsion against the parliamentary régime.

During the early eighties the enemies of the *parliamentary* republican order capitalized their strength. They included the advance guard of those who declared that the shifty opportunists governing a parliamentary republic were devoting themselves to selfish interests and sacrificing the pride of France, after defeat by Germany, to ignoble peace. They were the first preachers of *la revanche*, and wanted a revision of the constitution to secure a plebiscitary republic with a strong leader,—a thing which their enemies said meant Cæsarism and a military dictatorship. This was the group destined to grow in strength under the name of Nationalists, having as chief leader Paul Déroulède, poet and tribune, nephew of Emile Augier, incarnation of the spirit of *revanche*, stagy and bombastic but sincere, with a not infrequent French combination of Cornelian heroism and inability to distinguish the sublime from the ridiculous. The party was led, partly by the chance of a popular song, to the choice of a sorry leader. General Boulanger, though a shifty and superficial individual, was an attractive blond-bearded warrior on a black horse, and the tuneful melody of the *café-concert* singer Paulus, *En revenant de la revue*, mentioned "le brav' général Boulanger".[1] It was not long before bands of men began to parade the streets, proclaiming in rhythmic cadence:

> C'est Boulange, Boulange, Boulange,
> C'est Boulanger qu'il nous faut.

The monarchists saw their chance and secretly joined forces with Boulanger. When people succeeded in penetrating behind the scenes into the *coulisses du Boulangisme*, and it was discovered that, through the agency of an anti-republican duchess, Boulanger had been subsidized by the royalists, the *fiasco* came. In 1891 Boulanger committed suicide in a cemetery in Brussels, on the grave of a woman he had loved. This downfall of Boulanger had again turned some revisionists into still more ardent socialists.[2]

The Panama Affair of the early nineties was the revenge of defeated Boulangists, especially the conservatives. Evidence becoming clear of incompetent management of the French company organized to construct the Panama Canal, and of efforts to influence newspapers by graft and to bribe members of the Chamber of Deputies, a tremendous scandal followed. The term *chéquard*, given to those accused of receiving cheques, be-

---

[1] This is why Jules Ferry called Boulanger a "Saint-Arnaud de café-concert", thereby comparing and contrasting him with Louis Napoleon's chief agent in the *coup d'état* of 1851.

[2] For Boulangism in its relations to men of letters see the writings of Maurice Barrès and Paul Adam.

came synonymous with "grafter". Disaster fell not only on some of the culpable but on those who had been guilty only of hushing matters, and especially on the helpless investors. The result was a temporary check to radical republicanism and the conservatives regained a little of the influence they had lost.

The supreme conflict came in the late nineties and the early years of the twentieth century, in the prolonged Dreyfus Case, which created dissensions as bitter as those of civil war, exposed France to angry foreign criticism, and brought the Third Republic to its lowest level of prestige. The protagonist Dreyfus became an insignificant pawn in a greater game, in which the opponents were, on one side the partisans of the existing régime, on the other the various foes of democracy, especially the traditionalists. The Dreyfus dispute affected not only politics but society and the whole intellectual and literary order.

For several years the Catholics had been quietly regaining some of the influence lost by the establishment of public instruction divorced from clerical authority. They had strengthened their own schools, the Jesuit and Assumptionist orders were particularly strong, and the army officers were still largely anti-republican and contemptuous of the "ignoble" pacifism of a democratic government. There had existed, also, for nearly ten years, a rising tide of anti-Semitism, with the opprobrious hurling of the terms *youtre* and *youpin*, for Jewish names had been involved in the Panama scandals. The Jews were blamed, as well, for a sensational bank failure, by which thousands of investors had been fleeced, and they were considered international Shylocks without patriotism, ready to betray France to Germany. Morbid fear of treachery and the persistent cry of "traitor" form, in the eyes of the foreigner, a prominent emotional trait of the French temperament.

In December, 1894, a Jewish army officer, Captain Alfred Dreyfus, was condemned through illegal processes by court-martial for an offense he had never committed,—that of selling to Germany military documents. Before long, doubts arose among some isolated but sturdy lovers of justice, and a campaign was inaugurated for a revision of the trial. Unfortunately this could not be brought about without the admission that military justice was fallible, and efforts for revision were distorted into an attack on the army as incarnation of French patriotism.

The first impressive connection between literature and the Dreyfus Case came when, in 1898, the novelist Zola, democrat and semisocialist, published in Clemenceau's newspaper, *l'Aurore*, his famous letter, *J'accuse*. By 1899, when military influence was still great enough to cause a second condemnation of Dreyfus by court-martial, with a still greater travesty of justice than before, the great cleavage was formed. On one side were the liberals, including genuine republicans, both moderates and radicals, and some conservatives who put conscience above party,[1] together with Protestants and Jews, under the leadership of a group of writers and university professors, scoffingly known as *les intellectuels*. The socialists, whose gradual rise to influence we have still to treat, for the most part joined in time the revisionists, and the radical, Clemenceau, in his *Aurore*, was one of the chief spokesmen of the movement. On the other side were to be found the army hierarchy, the vast majority of conservatives, republicans or monarchists, and the clergy, the whole forming the Nationalist group. The "dreyfusards" were accused of being traitors, corrupted by Jewish money, and *vendus*. The anti-Dreyfusites were charged with a base alliance between "the sword and the holy-water sprinkler" (*le sabre et le goupillon*).

The part played by the Dreyfusite "Intellectuals" and by the intelligent, though prejudiced, leaders of the Nationalists brings the whole controversy out of the field of political strife into one which is of immediate importance to the student of literary movements. The Dreyfusite *intellectuels* were partisans of reason. They had the cult of abstract justice, and in determin-

---

[1] One of the two officers who, at the second trial in 1899, at Rennes, voted for acquittal was the Commandant de Bréon, an ardent Catholic, whose brother was a priest.

HISTORICAL AND POLITICAL SETTING 253

SECOND CONDEMNATION OF DREYFUS AT RENNES IN 1899
Colonel Jouaust, hated by the Dreyfusites for his brutality, really voted for acquittal. (From *l'Illustration*)

ing innocence or guilt they balanced the respective arguments for and against, and came to a mature judgment, particularly in the matter of forged documents. The anti-Dreyfusites were swayed by a sort of emotional mysticism, which took the shape, as we have seen, of a cult of the army as the only weapon with which to resist Germany, for the fear of that country had not vanished after twenty or thirty years. In addition to the military hierarchy, the chief civilian Nationalist organization was the *Ligue de la patrie française*, opposed to the Dreyfusite *Ligue des droits de l'homme*, the name of which harked back to memories of the Revolution. The *Patrie française* had among its leading spokesmen Maurice Barrès and François Coppée, and many of its schemes were devised at the home of the intimate friend of Jules Lemaître, the comtesse de Loynes. She was a remarkable woman of obscure origin, a former *protégée* of Prince Jerome Napoleon, who succeeded in making her *salon* a center of political intrigue and of the literary wire-pulling which led to election to the Academy.[1]

The second trial of Dreyfus had again ended with a condemnation, but in the end republican strategy proved effective. In the early years of the twentieth century the *bloc des gauches*, in which the radicals predominated, brought about the annulment of the conviction, and also the separation of Church and State.[2]

Meanwhile the *Patrie française* seemed too cumbersome to a certain number of Nationalists, who founded the *Action fran-*

[1] Contrast Anatole France's *Histoire contemporaine* and Maurice Barrès's *Déracinés* and *Scènes et doctrines du nationalisme* for the liberal and the nationalist-traditionalist points of view respectively. Zola's *Vérité* deals with the Dreyfus Case, and Roger Martin du Gard's *Jean Barois* is one of the most thoughtful works of fiction produced by the *Affaire*. André Beaunier's *les Dupont-Letellier* was written before the agitation was over. Alfred Capus's *Scènes de la vie difficile* portrays life during Boulangism, Panamism, and the Dreyfus agitation. Marcel Proust's *le Côté de Guermantes* touches upon Dreyfusism.

[2] The term *bloc* had its origin in a saying of Clemenceau, in 1891, that "la Révolution doit être acceptée en bloc", its evils being outweighed by its good results. The word "bloc" has entered American politics, though with a different shade of meaning. In France, a country of numerous parliamentary groups, the expression suggests the idea of union; in America, a land of two-party rule, it is applied to the separate groups into which parties many subdivide, probably through the influence of the English word "block".

çaise. This little group represents only a fraction of those in France who were recovering from the discouragement of the Franco-Prussian War, and it embodied the pride of a country again risen to power and by successful colonization creating a new empire.

In the early twentieth century the radical republic was victoriously established and the battle lines had shifted. It is interesting to surmise what might have been the evolution of the country if the World War had not broken out. The radicals were in real control and seemed to be making poor use of their power. There were bitter criticisms of the incompetence of the régime, and charges of parliamentary "Byzantinism", a term by which the futile political harangues were compared to the talk of the Byzantine rhetoricians quibbling over abstractions while the Moslem invaders were at the gates.

Georges Guy-Grand, in a lucid article in the *Mercure de France*,[1] summarized the conditions of French politics at the end of the nineteenth century, and characterized the three great divisions as follows:

1. The Conservatives, consisting chiefly of the *grande bourgeoisie*, with the remnants of the aristocracy. The *bourgeoisie* was the class successful through business and speculation. It supported the parliamentary régime which had brought it prosperity, and advocated economic liberalism. Its chief political party considered itself liberal and called itself *progressiste*. The republican conservatives were themselves opposed by the *réactionnaires*, of whom the noisiest and most amusing group were the neoroyalists, who pretended to support the claims to the throne of the incompetent Duke of Orleans. To these neoroyalists democracy meant decadence, and it had, under the influence of money, brought about the rule of Jews, Protestants, Masons, and *métèques*, or "metics", hyphenated citizens still more foreign than French. The conservatives as a whole supported with aggressive patriotism a policy of Nationalism, and many rallied round the Church attacked by the radicals.

[1] Vol. CXXXVI.

2. The Radicals, and the *radicaux-socialistes*, either destructive critics, like Clemenceau, or Jacobins, like Combes. But they were so centered on their anticlerical policy that with the achievement of the separation of Church and State they had no more *raison d'être*. Yet they still survive.

3. The Proletarians, who were Socialists or Syndicalists. The Socialists were hostile to free democracy and convinced that the radical anticlericalism was a means of throwing dust in people's eyes. They advocated the overthrow of capitalism and the seizure of the state, some being *réformistes*, others *intransigeants*. The Syndicalists were revolutionary and opposed to the whole idea of the existing state, *bourgeois* or socialist. They were destructive and not constructive, hostile to capitalism, to the parliamentary government, to the notion of patriotism. They were chiefly industrial workmen or agricultural laborers in the south of France. They formed the nucleus of the *Compagnie Générale du Travail*, and their chief intellectual exponent, but not executive leader, was Georges Sorel.

After the second trial of Dreyfus the political coalition known as the *bloc des gauches* was in control for a number of years. The radical, Combes, behind whom the reformist socialist Jaurès was a power to be reckoned with, carried through disestablishment. Unfortunately the Dreyfusite coalition had not consisted entirely of lovers of abstract justice. Many of its members used the agitation as a tool to further special interests, chiefly hostility to the Church.

The Church had been waging, on the whole, a losing fight since the establishment of the Third Republic, beginning with the weakening of control in education. Gambetta, the popularizer of the phrase "le cléricalisme, voilà l'ennemi", had not attacked it everywhere. Remembering that France, the "eldest daughter of the Church", was protector of the Catholic missions in the Orient, he had kept anticlericalism for home consumption ("l'anti-cléricalisme n'est pas un article d'exportation"). At one time in the quest for conciliation his follower Spuller tried to give currency to the term *l'esprit nouveau*. In the early nine-

HISTORICAL AND POLITICAL SETTING 257

ties Leo XIII had tried to "rally" the Catholics to the republic (*les ralliés*), but his scheme had been thwarted by the French clerical leaders themselves. The machinations of religious orders, and the suspected influence of the Jesuits upon certain generals during the Dreyfus campaign, embittered the radicals still more, so that disestablishment was put through in 1905. By this measure France gave up the associational control with Rome of the *Concordat*, which had lasted since the days of Napoleon I. It adopted, on the whole, the American policy of a Church independent of the State. The Church was deprived of government aid and had to rely henceforth on private initiative, but it gained freedom of action. Its bishops and priests were no longer under the supervision of the authorities and could not be penalized by them.

The great criticism that we meet in literature concerning the France of the early twentieth century, during the radical régime preceding the outbreak of the war, is the lack of idealism and the prevailing selfishness. Zola's *Paris* is a general indictment of social conditions in the great city, and the amusing farce by Flers and Caillavet, *le Roi*, is a laughable satire of politics and manners at the time it was played. But one of the fullest and most specific criticisms is in Romain Rolland's *Jean-Christophe*, in the volume called *la Foire sur la place*. The author assails an administrative overcentralization, forming a sort of republican imperialism, on which was grafted an atheistical organization, with its secret orders like the Masons, as baneful as the religious ones which they opposed, political fanaticism, and a spirit of espionage terrifying the army, the university, and every branch of the state. The politicians were chiefly dilettante socialists, really selfish opportunists, seeking a maximum of pleasure with a minimum of effort. In spite of centralization there was governmental anarchy,—an aggressive Department of Foreign Affairs, though pacifist heads of the army and navy sapped the national defense. It was a republic without republicans, in which the politicians had a fine time. Of the three estates of 1789 the first was extinct, the second proscribed, and the third gorged and stupefied by victory. The politicians in office tried to lure away the leaders of the proletariat and fed the country with indigestible science and middle-class culture.[1] There was maudlin humanitarianism everywhere, and the intellectual leaders themselves justified this national decline by the right to be happy.

Yet, in spite of the wrath of the censor, no country was more prosperous and more happy, picayune politics aside, than France at the opening of the war, in spite of the dearth of moral enthusiasms. It is true that there was a large intellectual proletariat, owing to the overcrowding of the professions by the increase of educational opportunities under a democracy. Apart from this, France was a land in which, though their margin was small, people lived and saved on their incomes, where life was comfortable and food good, in which parasitic middlemen were less numerous than in the United States to irritate both producer and consumer, a nation of agriculturalists and manufacturers on a small scale, and of *petits rentiers*. In spite of much useless state interference in the shape of red tape each one was free to enjoy his tastes if he could find happiness without the extravagance deemed essential in America.

During the decade preceding the outbreak of the World War we witness, in the new generation, a reawakening of national pride in realization of renewed strength. It was stimulated by diplomatic clashes with Germany, the feeling of power resulting from the alliance with Russia, and the *entente cordiale* with England. Names such as Tangier, Agadir, and Casablanca mark stages in its development. It took the form of an intensified cult of the national soil, of the army and the flag. It was foreshadowed by Barrès's "réveil de l'énergie nationale". It expressed itself in books with significant titles, like *la Renaissance de l'orgueil français*. Unfortunately it expressed itself also in patriotic

---

[1] The *universités populaires*. After the Dreyfus Affair there was a temporary union between intellectuals and working-men by means of evening schools. They failed because the *ouvriers* were too tired to study and disliked being patronized. See Bourget's *Etape*.

HISTORICAL AND POLITICAL SETTING 259

exclusivism, in dislike for the foreigner.[1] The French were made anxious by the growth of a similar nationalism in Germany, which was correspondingly suspicious of the revival in France. The results in France and Germany were forms of that spiritual "Imperialism", such as all the great powers have manifested in the twentieth century, which in Germany may be described as *militaristic*, which in France we can call, not militaristic but *militant,* especially when people's hearts reverted with Barrès and Bazin (*les Oberlé*) to Alsace and Lorraine. Significant of this new feeling is the following, written in 1913 by "Agathon": "It would be easy, for instance, to determine exactly the date when the word *français* acquired the more strict, defensive and almost martial meaning, which the youth of to-day attributes to it."[2]

Consequently the romantic dashing and chivalrous aspect of the warrior became again prominent. Paul Acker's *Soldat Bernard*, in 1909, marked a reaction in fiction against the disparagement of the army. Ernest Psichari, grandson of Renan, expressed a mystic glorification of the army and of war. Already, a number of years before, Rostand, in his *Cyrano de Bergerac*, had glorified *le panache*, which he himself defined in his speech of admission to the Academy as "l'esprit qui assaisonne la bravoure". The soldier was now eulogized for his *crânerie*, his dashing boldness. Stereotyped expressions came into vogue, such as *beau geste* for any sort of praiseworthy action whatsoever,[3] and *geste à la française* to characterize a combination of elegance and heroism. Rostand's *Chantecler*, though not a genuine literary or dramatic success, glorified the strut of the Gallic cock,—that strut which the Englishman, who

---

[1] See the extract from Anatole France on page 204. After the defeat of 1870–1871, the French had the feeling that, though Germany was victorious, France was intellectually superior. Since the victory of 1918 this intolerance has with some people grown to include others besides the Germans.

[2] *Les jeunes gens d'aujourd'hui*, p. 99. See also (p. 129): "C'est cet esprit guerrier qui se réveille", etc.

[3] See the passage in the first act of *Cyrano de Bergerac* ("Jeter ce sac, quelle sottise!"—"Mais quel geste!"), a passage undoubtedly suggested by the anecdote of Laurent Tailhade recorded in this book. See below, p. 264.

poses as phlegmatic, cannot take seriously, and which is to a great degree responsible for misunderstandings between the two countries, but for which the more expansive American is ready to make allowances.

The *Action française*, already mentioned, is numerically insignificant, being chiefly monarchical, but it has been in the foreground in French nationalism. The behaviour of some of its henchmen, the *camelots du roi*, at one time, aroused the ridicule of sensible Frenchmen, but because of the literary ability of its leaders its prominence is greater than would otherwise have been the case. It was launched chiefly by some ambitious *lycée* professors,—Vaugeois, Syveton, Dimier, Lasserre, and others. It has had as intellectual leader Charles Maurras, as inspiration Barrès, as militant spokesman Léon Daudet, son of Alphonse Daudet. The influence of Barrès attaches this school to the cult of the fatherland conceived as the spirit of tradition, gifted with a sort of unifying personality. The political philosophy of Maurras turns this Traditionalism into something positivistic, harking back through Taine to Comte. Society is conceived as based on inheritance and custom, and men reëcho the transmitted legacies of soil and of ancestry. The theory harks back, also, to Bonald and Joseph de Maistre, opponents of the Revolution, because a king best represents the continuity of French tradition. Therefore the *Action française* not only is monarchial and advocates the closest alliance of king and Catholicism, even though Maurras be himself an unbeliever, but is antiparliamentary, because parliamentary government is Anglo-Saxon. It preaches decentralization and "regionalism", the restoration so far as possible of the old regions and provinces which the Revolution destroyed. Incidentally it helped, without creating it, the praiseworthy literary regionalism of novels about different parts of France. In literature also the *Action française* implies classicism, because the age of Louis the Great was the apogee of classicism, and Louis XIV is the typical French hero to such a nationalist as Louis Bertrand.[1] Ardent classicism

[1] See his *Louis XIV*.

involves hostility to romanticism, and the severest onslaughts on romanticism during the last twenty years have come from followers of Maurras, such as Pierre Lasserre. The *Action française* preaches anti-democracy, anti-Semitism, anti-Protestantism, anti-romanticism, hostility to all foreign influences, and erects national selfishness into a duty. Yet in spite of the literary classicism of this particular school the tendency of French Nationalism as a whole has been, through the religion of patriotism, to revert to the cult of instinct and to anti-rationalism,—a tendency which harmonizes with Bergsonism.

A captivating outward symbol of the new spirit in the country is found in the idealization of Jeanne Darc. France lacked what writers have called a "tribal deity" such as the Teutonic nations possess in Columbia, Britannia, or Germania. A man cannot feel for allegorical figures of "Liberty, Equality, Fraternity" on a five-franc piece, or for an abstraction like the "Droits de l'homme", the same thrill that he may experience for a beautiful woman, even though it be only the mystical worship of a symbolic being. In Jeanne Darc there was a splendid opportunity for such a token of national unity, and a bond between clericals and anticlericals in the name of patriotism. The unorthodox religiosity of writers such as Barrès contributed to the growth of the new reverence. She could be interpreted as the incarnation of the French national spirit. She could appear as the one who expelled the foreigner from French soil. To the traditionalist she was the defender of the king and therefore of the national Church, linked with the monarch. In her name could be effected a mystical synthesis of the religions of God and of country. The modern Clœlia on horseback appealed to the martial ardor even of the nonreligious, and the tinted statuettes of Jeanne in shining armor, with the upturned eyes of ecstatic vision, stirred the love of the faithful in the churches. In processions at Orleans prelates in their robes and the officials of an anti-ecclesiastical republic joined together almost for the first time. Jeanne Darc was canonized and became to many French people a sort of national goddess. The *Mystère de la charité de*

Jeanne Darc of Péguy and the life of Jeanne Darc by Anatole France represent respectively the mystical and the rationalistic interpretation of her character.

Socialism under the Third Republic, although illustrated by numerous novels, is less literary than before 1848. It is chiefly economic and the romantic utopianism is gone. The downfall of the Commune, and the drastic methods employed against its leaders, put an end for nearly ten years to labor unrest. By 1880, however, amnesty brought the exiled Communards back and they began their ultraradical agitation, into which bitter memories of men sent to New Caledonia and of women reduced to poverty and prostitution paved the way for an acceptance of the Marxian idea of Class War in competition with a more gradual Proudhonism. France became, if we omit the Blanquists, the battle ground of two theories of social renovation, French and foreign, reformist and Marxian, of "possibilists" wanting a gradual conquest of public power versus the fatalistic theory of a gigantic proletariat growing strong enough to avenge its wrongs, —catastrophic instead of evolutionary. Marxism boasted of being historical, scientific materialism, proscribed sentimental justice, and declared that society tends inevitably to communism. The genuine French tradition tried to keep something of the spirit of 1848, to appeal to altruism and human brotherhood, and, under the influence of Proudhon's "anarchism", to work toward coöperation rather than the tyranny of the proletariat.

During the second decade of the Third Republic the socialists became more outspoken. They complained that the republic was reverting to *bourgeois* capitalism, but their divergent views long caused their weakness.

During the great formative periods of the movement there were three chief groups, forming in reality two tendencies: the Marxians, led by Jules Guesde; the Blanquists, merging into militant Marxism; and a third group in which Benoît Malon sought to diminish the harshness of Marxian materialism by metaphysical and moral conceptions of justice instead of necessity.

Later the great leader of this tendency was Jean Jaurès, murdered by a fanatic at the outbreak of the war, who did not disdain parliamentary methods to attain his ends. During the decade preceding the war, after 1905, the socialists achieved at least outward unity, the extremists having forgone something of their violence of method, and they were making progress by legislative influence toward the goal to which Jaurès, now entombed in the Panthéon, aspired. At the beginning of the war most of the socialists rallied to the *union sacrée*, but dissensions reappeared and, with the return of peace, a section actually accepted the doctrines of Moscow.

Proudhon, because of his great mental richness and even because of his contradictions, proves to be one of the most fertile initiators of modern thought, though his successors have gone beyond his position. Not only was this individualist the forerunner of much of French evolutionary radicalism and socialism, but also from him are descended the Anarchists and, in part, the Revolutionary Syndicalists.

The individualism of Proudhon found favor with those who feared lest socialism prove as tyrannical as *bourgeois* government. The Russian Bakunin broke away from the International in 1872, and after 1878 anarchism became more pronounced. It took, as usual, two forms, evolutionary and revolutionary. With the Russian Kropotkin and the Frenchmen Jean Grave and the geographer Elisée Reclus it became propaganda by newspaper, pamphlet, and harangue against an opportunist or radical capitalism, and sought the abolition of governmental tyranny and the liberty of the individual tempered only by the consciousness of social obligation.

The revolutionary anarchists were the unreasoning, sometimes mentally subnormal, hotheads who discredited the whole movement and used murder to destroy civilization. These were the Russian political murderers, the Nihilists, or the assassins of Carnot and McKinley. Examples of this class in France were Ravachol and Henry, degenerate and unrecognizable descendants of Proudhon, who threw bombs.

The whole evidence of the preceding pages of this volume has shown that it is the supreme privilege of the French literary intellectual to rebel against the *bourgeois*. Zola makes one of the characters in his *Paris* say: "It seems to me that, in these days of universal baseness and ignominy, a man of any distinction can only be an anarchist."[1] Consequently, at the time of the throwing of bombs by anarchists in Paris during the early nineties, some men of letters, especially youths, were anarchists as a literary pose. After one explosion Laurent Tailhade remarked: "Qu'importe le crime pourvu que le geste soit beau", bestowing æsthetic approval upon the deed, though he was probably less enthusiastic when, by a queer coincidence, he was himself wounded and disfigured in another explosion. Anarchism seemed a way by which the youth of 1892 could express its noble indignation. Camille Mauclair, in his recollections, says: "People were anarchists because it seemed dashing and romantic, because the attitude fell in with our position as spurned writers, and because the label covered all our motives for dissatisfaction." He adds that Ravachol, the foe of society, seemed to have the build of a character of Balzac. Marcel Schwob compared the death of this degenerate criminal to that of Socrates, and Paul Adam wrote of him: "Un saint nous est né."

In the school of violence known as Revolutionary Syndicalism there is a synthesis of the teachings of Marx, Bakunin, and Proudhon, and for it the brilliant but erratic thinker Georges Sorel tried to evolve a philosophical basis by seeking one in Bergsonism.

Syndicalism as a form of socialism to remedy labor grievances is too predominantly economic to enter largely into the present study, which is chiefly literary. Syndicalism is the development of the theory of organizations resembling labor unions, and can be pushed either by *peaceful* or by *warlike* methods. These two tendencies have opposed each other in the great French union, the Confédération Générale du Travail, known as the "C.G.T.", active since 1892.

[1] Chap. ii.

The syndicalism of Sorel, whose imaginative theories probably had little concrete effect on the actions of the C.G.T. and of the proletariat, of which they are an interpretation, is opposed to *bourgeois* socialism, which is "rationalistic". His philosophy rests on the idea of the *spontaneousness* of the working classes, and results from applying the intuitionalism of Bergson to economics and sociology. He was hostile to all intellectual workers as parasites, and he wished to undermine *bourgeois* democracy and culture, which has resulted in a degeneracy as pronounced as that of the aristocracy in the eighteenth century. Producers live by intuition; life is incommunicable by language and impenetrable to discursive reason. The motive impulse of humanity is the Myth, having a creative power and exerting dynamic force on the collective masses. The myth is the expression in imagery of the way in which the new civilization shall come about through violence, by class war, "direct action", and the general strike. The myth may be vague and work out very differently from its original conception, and it is very remote from the rationalistic though imaginative utopias of the older socialists. Through the myth of class war real civilization will not be destroyed, but the old one will go for good. The revolution of the proletariat will create a new civilization, with nothing of the old institutions and traditions. The virulent criticisms of democracy by Sorel caused the paradoxical neo-royalists to welcome some of his teachings, and it is amusing to see Sorel before his death becoming himself sympathetic to nationalism.

Socialism and industrial problems, the relations of capital and labor, are prominent in France earlier than in the United States, as we realize when we remember the discussion aroused by such an innovation as Edward Bellamy's *Looking Backward*. Novels and plays portraying the sufferings of the working classes are too numerous to record fully. Zola progressed from the inchoate surge of humanity in *Germinal* to the Fourierism of *Travail*; the intellectual aristocrat Anatole France is an ironical socialist, and his brief *Crainquebille* brands the injustice

of Law to the weak and ignorant; some of the novels of
J.-H. Rosny introduce noted labor leaders only slightly disguised; Gustave Geffroy's *l'Apprentie* and *Cécile Pommier* picture the clash of castes under the Third Republic; Octave
Mirbeau is bitter against the evils of modern society. On the
other hand, Donnay and Descaves's play *la Clairière* gives an
amusing picture of the impracticability of regenerative utopias,
and Paul Bourget's dramas, such as *le Tribun* and *la Barricade*,
preach open resistance to the encroachments of socialism and
collectivism, and to every effort to subvert the existing social
hierarchy. *Chansonniers*, some of them, like A. Bruant, themselves near the people, have told the hardships of the oppressed.
Finally, it was a Frenchman, Eugène Pottier, an ex-Communard,
who wrote *l'Internationale*, that song which has replaced the
Marseillaise, now turned over to the *bourgeoisie*, as the war song
of communist revolutionaries all over the world.

CHAPTER XVI

THIRD REPUBLIC. VARIOUS SOCIAL TYPES

UNDER the Third Republic Paris continues to dominate France and French literature, though after a while the regionalistic tendency in fiction gives variety and relief. But Paris was the cosmopolitan center of Europe, and to most foreigners Paris was France. To the provincials it was the magnet that drew them from the monotony of their existence.[1] On the other hand, such becomes the hectic activity of Paris life, with its constant interruptions, that today serious writers more and more seek the country for the leisure of composition.

For a number of years after the Franco-Prussian War Paris was outwardly much the same, although the gaunt and blackened ruins of the Tuileries remained to testify to the destruction wrought by the Commune. Plans for the embellishment of Paris begun under the Empire were continued, the Opéra was dedicated and the few Jablochkoff electric lights scattered along the new avenue de l'Opéra seemed more gorgeous than a Great White Way does at present. The operetta was still at the height of its popularity, and the spectator at *la Fille de madame Angot*, of which the scene was supposedly under the Directoire, could apply to the present the words of the song:

> C'n'était pas la peine,
> Non, pas la peine, assurément
> De changer de gouvernement!

The exposition of 1878 showed France making a brave display to the world, and the succeeding great fairs of 1889 and 1900 marked stages of the return to prestige and splendor. But the

[1] Bazin's *la Terre qui meurt* shows the lure of town in general upon the countryman and peasant.

exposition of 1900 is roughly a dividing line between the individual Paris of the past and the denationalized cosmopolitan center of today. The quaint musical street-cries commemorated in Charpentier's opera *Louise* became rare, and Paris catered to the foreigner. Even the artists of Montmartre were driven to remoter sections of the *butte sacrée*, and the neighborhood of the place Pigalle was commercialized into show places for people in quest of Gallic wickedness. In time, also, the underground trains and the development of quick transit, enabling one to go from Montmartre to Montrouge in a short time, broke down the barriers between the quarters. Yet to the Parisian Paris is still lovable, and the spirit of Paris, its charm amid its alluring dangers, is expressed in the duo of Louise and Julien in *Louise*, or in eloquent pages of Anatole France, especially the following in *le Crime de Sylvestre Bonnard*:

old and venerable Paris with its towers and its spires, all that is my life, it is myself, and I should be nothing without those things which are reflected in me with the thousand shades of my thought, which inspire me and urge me on. That is why I love Paris with a mighty love.

Connecting links between various sections of Paris often mentioned by story-tellers are the omnibus lines Passy-Bourse and Batignolles-Clichy-Odéon, cleaving the metropolis, the one horizontally, the other nearly vertically. They suggest by their names typical quarters of prosperity, money-making, middle-class mediocrity, and the toil and pleasure of the university district. Fernand Vandérem, in his novel *les Deux rives*, tried to characterize the two great sections on the right and the left bank of the Seine. In the former is a restless mob of unprincipled men and women, adulterous and dishonest; in the latter, the serious and honest part of the population. It is true that the busy right bank affects to scorn the quiet streets of the left bank, and the term "rive gauche" is sometimes used to characterize literature which lacks the sparkle of the boulevards; but a classification of the quarters of Paris under the Third Republic is not so simple. The boulevards retain their prominence,

BETTING AT THE RACES

though sadly shorn of their former glamour, the great restaurants which made life there worth living having one after another closed their doors. In the early days of the Republic the *gommeux*, representative of *la haute gomme*, or smart set, was still to be seen. But his successors, the inane *mufle* of Lavedan and Gyp, with his tittle-tattle, the *fêtard* of Lavedan's *Nouveau jeu* and the older *vieux marcheur*, have migrated elsewhere. Especially in the west, in the quarters of the Champs-Elysées, Chaillot, Monceau, and Malesherbes, they fain must associate with the foreigners to whom Paris is a magnet, the sallow Argentinian *rastaquouère* in patent-leather boots, who has replaced the swarthy Brazilian of the Second Empire, and who has brought with him the tango; the rich North American idler and his cakewalk. This was the Paris of the *Transatlantiques* and *Trains de luxe*,[1] of people belonging to the "monde des palaces" (expensive hotels), to the "monde des wagons-lits européens" (who travel luxuriously), and of *orchestres de tziganes*. In these quarters were situated the luxurious *garçonnières*, or bachelor apartments where the heroes of fashionable novels received the wives of their friends. Truer elegance sought quieter neighborhoods in Passy or outside the city in Neuilly. To the north and northeast the peripheral districts and *quartiers excentriques*, away from the center, became in literature more connected with the lower classes, even the criminal population. Montmartre, losing its prestige as the home of artistic bohemianism, is a background for the *littérature apache*, tales of hoodlums and malefactors to whom the French have given the name of the American Indian tribe. Belleville is frankly proletarian, with its rough street navvies, or *terrassiers*, in loose corduroy trousers, short jackets, and flat caps, among whom the sturdiest and roughest, the *Costaud*, is the woman's "cave-man" and darling. In the faubourg Saint-Antoine and in the downfallen Marais quarter socialism and communism seethe, but the workmen still have pride in their skilled craftsmanship and give to their products an individual touch that the

[1] Novels in dialogue by Abel Hermant.

products of American standardization do not show. Across the river the nobility long sulked in the dead streets of the faubourg Saint-Germain, or, until the aftermath of the war made it seek wealth by business, like other people, tried to recoup its fortunes by marrying a Jewish heiress or a rich American girl, generically described as daughter of a "marchand de cochons de Chicago". The Latin quarter and university district is the home of study and pleasure; students saunter through the garden of the Luxembourg, and the children of the *petite bourgeoisie* play on its graveled walks or near the statues of the queens of France. Montparnasse is getting the reputation for artistic eccentricity that once belonged to Montmartre. The outer districts on the south, again, are the homes of toilers, *les humbles*, and of the "petit épicier de Montrouge" whom François Coppée made famous long ago, "with a chill on his heart and chilly feet!" If we read some novelists we imagine that Paris is given over to dissipation, *la noce*, but this is the penalty which results from distorted emphasis. In the humdrum lives of the great multitude whose adventures are not spicy is to be found the spirit of labor, thrift, and endurance which characterizes the genuine Parisian as well as the provincial.

NEWSPAPER HAWKER
"Paris-Speu-r-r!"

Paris, however, is far from being France, and regionalistic literature gives increasing evidence of the fact. In a narrow sense Regionalism is an expression of a political theory. But in a broader sense, as a revolt against bureaucracy, as an endeavor to revive the local spirit of different districts, and as expressed in the development of provincial universities, regionalism is nonpartisan and to be commended for its picturesque discoveries. The early pages of this work have indicated various writers and the sections they have described; but, more than that, some authors like E. Pérochon (*Nêne*) and A. de Châteaubriant (*La Brière*) have revealed to the French remote or hidden landscapes and types of which they themselves were scarcely conscious.

It is, however, the provincial small city or town which generally forms the most effective contrast to the pictures of high-strung Parisian life. In spite of divergences of temperament between the parts of France, there are recurrent types and themes. The *pharmacien* Homais of Flaubert's Norman Yonville-l'Abbaye and the Bézuquet of Daudet's southern Tarascon belong to the same semieducated class that the satirist likes to ridicule. Scheming prelates did not pass away with those of Balzac's *Curé de Tours*, but are still in Anatole France's *Histoire contemporaine*. What the novelist particularly portrays is the drab monotony of provincial life; its uneventful routine; the cheap gaudiness of its bazaar or *Grandes Galeries*; its petty rivalries and jealousies, social, political, and religious; its society of officeholders, from the *sous-préfet*, reflecting the glamour of governmental authority, to the *percepteur* and the *receveur de l'enregistrement*, hobnobbing at the hotel restaurant where they take their meals; the *petit rentier* reading his daily paper at the *café*; Anatole France's Monsieur Bergeret under the *orme du mail*, or the priest reading his breviary in the *allée des tilleuls* as he passes and repasses the retired *fonctionnaire* in short black alpaca coat, with a rosette in his buttonhole, sauntering to and fro in his daily stroll and holding his walkingstick in both hands behind his back.

In the background of the picture is the vast countryside, where descriptions of the uniformity of life are varied by the landscapes of beautiful France, a countryside of which Zola gave such a distorted view in *la Terre*, and Emile Guillaumin such a vivid one in *la Vie d'un simple,* where the small proprietor and *cultivateur* clings with devotion to the soil, but where subsist eternal human rivalries and the parochial jealousies and *haines de clocher* between the *curé*, agent of Rome, and the *instituteur*, servant of a radical government, both of them of peasant origin and equal intellectually, yet unable to find a common meeting-ground.

The pictures of the social classes under the Third Republic, as given in literature, are too varied for exhaustive treatment. We can at most touch here on some of the most striking aspects, *always bearing in mind the exaggerations of the writers.* In rank the nobility heads the roll, but the novelists and dramatists, particularly of the eighties and nineties, liked to portray the aristocrat as a degenerate, morally, mentally, and spiritually, the last result of worn-out families, or a "fossil", as in the play of Curel, often a neurotic pervert like Huysmans's Des Esseintes, leading a life of boredom in the provinces or of dissipation in Paris. Such men are what in Lavedan's *Prince d'Aurec* are called "Folly's bells" (*grelots de la folie*). More in accordance with truth, the titled Frenchman continued the foolish inherited fashion of sulking against the times. Through dislike of work and consciousness of social superiority he condescended only to military service in a smart cavalry regiment for an occupation, or spent his time hunting and lounging at his club, grumbling against the republic. Some of the men, willing to corrupt the blood of the crusaders for money, married the daughters of middle-class business magnates, or American or Jewish heiresses, and consorted in patronizing scorn with flashy Hebrews and successful journalists. The novelists, like Bourget and Maupassant (*Mont-Oriol*), show them thus occupied in the cosmopolitan life of Paris, or at the seaside resorts and water cures. The French nobles, we are told in the *Prince d'Aurec*, "are useful today only for the names of dishes. The French aristocracy peoples the bills of fare." The poorer nobility retired to the country in straitened circumstances, and the women, without dowries, grew into crotchety spinsters.

This whole picture by writers of a generation ago, which was exaggerated and unfair to many of the aristocracy then, would be quite untrue of the nobility of today, which, like the rest of France, has put its shoulder to the wheel. Apart from some seniors too old to change their ways, the after-war *noblesse* is at work.

Next to the aristocracy we are shown the three divisions of the middle class: the *haute*, the *moyenne*, and the *petite bourgeoisie*. The first contains the rich industrialists and capitalists; the second, the officeholders and professional men. In these groups are the financier, meddling in politics, often vulgar and pushing (an *arriviste*) or a business promoter (a *brasseur d'affaires*).[1] To Paul Hervieu money is the framework (*armature*) of society. Here belongs also Anatole France's Monsieur Bergeret, the naïve yet philosophical observer, a good example of the intellectual Voltairian, representing the average intelligent opinion, disabused, good-naturedly satirical, but unorganized and, with a shrug of the shoulders, letting things take their course. Here we find the intriguing side-whiskered magistrates and lawyers of Brieux's *Robe rouge*, Lemaître's politician, the Député Leveau, successor to Sardou's Rabagas and Daudet's Numa Roumestan, as well as Courteline's grotesques. The third division is the lower middle class, varied in its examples, thrifty, niggardly, scheming to better itself or to save for old age and for the *dot* of the only child, eager to graduate from a *petit commerçant* to a *petit rentier*, and so be able to apply to others the familiarly patronizing "mon ami" which it resented when applied to itself. Here comes Courteline's Boubouroche, the great example of the *petit bourgeois célibataire*, victim of tricky women in his incorrigible dullness of perception. Here come Courteline's other types of human stupidity, the *rond de cuir*, incarnation of red tape, so named from the round leather office-stool cushion on which his life is spent. Here, too, we can place the famous example of patience and of vacuous

---

[1] See Octave Mirbeau's *les Affaires sont les affaires* and the character of Isidore Lechat, or Maupassant's *Mont-Oriol*.

placidity, the solitary fisherman under his broad-brimmed hat, or *chapeau parasol*, waiting imperturbably with rod and line for the fish that never bites. As Jean Richepin wrote:

> Tout le long de la journée,
> O destin, tu leur promets
> La douce proie ajournée
> Qu'ils n'attraperont jamais.
>
> Et pas un ne s'en indigne,
> Pas un ne songe à partir!
> Car le pêcheur à la ligne
> Vit et meurt vierge et martyr!

At the bottom of the scale come the working classes, those who toil with their hands; the *ouvrier* embittered by industrialism and gravitating to socialism; the peasant, on the other hand, an intense individualist, miserly and loving his land, with superstitions harking back to paganism, not necessarily truly religious. The novel, and especially the short story and farce, present the tyrannical *concierge*, female Cerberus of French apartment houses; the *garçon d'hôtel*, or male chamber-maid, with his big feather duster; the buxom wet nurse, or *nounou*, in elaborate ribbons, from le Morvan; the shrill-voiced street huckster, or *marchand des quatre saisons*, with pushcart; the Dogberry *sergent de ville*. The ponderous and surly driver, the *cocher de fiacre*, in flamboyant *Jeune-France* waistcoat and shiny tall hat of *cuir bouilli*, Diogenes on the driver's seat, has perforce yielded to the more alert automobile driver; and instead of Mimi, the pretty *grisette* of olden times, we now see the busy *midinette*, shop girl or seamstress's worker; the stately *mannequin* of expensive dressmaking establishments in the rue de la Paix, whose form and style, as much as her face, are her fortune; or the twentieth-century stenographer, the *dactylo*.

In the aura surrounding these types, and not within the limits of any class, are the bohemians and the actors and actresses: Daudet's Delobelle, the perpetual *cabotin*; the characters of Anatole France's cynical *Histoire comique*; Ludovic

Halévy's Famille Cardinal, of the world of ballet dancers, and Madame Cardinal, so virtuously unmoral; the café-concert singers like the "vagabonde" of Colette. In the outer darkness wander the *noctambules* commemorated in Richepin's *Chanson des gueux*, impecunious night-wanderers and bohemians, seething with ideas, to some of whom, perhaps, fame and glory may, indeed, come.

The most savage and the most foul of the types of social satire is Ubu roi, an Aristophanic and Rabelaisian character, embodying grotesque cruelty, cowardice, and coarseness, from a farce by Alfred Jarry, said to have been merely a schoolboy's caricature of his teachers. Ubu was by some people accepted as a successor to Mayeux, Robert Macaire, Prudhomme, Homais, and Tribulat Bonhomet as a truculent satire of human imbecility.

STREET PEDDLER

The French conception of the Englishman has so often been alluded to in this volume that it is not out of place to add the portrait of the American. Down to the time of the Monarchy of July the idea of the American as a political sage like Franklin was still prevalent: the liberals eulogized Washington, and Tocqueville studied sympathetically American democracy. Then the vogue of James Fenimore Cooper in translation, which lasted for a full half century, created a picture of America as the land of Indian adventure and of *Bas-de-cuir*. The United States appeared to many a narrow strip of civilization on the Atlantic coast, back of which were the vast plains where roamed the buffalo. Under the Second Empire and the early days of the Third Republic society and men of letters often adopted a superior moral tone. Sardou, in *l'Oncle Sam,* treated the Ameri-

MILITARY DRILL
Drawing by Guillaume

cans in the tone of Dickens's *American Notes,* and Dumas's Mistress Clarkson, in *l'Etrangère,* was an adventuress. The American girl long seemed reprehensible by the freedom of her ways, as compared with the sheltered French girl, and was held up to criticism until later times brought better acquaintance. To the vivacious Frenchman Yankee self-restraint was striking, and Jules Verne's Americans are all cast in the same mold. His President Barbicane of the *Voyage autour de la lune* is an interesting contrast to his excitable Frenchman, Michel Ardan. At the time of the outbreak of the war the attitude in literature toward the American was friendly and appreciative, as in the comedy *Mon ami Teddy.* The French were, at the same time, worried lest Americans fail to appreciate the virtue of their women, because of the false impression created abroad by French fiction. Of this feeling Brieux's *la Française* is an illustration.

Two elements of the social structure vastly more important to the Frenchman than to the American are religion and the army. The black and the red are no less significant than in the days of Stendhal. Both constantly recur in literature, and because of universal military service the officer and soldier are even more frequent than the priest.

Obviously the portrait of the priest varies much, according to the political or philosophical bias of the author, or the public for which it is intended. In literature the French reader can, today at any rate, be more detached in spirit in his clerical studies than one might imagine from the virulence of Michelet and other early democratic writers. Anticlericalism at present is to a considerable degree political, a radical campaign slogan, more than a movement against anything really dangerous. The men of the French *bourgeoisie* still cling somewhat to the Voltairian irony, and the contrast between the number of men seen praying in French and in Spanish churches is striking. They are, therefore, on the whole, indifferent, whether intellectuals, half-educated successors of Homais, proletarians, or the shrewder, materialistic members of the peasantry. In the struggle between the two organizations, State and Church, they incline rather to the State, whereas the women are more guided by their confessors and the priests in general. Romain Rolland, in *Antoinette*, says that the anticlericalism of the small towns of France is always more or less an episode in domestic warfare, and is a subtle form of the "silent, bitter struggle between husbands and wives which goes on in almost every home."

As a result the cleric is sometimes hypocritical and debauched, particularly in older portraitures written in the tradition of virulent warfare and with memories of *Tartuffe* as a political document. At other times he is the good-natured semi-skeptical Frenchman, the priest of Béranger's "Dieu des bonnes gens"; at other times, the good *curé de campagne*, father of his flock, of which type the abbé Constantin is the climax. But French writers are particularly skilled in delineating the subtle intrigues of religious politicians and timeservers for power and influence: Ferdinand Fabre's abbé Tigrane, "candidat à la papauté"; the abbé Guitrel, of Anatole France's *Anneau d'améthyste*, scheming to be bishop; "ces messieurs" of Georges Ancey, and especially the Jesuits of Estaunié's *l'Empreinte*, stamping their impress on plastic youth. The satanism of Huysmans's *chanoine* Docre, in *Là-bas*, is, of course, an aberration.

When, at the downfall of the Second Empire, the National Guard, so long an inherent part of the French military organization, disappeared, when the idea of a professional army was discarded and universal service was gradually introduced, then army life became more prominent. In the days of the antimilitarism of the eighties life in the barracks is pictured as corrupting and degrading. To that period belongs the famous character, Colonel Ramollot, a *vieille moule*, an imbecile endowed with the authority of his uniform. Of a like nature, but portrayed in a good-natured spirit and understood to be merely examples of general human stupidity, are characters in Courteline's inimitable farces. The young officer is nearly always a gay Lothario, aided by his smart uniform in the quest of amorous intrigue, unless he be a virtuous exception, like the lieutenant in *l'Abbé Constantin*. Above all, the happy-go-lucky experiences of an army service performed by everyone made military farces dear to the populace. No form of comic play was more enjoyed in the decade preceding the last war than that in which the chief characters were red-legged troopers, or which portrayed the adventures and misadventures of the reservist back in uniform for the training of his annual "vingt-huit jours".

CHAPTER XVII

THIRD REPUBLIC. LITERARY AND ARTISTIC TENDENCIES AND TYPES

IF WE examine closely the literary schools and their leaders under the Third Republic, we find that the first decade shows the growth of realism into naturalism in fiction, and, on the stage, the prestige of the dramatic moralists. The height of the influence of Zola is from about 1877 to 1887; the great popularity of Augier at the Comédie française lasts until about 1880, prolonged for another decade by that of Dumas.

Important above all as influences in fiction are the Goncourt brothers, who had much to do with shaping the course of the novel in France. To these two authors and to their influence on the period from 1870 to 1890 France owes much of the evil reputation which the moral standards of its literature have acquired abroad. The Goncourt brothers were morbid valetudinarians who introduced mannerisms into style, neurosis into their pictures of life, and in art the dilettante taste for the out-of-the-way and the exotic. Familiar only with certain narrow phases of modern civilization, they tried to show that all humanity was as corrupt. Under pretext of bringing literature nearer to life they chose their "human documents" in the crudities of low life and paved the way for Zola. To the Goncourt brothers more than to anyone else is due the concentration of writers for so long on feminine perverts and prostitutes. The literature of the Third Republic assumes a greater freedom of speech, a right to audacious descriptions, and the free discussion of topics hitherto glossed over.

Students of the Goncourts collectively and of the surviving brother classify their influence under four heads:

1. The school of *Germinie Lacerteux*.
2. The school of *la Faustin*.
3. Stylistic nervousness.
4. The school of the *Grenier*: impressionism in art and criticism, the taste for bric-a-brac, *bibelots*, and exoticism, such as the art of Japan.

The first two only are important to us here. The fourth we shall speak of under Art.

Germinie Lacerteux foreshadows "putrid literature". By this novel fiction and the stage are familiarized with the brutalities of the underworld. Prostitution becomes a common theme. The *femme entretenue* of the Second Empire gives way to the woman of the streets and her associates who live on her earnings. The reader is taken to disreputable dance halls in the working quarters, to scenes of drunkenness and of debauchery, to the horrors of the hospital and the dissecting-room. The writer sets down for him the brutal and cynical language of such places, and Zola's Naturalism emphasizes the filth of it all. Maupassant sometimes shows the sardonic humor found in the paradoxes of such themes, and devotes a whole story, *la Maison Tellier*, to the holiday of the inmates of a house of ill fame. In some naturalist writers the crude treatment of women is a reaction from the exaggerated idealism of earlier schools. Some, as Zola, justify naturalism as a form of "*democratic art*", because it is "scientific" and "positive", and its themes of poverty, suffering, and social injustice are in contrast with scenes from aristocratic or wealthy life.

In addition to their brutal pictures the Goncourts maintained that the hothouse life of Paris had developed a new disease, "Parisianism". They prided themselves on being the pathologists of this disease, for which they were well fitted by their natures, and Edmond de Goncourt, the surviving brother, made it his literary domain. In the famous Goncourt diary[1] he calls his brother and himself "les Saint-Jean-Baptiste de la nervosité moderne", and boasts that they were the precursors of modern

---

[1] Vol. VI, p. 19.

novelists, writing with their nerves more than with their brains. In their enumerations of plastic detail they make their characters supersensitive and responsive to stimuli which usually belong to the subconscious. By their analysis and vivisection they not only are the precursors of a numerous school in the Third

THE *MOULIN DE LA GALETTE*, A PUBLIC DANCE HALL, BY RENOIR
(LUXEMBOURG)
Example of Impressionism

Republic but they reacted on life. In the bizarre Russian girl of Paris in the eighties, Marie Bashkirtseff, whose high-strung Slavic temperament quivered and throbbed in response to all that was most artificial in French morbid intellectualism and emotionalism, is seen the full flower of the type of woman the Goncourts portray.[1]

[1] She becomes a character in fiction in Albéric Cahuet's *le Masque aux yeux d'or*, 1924. Bataille had already disguised her in his play, *le Phalène*.

The souls of men and women became, under the spell of the Goncourts, tainted, like game that is high (*faisandage*). Women in Paris, says Edmond de Goncourt in *Chérie*, mature to sex consciousness much earlier than in the provinces. Their life is one of distractions, elegant lassitudes, and the overstrain of an artificial existence. Novels are in time penetrated with allusions to the "odeur féminine" and "voluptés cachées". In the seventeenth chapter of *la Faustin* (1882), Edmond de Goncourt writes this strange passage:

"Society women, the society women of to-day," exclaimed the first speaker interrupting, a celebrated author, "women who are thin, fleshless, flat, bony, with so little body, so little room for love, women with complexions suggesting chlorosis and disease, with poorly painted lips and eyes, beings of spectral and unhealthy appearance, of whom one asks only clever looks, smartness, spirit. Certainly it is not the standard of beauty of primary school drawing-classes; but it must be admitted that, in the condition of tainted game which the passions of nineteenth-century man have reached, this type is deucedly stimulating."

Whatever justification, if any, there may be for this analysis of the modern Parisienne, the type has, with variations, been constantly repeated. Novelists like Paul Bourget in his first period, and Marcel Prévost, depict the French woman as shallow, sly, coquettish, and sensual, unable to resist her impulses, devoted to flirting and adultery, hastening from one *garçonnière* to another. Even a sober realist like Maupassant, at the base of whose monument in the Parc Monceau the Parisienne reclines, depicts woman as a being of overwrought sensibility, whose restless and wavering nature is incapable of self-mastery. Becque's *la Parisienne* shows her passing from lover to husband and back again indifferently. Encouraged by such examples women writers themselves went still farther and seemed to justify by their exhibitionism the accusations of the men. But the climax is found in the women of the plays of Henry Bataille.

As a reaction against the pseudo-science of Zola's naturalism, and in the spirit of *la Faustin*, there comes in the eighties the vogue of the *roman mondain*, or society novel, illustrated by the

L'ABSINTHE, BY DEGAS (LOUVRE)
Naturalism in art. Photograph by Giraudon

early writings of Bourget, Prévost, some of those of Maupassant, and Goncourt's own *Chérie*. More sophisticated and outwardly less "brutal" than the woman of naturalism, the heroine is not more alluring. The emphasis of Taine on psychology reaches fruition, and the novelist devotes himself to subtle pseudo-psychological analysis of *états d'âme*, or "states of feeling", which the influence of the Goncourts had already directed toward perverseness and maladies of the will.

The popularity of Renan's indifferentism, and the added cosmopolitanism of the nineties, bringing with it the morbidness of Ibsen, explain the appropriateness of the term *veule*, suggesting mental and moral flabbiness, applied by critics to the pictures of *fin-de-siècle* society. In novels, in comedies, in the smart and flashy dialogues of Lavedan and others, the assumption is constantly of adultery and the *ménage à trois*. The well-to-do classes are idle and profligate. Man may make it his purpose to victimize women, like Lavedan's marquis de Priola, or a woman may be helping to support her lover, as in Maupassant's *Bel-Ami*. The *bourgeoisie* is still the butt of cynical writers who do not forgive it for being thrifty and unimaginative. The *comédie rosse* of the Théâtre-Libre, purporting to represent cross-sections of life (*tranches de vie*), concentrates on the turpitude of conventional respectability. A husband and father is apt to be unfaithful or an old idiot, a *gâteux*; the mother is avaricious and scheming; the children are involved in corrupt intrigues. The *blague* of other days has here turned to gall and wormwood. The Théâtre-Libre and some novelists still preserved also the naturalist tradition with its scenes of drunkenness and of life among the criminal classes. The earlier crudeness of portraiture was now often veiled by literary craft. Maupassant, out of contempt for the *bourgeoisie*, excuses the peasant girl who goes wrong, for disregarding the red tape of marriage; and in *Boule-de-suif* his sympathy is with the fallen woman and his scorn for the respectable fellow travelers for whose sake she sacrifices herself. With the advent of the Russian novel and doctrines of humanitarian sympathy and brotherhood the street-walker is made out to be entirely the victim of society, and Charles-Louis Philippe, a pupil of Dostoevsky and Tolstoy, in *Bubu de Montparnasse*, calls her a "pauvre petite sainte."

Inasmuch as the *bourgeoisie* is, after all, still the class by which France is characterized, and inasmuch as the *bourgeoisie* of France is not addicted to persistent violation of the marriage tie, the inaccuracy of these pictures of life is obvious.[1] There is this to be said: the administrative complications incident upon marriage make many people of the lower classes neglect it entirely and do without legal sanction; the fact that unmarried men who violate the moral code are not punished to the same degree as in countries of puritanical tradition by loss of position or of social esteem makes more of them live in celibacy or flaunt their mistresses more openly. By tacit convention the fact that an unmarried man has a mistress is overlooked and occasionally he weds her even when she is vastly his inferior. Whether the Anglo-Saxons are in this respect merely more hypocritical, as the French say, or not, is not to the point.[2] In social convention in France there is not the same emphasis on self-restraint for young men as in America. A revelation of this is found in a recent work of fiction, *Oxford et Margaret*, by Jean Fayard, a young man:

> His experiences had been those of a young Frenchman; that is to say, that without thinking sexual enjoyment a superior pleasure, he did not consider it degrading: it was a pleasure, that is all; and it is silly to deny oneself a pleasure.

[1] Professor Baldensperger, in his volume *l'Avant-guerre dans la littérature française*, quoted the theory of the late Edouard Rod that the frequency of adultery in modern fiction is due to so many bachelor novelists, the absence of home life, the nonexistence of immediate social responsibilities. But see above, p. 142. Literature would seem to justify the cynic that "a Frenchman will never steal his friend's mistress, but will always try to steal his friend's wife".

[2] "Sa fortune personnelle lui avait permis de rester célibataire" (O. Méténier, *les Demi-Castors*, p. 100); that is to say, firstly, he had not been obliged to marry a *dot*; secondly, he had money of his own to spend on what would cost more than a lawful establishment. An American writer would have probably put it: "His private means had enabled him to marry young."

Adultery is, then, more literature than life.[1] Yet, such is the frequent treatment of this theme, and of other traditional ones already enumerated, that one is not surprised at the tirade of Romain Rolland, in *la Foire sur la place*, against Paris society, its emptiness, moral impotence, neurasthenia, pointless, self-devouring hypercriticism, and stagnant atmosphere of art for art's sake and pleasure for pleasure's sake.

Novelists and dramatists, either for commercial reasons or because they are carried away by the apostolic ardor with which they preach a cause, are, to mention at random some of the important tendencies, stern moralists, like Brieux and Paul Hervieu, supercilious aristocratic traditionalists (Bourget's later manner), supersensitive impressionists (school of Loti), realists whose frankness sometimes has a touch of sadism, as with Octave Mirbeau. In some the brutality of Zola and the sentiment of Daudet have been replaced by a combination of cynicism and tearfulness characteristic of the new realists just before the war. As propagandists they preached, not only social reform in general and the emancipation of the proletariat, but free love, the *union libre*, the *droit au bonheur*, and many forms of ultrafeminism to which Frenchwomen, as a whole, are supremely indifferent. In addition to sinning married men and women, they portray the vampire, the *femme à collage* after the pattern of Daudet's Sapho, the *demi-mondaine* or *demi-castor* and frequenter of flashy night restaurants, like the *Dame de chez Maxim*, the music-hall actress, whose charm must not be aristocratic but alluringly vulgar (*canaille*). In the general release from older social ideas even the young girl in Parisian

---

[1] "Below one hundred thousand inhabitants there is nothing for adultery to do. There remains for it literature. Do not laugh; it is an absolute fact. No souls are more wildly smitten with literature than the souls of those misunderstood little *bourgeoises*, ill-adapted to such environments, who avenge themselves by a debauch of reading suited to their sentimental or sensual disappointments. It ranges from the lower *bourgeoisie* to the aristocracy, and is almost always expressed by the same authors. Much Parisianism, a little viciousness, a little sentimental touch, such is their formula."—BERTAUT, *Ce qu'était la province française avant la guerre*, p. 180.

literature becomes more emancipated. The *ingénue* has opened her eyes. Where the younger members of the Benoîton family in Sardou's play were colloquial and slangy, the new generation is plain-spoken and specific. The overknowing girl Claudine, in black pinafore, broad white collar, bow tie, and hair ribbon, created by Colette and "Willy", had considerable vogue among readers of novels. The *demi-vierge* of "moralists" like Marcel Prévost no longer startles those who can stand the stronger food set before them today in *la Garçonne*. Here, again, literature has run ahead of life. Romain Rolland, to whose criticisms we have several times referred, characterizes the French drama of the early twentieth century in *la Foire sur la place*, and what he says is applicable to the presentation of life in fiction as well. Contemporary French drama, he says, consists of vulgar farce in the *genre gaulois*, with barrack-room jests, underclothing, and scenes in private rooms at restaurants; "modern style" drama, the unmoral theater of Judaicized Christians and of Parisianized Jews, where vice has a flavor of virtue and virtue a flavor of vice, where every relation of age, sex, and affection is turned upside down; the ponderous problem plays of the Théâtre-Français, and the poetic drama of sexual immorality and Cornelian heroics combined. Even religion is dragged in: "Jewish authors [Catulle Mendès] wrote tragedies about St. Theresa for Jewish actresses [Sarah Bernhardt]." In all this Romain Rolland is emphasizing the Jews, and it is undeniable that many of the most flashily brilliant and insincere of the contemporary French plays have been written by Jews. But it must not be forgotten that Rolland is here speaking in superlatives, and that the modern French drama since 1890 contains a goodly proportion of what may be described as "pièces de haute allure" by men like Brieux, Hervieu, and Lavedan.[1]

The earlier years of the Third Republic have little to show in poetry that is new. The Parnassian impeccables stood too

[1] Compare the passage from Romain Rolland referred to in the preface of this book.

far aloof to have much vogue, and Hugo was old. Gradually, however, the influence became pervasive of a most significant poet, Charles Baudelaire.

Baudelaire, like so many others, had reacted against the sordidness and materialism which he saw in the civilization of the nineteenth century and had assumed toward it the superior attitude of intellectual "dandyism". Scorning his age, he deliberately undertook, again like many others, to cultivate that which would shock the *bourgeois*, and the grain of madness in his own artistic temperament led him, in rebellious disillusionment, to the morbid and the perverse. Gifted as he was with the power of rhythmic effect and melodious suggestivity, he made the two elements, the *macabre* and the musical, powerful in the generation following his own.

PROLETARIAN TYPE

It may readily be guessed that the outwardly shocking was what had the more immediate effect. The *poncif* of Baudelaire, as it was called, the corrupt and perversely evil, accompanied by discouragement and *spleen*, took hold of the youth of France, made melancholy by the defeat of 1870–1871, prone to react against moral conventions which had hitherto restrained it, and succumbing, as a vanquished nation sometimes does, to reckless indulgence of the passions. The morbid pose of Baudelaire was especially borrowed by the literary and artistic æsthetes who dissociated art from morality.

The influence of Baudelaire grew during the eighties and the nineties, reaching a climax when, as we have already pointed out, the term *fin-de-siècle* suggested the death of a period of civilization. The bohemian and literary *cafés* and *cabarets* of Montmartre were thronged by art students with huge neckties, unappreciated poets with unkempt hair and downy chins, and their women associates in æsthetic pre-Raphaelite *coiffures*, their hair plastered over their ears like maidens of Botticelli. In these resorts the entertainers declaimed or sang verses suggestive of physical decay and moral corruption, sepulchral, satanic, erotic. Impecunious poets, jealous of the prosperous, outvied each other in the crudity of their realism, and evoked scenes of poverty, the grimy *hôtel garni* and night lodging, and suffering in the underworld and on the desolate slopes of the fortifications, refuge of the homeless. The *genre macabre*, school of blasphemy, of lassitudes and pagan vices, of "chlorotic" loves, acquired some impressiveness by its numbers, by its assumption of artistic superiority, and by one or two really significant exceptions, such as Maurice Rollinat and the group of the *Chat noir*. But many of its members died or went insane from vice or dissipation, thus seeming to verify the term *décadent*. In some of the taverns of Montmartre, designed for naïve foreigners, like the *Cabaret de l'Enfer*, with its waiters dressed as devils, Baudelairism was commercialized for tourists. Meanwhile poetesses, leaving to the men Baudelaire's lassitudes, chlorosis, and brooding over shades of feeling, borrowed his erotic "mysticism" and sang fiercely and unblushingly of the "trouble de la chair".

Some early symbolists were decadents, many decadents were symbolists, and the general public of the nineties lumped them together. Symbolism began about 1885 and was one of the forms of reaction against pseudo-scientific realism. Whereas many novelists turned to complex psychological analysis, the poets sought refuge in a mystic, sensuous, visionary world, in order to bring back the thrill, the *frisson du mystère*, banished by the Parnassians. Symbolism borrowed from Baudelaire rhythmic effects and melodious suggestivity, reënforced by other tendencies in art and music, English æstheticism, going back through Ruskin to the pre-Raphaelites, and German Wagnerian romanticism. The sinking in national self-esteem coincident with political conditions made men of letters susceptible to foreign tendencies. Symbolism appeared a new form of cosmopolitan romanticism, belonging once more to the few rather than to the philistines, manifesting familiar themes of pride, pessimism, mystical sensuality, and scorn for what Jules Laforgue called the "eternullity" of life. The new poets veiled the clarity of their thought by suppressing the connection of ideas, and some of them, as has been said, by suppressing punctuation. They reveled, like the pre-Raphaelites, in peacocks, swans, and lilies, and, like the Wagnerians, in pictures of princesses with jeweled fingers and knights in shining mail. Audiences at tiny theaters such as the *Théâtre de l'Œuvre* first applauded Maeterlinck's *Pelléas et Mélisande*.

Two poets influential in setting the stage for later writers were Paul Verlaine and Stéphane Mallarmé. Verlaine was the leader of what has been called the *art flou*, of vague and indeterminate prosody and feeling. He substituted *la nuance* for clarity of expression and sharp imagery, and reacted against Parnassian perfection of form and conventional poetical rhetoric. Mallarmé taught by example to his band of devoted admirers the *art sibyllin*, so obscure as to be hailed with delight by many minor imitators because of the opportunity presented of saying nothing in sonorous terms. Mallarmé was an important influence on the *décadents*, and the whole spirit of the decadent and symbolist poetry is delightfully parodied in the so-called *Déliquescences d'Adoré Floupette*, by Gabriel Vicaire and Henri Beauclair.

With greater maturity many symbolists did as the Parnassians and romanticists had done before them, and became more conventional and *assagis*. But the whole tendency of the early twentieth century away from discipline in life and art encouraged a disintegration into small schools and groups, each with a battle cry and a manifesto, professing to interpret life from a single angle, which was, after all, the only true one. The result is seen in the numerous sets, "chapels", and "isms" of contemporary literature, remote from the comprehension and the enjoyment of the majority of presumably intelligent people.

THE HAY-MAKERS, BY BASTIEN-LEPAGE (LUXEMBOURG)
Open-air realism

In art the early Third Republic, after the interruption of the Franco-Prussian War, continued many of the past tendencies. The "official" theories were taught in the national academies, and Gérôme was the bitter foe of the impressionists. The word "academism" became the cant term by which the innovators designated as mediocre and unoriginal the art which followed tradition and rules. The schism grew and the rebels had admirers, some out of conviction, some for no other reason than that they were rebels and *ipso facto* liberal and progressive.

We have seen that even under the Empire the "Salon des refusés" suggested an opposition strong enough to be vocal. Out of the medley are formulated the movements of realism and, later, of impressionism, which many realist painters joined. Realism called itself democratic, and the realist Courbet was a Communard who helped to pull down the imperial Vendôme Column. Monet and Manet were important names in the reaction against academic art, and Manet had successive stages of realism and of impressionism.

The objects of attack in academic art were the theatrical gesticulations and conventional postures of the models; the black and brown shadows expressed by bitumen, a pigment which, it was argued, gave no valid tones; as well as the uniformity of the studio north light. The result of realistic democratic art was to diminish dignity, to heighten pathos and effect, and to substitute character for the *beau proportionnel*. Modern art, relieved from old traditions and conventions, became more vivid, and pictures no longer to the same degree fitted into uniform schemes of wall decoration. The realists painted scenes of industrialism and commercialism and the platitudes of everyday life, often with hints of social propaganda, or depicted the "naturalism" of rustic trivialities, like dirty stables, and farmyards with their piles of manure and dull-faced peasants. The term "école du plein air" came into vogue to designate the blunt portrayal of figure and landscape.

The reaction against dull shadows developed also along different lines into impressionism. It was argued, for the artists were vociferous theorists, that the painter should not *cuisiner*, or mix, his colors for the observer. They said further that there is no such thing as a sharp defining outline to an object, but that the object, through effects of light, merges into its surroundings. The artist, then, sacrificing story or anecdote in painting, emphasizes atmosphere, and, putting before the spectator the elementary tones which the latter may not himself

LE BOIS SACRÉ AUX ARTS ET AUX MUSES, BY PUVIS DE CHAVANNES (LYON CITY HALL)
Symbolism in art

have realized, leaves it to him, by standing far enough away, to recompound the hues. Pictures no longer presented solids, but landscapes volatilized and made fluid,—"symphonies" of colors like the harmonies of music, of which art the American Whistler was one of the most noted exponents.

There was close contact between artists and men of letters. Zola, the literary naturalist, sympathized strongly with realistic democratic art. In his art criticisms he was a great advocate of Manet; his novel, *l'Œuvre*, is important for the literary study of art, and the hero, Claude Lantier, is partly drawn from Manet and Cézanne. *Manette Salomon*, by the Goncourt brothers, is another significant work, and their diary is full of impressionistic art criticism. The interest of the Goncourt brothers in Japanese art, with its sharp contrasts and neglect of dark shadows, brings impressionism into connection with their *grenier*, and with their usual self-esteem they emphasize their influence to the full in their journal.

Thus, by the second decade of the Third Republic art was experiencing diversity and confusion. Academic art, favored as it still is today by the prestige of state favor and the terms of competitive awards like the *prix de Rome*, was the butt of satire by those who had not won its rewards, and the recurrent examination *poncifs* excited journalistic mirth. The new painters laughed at those of the old school, and their studios littered with panthers' skins, armor, Oriental draperies and costumes, and bric-a-brac. Democratic art sought the effects of urban as well as of rural life,—streets, railway stations, and the smoke of factories. Naturalism decorated town halls and public buildings with appropriate but unpoetical themes,—marriages and christenings, or huge processions of toilers suggesting the surge of democracy. Some painters expressed the unorthodox democratic religious mysticism by biblical episodes in modern costume, which sometimes startled by their incongruity.

With the reaction against naturalism in literature came a corresponding one in art. Imagination, using sober colors,—pale blues and grays,—again had its day, and symbolists like

Puvis de Chavannes were in vogue. Others, less subdued than he and less respectful of classic tradition, expressed themselves in decadent cerebral eccentricities or in deliquescent religious mysticism like the literature of Huysmans. Finally, pariahs (were it not for the successful advertising of art dealers) known as *indépendants*, specialized in obese and misshapen female nudes, hideous and grotesque in form and coloring, what the painter Cézanne, dropping into verse, called "fine meat".[1] Some corresponded to the writers of life in the underworld and were artists of the lowest depths, or *bas fonds*, of Parisian life and the hideousness of the bohemianism of Montmartre and its dance halls, intensified in their rendering of the *fumier humain*. In the days of disillusion the sketches of newspaper caricature too grew bitter. Society was represented as permeated with the spirit of caddishness (*muflerie*), with administrative and financial corruption, with sordid middle-class materialism. The sentimental *grisette* of older times, here as elsewhere, was replaced by the venal woman. In the early Third Republic A. Grévin had specialized in the sprightly but cold-blooded *cocotte* victimizing the idiotic *gommeux*. Now the cruel sketches of Forain and the like corresponded to the most bitter literary descriptions of the *fille*. On the other hand, the tradition of gayety happily still survived in the fantasies of Willette.

An important tendency of modern French art is expressed in the "academic nude". It is a phase of a tradition going back through Ingres to David, under the protection of the Institute and the academies. The nudes of David had been for the most part male, but the sensuality of Ingres encouraged the popularity of the female nude, and it was taken up by painters and teachers such as Cabanel, Bouguereau, and Gérôme. It was a convenient reaction against the picturesque accessories of romantic local coloring to concentrate attention on figure study, and

---

[1] The lines are quoted in Vollard's study of Cézanne. They conclude:

> La couleuvre n'a pas de souplesse plus grande,
> Et le soleil qui luit, darde complaisamment
> Quelques rayons dorés sur cette belle viande.

the sensuous spirit of the Second Empire, especially during the latter half, popularized in the annual *Salon* female nudes with a few mythological trappings to make a Venus, a Diana, or a Truth. They were sufficiently numerous to make possible that annual volume of reproductions, *le Nu au Salon*. Study of the *tout ensemble* was the important occupation of all those *ateliers* that became so familiar to England and America in Du Maurier's *Trilby*. The world at large was made intimate with the female figure through the story writers who consorted with the artists and frequented their haunts. A daily paper, the *Gil Blas*, to which Maupassant contributed, was started to specialize in spicy stories, like the "histoires grasses" of Armand Silvestre, and was the chief specimen of the "pornographic press". Every public monument or portrait statue had to have one or more nude or seminude women clinging to the pedestal, in contrast to the Libertys and Columbias in demure *peignoirs* of American art. The border arabesques of illustrations and of engravings introduced the undraped anatomy. The decorator, instead of following a geometrical curve, fell naturally into the sinuous outline of full hip or bust. Says Remy de Gourmont in *le Livre des masques*: "To be fond of the nude, and especially the feminine nude, with its graces and insolences, is traditional in races which have not been completely terrorized by the harsh Reformation." Though the thing cannot be proved by chapter and paragraph, there is no doubt that the influence of artists favored the increased frankness of scenes of *déshabillage* and recurrent descriptions of the body in novels, the undress of modern *revues* in music halls, first of Montmartre and its art quarters, then of the rest of Paris. It explains also how the decadent pseudo-Hellenism of Pierre Louÿs's descriptions could be judged as art dissevered from morals, and how his *Aphrodite*, after success as a story, was turned into an opera.[1] The nonacademic painters, such as the realists, could not very well use

---

[1] "A family poet, *bourgeois* and Catholic [François Coppée], gave his artistic blessing to a very detailed description of perverted Greek morals."— R. ROLLAND, *la Foire sur la place*

THE WEDDING, BY THE *DOUANIER* ROUSSEAU, WHO WAS "DISCOVERED" BY G. APOLLINAIRE, A. JARRY, AND THE "INCOHÉRENTS"

Ignorance of art glorified as genius. Photograph by Giraudon

the fiction of "Venus" or "Truth", but an unending procession of unclad bathers, or *baigneuses*, still troops through the exhibitions. Degas was the precursor in art of the *genre rosse* and the ironic treatment of the nude, and the independents, we have seen, present not the human form divine but the nude hideous.

In two important ways French literature has been both dissociated from national life and an influence on other countries, by literary cliques and by Montmartre. Many modern exaggerations owe their success to "log-rolling" and to the cohesive effect of what have in recent years been called *chapelles littéraires*. No publishers in the world are greater adepts than those of Paris today in creating "best sellers". Consequently various quickly passing fads for second-rate books have been successfully launched and sometimes boomed by multitudinous literary prizes. They have been naïvely accepted abroad.[1] Many of the artistic aberrations of neo-impressionists, cubists, and the like owe their notoriety to exhibitions got up by picture dealers, as of a new and original genius. Similarly, the exaggerations of modern Montmartre have been considered by foreigners more serious and more representative of France than they have been by the French themselves.

Intellectual and literary groups are of time-honored vogue in France. The Pléiade, the Hôtel de Rambouillet, the *salons* of the eighteenth century, the *cénacles* of romanticism are but a few among many instances. The academies of the Institute, and particularly the Académie française, have been striking examples of the power exerted by official organizations, but even the Académie française is not held to be perfectly representative. The artificial limit of forty may both exclude merit for want of a vacancy and admit mediocrities when talents are few. The same limitation encourages intrigues and wire-pulling, as well as unfortunate compromises between the *parti des ducs* and the *universitaires*.

---

[1] Witness the recent case of the rich man who wrote a novel, established a literary prize through another name, and was charged with having himself awarded a distinction.

LITERARY AND ARTISTIC TENDENCIES

LE SECRET DU MANIFESTANT

Drame express en 7 tableaux et en vers de Jacques FERNY

Dessin de Fernand FAU

LE RÊVE DE ZOLA

Fantaisie en 10 tableaux

par Jules JOUY; dessins de Jules DEPAQUIT

REPRODUCTION OF A PAGE FROM A PROGRAM OF THE THEATER *CHAT-NOIR*

Unofficial gatherings have often had much hidden influence, particularly when grouped about a clever and energetic hostess. The *salon* of Mme Adam, frequented by Gambetta, helped to engineer the Third Republic; that of Mme Aubernon was political and dramatic; that of the comtesse de Loynes we have seen to have been a home of anti-Dreyfusite agitation. More than one *salon* has prided itself on being, like that of Mme de Lambert in the eighteenth century, an *antichambre de l'académie*, and the strenuous intellectualism of some of the *salons* of the early Third Republic, as that of Mme de Blocqueville, was amusingly satirized in Pailleron's *le Monde où l'on s'ennuie*. Often these gatherings became centers of *snobisme littéraire* and of pure dilettantism, opportunities for recitals by poets and poetesses,—what Camille Mauclair calls "afternoon-tea sirens" (*sirènes de five-o'clock*),—either at private houses or in doll theaters like the Bodinière, which long enjoyed a reputation in æsthetic circles. An excellent example of the literary dilettante, reflecting tendencies associated with the names of Renan, Baudelaire, and Huysmans, was Count Robert de Montesquiou-Fezansac, amusingly portrayed as the peacock in Rostand's *Chantecler* and the original in part of the M. de Charlus of Marcel Proust. The French fondness for literary discipleship, the "cher maître" attitude, results in many self-created immortalities, sometimes continued for a few years after death by a society of "les Amis de—". These leaders, with amiable altruism, sometimes unearth other immortals, as when the literary cubist Guillaume Apollinaire discovered a modest agent of the *octroi* of the city of Paris, a *douanier* named Henri Rousseau, who could neither draw nor paint, and as a joke proclaimed him a genius, keeping up the jest with such vigor that he was finally hypnotized by his own myth.[1]

Montmartre, before it became commercialized and some of its vogue transferred to Montparnasse, was famous for its art and its *esprit*. To some Americans Montmartre is France. As a type it is an exaggeration of both French qualities and defects. It has been called a *pochade*, a rough, offhand sketch,

---

[1] My authority for the interpretation as a *farce*, or practical joke, of Apollinaire's cult of Rousseau is an article by Sylvain Bonmariage in *les Partisans*, which I have not seen, but which is summarized in *l'Opinion*, May 9, 1924.

or draft, of the French spirit, characterized by bohemian good fellowship, recklessly fantastic criticism, and preoccupation with "la petite femme". For many years Montmartre and Montparnasse were rival art centers, nip and tuck, and in literature Montmartre was more whimsical than the left bank, which was a little steadied by the neighboring university quarter. The symbolists, says Camille Mauclair, were apt to be "left bankers". Montmartre was the home of literary practical jokers and of the artistic *cabarets* like the *Chat noir*. The *Chat noir* could be the foundation of solid fame, and Maurice Donnay, now of the Academy, began his career among the songs and genuinely artistic silhouette plays (*ombres chinoises*) of the Black Cat. Many an author who became noted later started at the Théâtre-Libre, which held its first sessions in one of the most obscure thoroughfares of Montmartre. The great days of Montmartre were from 1870 to 1900. Too often, since 1890, it has harbored *café* charlatans, sham artists and journalists, blackmailers, and *demi-mondaines*, until paradoxically it has ceased to stand for France at all, yet is by many tourists considered more typical than ever. The tradition of the *Chat noir* and of literary Montmartre is now to be found only in a few resorts of the Latin Quarter like the *Noctambules*. Certain *cabarets* of Montmartre are now visited almost wholly by foreigners. Montmartre and Montparnasse, both today commercialized, are largely responsible for Greenwich Village.

APPENDIX

The following pages contain four characteristic passages from French literature illustrating:

A. The *genre troubadour*.
B. Romanticism.
C. The *bourgeoisie*.
D. The intellectual proletariat: *la bohème*.

A. THE GENRE TROUBADOUR

L'ERMITE DE SAINTE-AVELLE

Aux rochers de Sainte-Avelle
La reine Berte autrefois
Fit bâtir une chapelle
A Notre-Dame-des-Bois.
Ce fut dans ce lieu sauvage
Qu'un jour, disant son missel,
L'ermite du voisinage
Reçut un beau damoisel.

Bien que le vieillard d'avance
Cherchât à le rassurer,
L'étranger en sa présence
Soudain se prit à pleurer.
"Mon fils, dit le solitaire,
Parlez; d'où naissent vos pleurs?
—Hélas, je n'ose, mon père
Vous confier mes douleurs.

Pour avoir de noble dame
Obtenu simple baiser,
Je vais brûlant d'une flamme
Que rien ne peut apaiser.

Oh! dites-moi, je vous prie,
Par quel charme si fatal
Le doux baiser d'une amie
Est cause de tant de mal.

Je ne saurais, la nuit même,
Reposer dans mon sommeil;
Et dès l'aube un trouble extrême
Précipite mon réveil.
Tout vient irriter ma peine ;
Tout m'offre le souvenir
De la belle châtelaine
Dont les baisers font mourir.

Mais un époux dans Grenade
La tient sous sa dure loi;
Et j'apprends qu'à la croisade
Il me faut suivre le roi.
Je viens donc ici, mon père,
Vous demander instamment
Ou croix bénite, ou rosaire,
Pour apaiser mon tourment.

—Mon fils, répondit l'ermite,
De Notre-Dame-des-Bois
Le pouvoir est sans limite,
Et le ciel s'ouvre à sa voix.
Mais, hélas! sur cette terre
Où l'homme ne vit qu'un jour,
Il n'est croix, ni rosaire
Qui guérisse de l'amour."

B. Romanticism

The following extract from the first chapter of Louis Reybaud's *Jérôme Paturot à la recherche d'une position sociale* is an excellent satirical summary of the themes of Romanticism:

C'était alors le moment de la croisade littéraire dont vous avez sans doute entendu parler, quoiqu'elle soit aujourd'hui de l'histoire ancienne. Une sorte de fièvre semblait s'être emparée de la jeunesse: la révolte contre les classiques éclatait dans toute sa fureur. On maltraitait Voltaire, on *enfonçait* Racine, on raillait Boileau sur son prénom de Nicolas, on infligeait à tous nos vieux et glorieux auteurs l'épithète un peu légère de *polissons*. Passez-moi le mot; il est historique. En même temps on disait à l'univers que le temps des génies était arrivé, qu'il suffisait de frapper du pied la terre pour en faire sortir des œuvres brillantes et colorées, où le don de la forme devait s'épanouir en mille arabesques orientales. On annonçait que le grand style, le vrai style, le suprême style allait naître, style à ciselures, style chatoyant et miroitant, empruntant au ciel son azur, à la peinture sa palette, à l'architecture ses fantaisies, à l'amour sa lave, à la jalousie ses poignards, à la vertu son sourire, aux passions humaines leurs tempêtes. La littérature que nous allions créer devait être une boîte à couleurs, bleue, verte, mordorée, profonde et calme comme le lac, tortueuse comme le poignard du Malais, aiguë comme la lame de Tolède ; elle devait réunir la fierté de la grandesse espagnole et l'abandon du polichinelle napolitain ; avoir des minarets comme Stamboul, ou des dalles de marbre comme Venise ; résumer Soliman et Faliéro, le muezzin et le gondolier des lagunes, deux types contradictoires : chanter avec l'oiseau, blanchir avec la vague, verdir avec la feuille, ruminer avec le bœuf, hennir avec le cheval, enfin se livrer à toutes ces opérations physiques avec un bonheur extraordinaire, vaincre en un mot, supplanter, et (passez-moi encore une fois l'expression) *enfoncer* la nature.

. . . .

Oui, monsieur, tel que vous me voyez, j'ai été une victime du sonnet, ce qui ne m'a pas empêché de donner dans la ballade, dans l'orientale, dans l'ïambe, dans la méditation, dans le poème en prose et autres délassements modernes. Mais mon encens le plus pur a brûlé en l'honneur de cette divinité que l'on nomme la couleur locale. A volonté mes vers étaient albanais, cophtes, yolofs, cherokees, papous, tcherkesses, afghans et patagons. Je faisais résonner avec un égal succès la mandoline espagnole, le tambour nègre et le gong chinois. Mes recueils poétiques composaient un cours complet de géographie. La feuille du palmier, la fleur du lotus, le tronc du baobab, les fruits de l'arbre de Judée y tenaient la place que doit leur accorder tout amant de la forme, tout desservant fidèle de la nature. Les costumes, les armes, les cosmétiques, les mets favoris des peuples divers n'échappaient point à ma muse : la basquine, le bournous, le fez, le langouti, la saya, le kari et le couscoussous, le kava et le gin, le kirsch et le samchou, aucun vêtement, aucun aliment, aucun spiritueux même n'étaient rebelles à l'appel de mon vers, et les trois règnes se défendaient vainement d'être mes tributaires.

C. The *Bourgeoisie*

In *Charles Demailly*, by the Goncourt brothers, the hero is described as planning a novel, *la Bourgeoisie*, to depict the evolution of society and manners in the nineteenth century:

Dans son roman, l'idée mère était la gradation et l'assemblage de trois générations de la bourgeoisie, montrée à ses trois âges et sous ses trois formes. D'abord, en bas à la souche, c'était le grand-père, l'acheteur de biens nationaux, l'homme du bien-fonds, le fondateur du patrimoine, et l'incarnation du sentiment de la propriété; amasseur de terres, se dérobant, en dehors de tout ce qui n'est pas l'impôt, aux grandes lois économiques de la circulation de l'argent; dur à lui-même, dur aux autres, de cette dureté de paysan qui rappelle en province Rome par Caton, et chasse vers le servage plus humain de la ville les populations des campagnes; l'homme absolument détaché de cette grande famille: la Patrie; l'homme assis dans un égoïsme brut et carré, sans une foi, et prêt d'avance à tout pouvoir qui n'inquiète pas son champ. Au milieu, Charles plaçait le père avec ces franchises, ces dévouements, ces générosités, ces aspirations, ces religions de solidarité humaine ou nationale, tous les élans, toutes les belles passions que lui avaient appris le métier de soldat de sa jeunesse, les guerres de l'Empire, puis les guerres de la paix, les luttes politiques de la Restauration; grandes guerres, nobles batailles qui avaient refait son sang, élargi sa poitrine, élevé son cœur, et mis en lui comme une cordiale majesté de l'honneur, comme la dernière restauration des plus saines et des plus belles vertus de la bourgeoisie du XVIIIe siècle. Le petit-fils de ce grand-père, le fils de ce père, homme hâtif, gangrené à vingt ans des sciences de l'expérience, sorte d'enfant vieillard, résumait dans sa personne les ambitions froides, les impatiences de parvenir, les sécheresses et le calcul des intérêts, le trouble du sens moral par les conseils et les tentations des fortunes scandaleuses, tous les scepticismes pratiques de la jeunesse moderne.

Un type de femme correspondait, dans l'œuvre de Charles, à chacun des types d'hommes, le doublant et le complétant par les passions ou les beautés de l'âme de la femme, montrées dans les trois successions de la famille bourgeoise. La grand'mère représentait la femme annihilée par le mari, tenue par lui hors de ses affaires, mais associée à son avarice, et n'accomplissant dans la maison que le rôle et les devoirs d'une servante maîtresse. La mère était l'épouse vivant dans la communanté de l'honneur, dans le partage de la belle et pure conscience du mari. Elle était cette femme sainte: la mère de famille,—la femme d'intérieur et de ménage, qui vit en ces enfants et avec eux, leur donnant son âme à toutes les heures, avec l'adorable compagnonnage d'une sœur aînée. Puis venait la fille, la jeune fille d'aujourd'hui sitôt femme. De ces caractères particuliers à notre siècle, de son enfance formée à la camaraderie de ses parents, de son père autant au moins que de sa mère, de son éducation égale et presque pareille à l'éducation de l'homme, de sa place nouvelle au salon, Charles faisait sortir deux races et deux espèces : l'une cachant sous les dehors de son sexe l'âme de son frère, ses maturités sans cœur, ses volontés enracinées, ses désillusions et ses irréligions précoces, surexcitées encore et raffinées par sa nature de femme; l'autre, ayant la liberté, la franchise, la grâce et l'élévation d'un cœur viril, montrait dans toute sa personne cette belle et grande chose : un honnête homme dans une honnête femme.

Tel était le dessin du roman où Charles voulait s'élever à la synthèse sociale, peindre dans son plein épanouissement la *ploutocratie* du XIXe siècle, et intéresser l'attention du public, non par la tragédie des événements, le choc des faits, la terreur et l'émotion matérielles de l'intrigue, mais par le développement et le drame psychologique des émotions et des catastrophes morales.

The touching *Aricie Brun, ou les vertus bourgeoises,* by Emile Henriot, which won the *prix du roman* of the Academy in 1924, carries out a somewhat similar scheme.

D. *La Bohème*

Une race nouvelle d'esprits, sans ancêtres, sans bagage, sans patrie dans le passé, libre de toute tradition, était parvenue à la publicité et à l'étalage. Montée derrière le livre charmant d'un des siens, le *Voyage autour d'une pièce de cent sous,* la bohème, ce peuple besogneux, bridé et fouetté par le besoin, n'entrait point dans l'art comme y était entrée la génération précédente, les hommes de 1830, dont presque tous, et les meilleurs, appartenaient à la bourgeoisie aisée : la bohème apportait les exigences de sa vie dans la poursuite de ses ambitions; ses appétits tenaient ses croyances à la gorge. Condamnée à la misère par la baisse du salaire littéraire, la bohème appartenait fatalement au petit journal et le petit journal devait trouver en elle des hommes tout faits, une armée toute prête, une de ces terribles armées nues, mal nourries, sans souliers, qui se battent pour la soupe. Le fiel dévoré, le pain dur mangé, les aigreurs, les froissements, les éclaboussades des succès qui leur passaient dessus sans les voir, la maîtresse sans châle, le foyer sans feu, le livre sans éditeur, les déménagements au mont-de-piété, les dettes hurlantes, tout à venger, tout à gagner, donnaient à la bohème les haines d'un prolétariat, et il y eut dans le mouvement qui la jeta au *Scandale* quelque chose d'un peuple qui monte à l'assaut d'une société, et comme un écho du cri de la journée du 16 avril 1848: *A bas les gants!*—From *Charles Demailly*

BIBLIOGRAPHY

Acton, Lord. Lectures on the French Revolution. 1910.
Adam, Ch. La Philosophie en France (première moitié du xixe siècle). 1894.
"Agathon." Les Jeunes Gens d'aujourd'hui. 1913.
Alexandre, R. Le Musée de la conversation. 1902.
Allard, L. La Comédie de mœurs en France au xixe siècle. 1923.
Alméras, H. d'. La Vie parisienne sous la Révolution. 1909.
Alméras, H. d'. La Vie parisienne sous le Consulat et l'Empire. 1909.
Alméras, H. d'. La Vie parisienne sous la Restauration. 1910.
Alméras, H. d'. La Vie parisienne sous Louis-Philippe. 1911.
Alméras, H. d'. La Vie parisienne sous la République de 1848. 1921.
Arvin, N. C. Eugène Scribe and the French Theatre, 1815–1860. 1924.
Aulard, A. Le Culte de la raison et le culte de l'Etre Suprême. 1892.
Aulard, A. Histoire politique de la Révolution française. 1901.
Avenel, H. Histoire de la presse française depuis 1789 jusqu'à nos jours. 1900.
Bachelin, H., et Dumesnil, R. "Le Cosmopolitisme dans la *Comédie humaine*", in *Revue de Paris*, 1924.
Baldensperger, F. L'Avant-guerre dans la littérature française, 1900–1914. 1919.
Baldensperger, F. Etudes d'histoire littéraire. 1907.
Baldensperger, F. Goethe en France. 1904.
Barre, A. Le Symbolisme. 1911.
Barron, L. Paris pittoresque, 1800–1900. 1899.
Bax, E. B. The Last Episode of the French Revolution. 1911.
Bénédite, L. Histoire des beaux-arts (1800–1900). 1909.
Benoît, F. L'Art français sous la Révolution et l'Empire. 1897.
Bersaucourt, A. de. Au temps des Parnassiens : Nina de Villard et ses amis.
Bertaut, J. Ce qu'était la province française avant la guerre. 1918.
Bertrand, L. La Fin du classicisme et le retour à l'antique. 1898.
Booth, A. J. Saint-Simon and Saint-Simonism. 1871.
Boschot, A. Berlioz : La Jeunesse d'un romantique. 1906.
Boschot, A. Un romantique sous Louis-Philippe. 1908.
Boschot, A. Le Crépuscule d'un romantique. 1913.
Bouglé, C. La Sociologie de Proudhon. 1911.
Boulenger, J. Les Dandys. 1907.
Bourgeois, E. Modern France, 1815–1913. 1919.
Bourgin, H. Fourier. 1905.
Boutet de Monvel, H. Les Anglais à Paris (1800–1850). 1911.

Bouvier, E. La Bataille réaliste (1844–1857).
Bowen, R. P. "An Analysis of the Priest Genre in the Modern French Novel", in *Publications of the Modern Language Association of America*, 1922.
Brenier de Montmorand, Vicomte. La Société française contemporaine. 1899.
Broc, H. de. La Vie en France sous le premier Empire. 1895.
Busson, Fèvre, Hauser. La France d'aujourd'hui et ses colonies. 1924.
Calmettes, F. Leconte de Lisle et ses amis. 1902.
Canat, R. Du sentiment de la solitude morale chez les derniers romantiques et les premiers Parnassiens. 1904.
Canat, R. La Littérature française au xixe siècle. 1921.
Carrère et Bourgin. Manuel des partis politiques en France. 1924.
Cassagne, A. La Théorie de l'art pour l'art chez les derniers romantiques et les premiers réalistes. 1906.
Celler, L. Les Types populaires au théâtre. 1870.
Champfleury. Les Excentriques. 1852.
Champfleury. Henry Monnier. 1879.
Champfleury. Histoire de la caricature moderne. 1865.
Champfleury. Les Vignettes romantiques. 1883.
Charles-Brun. Le Roman social en France au xixe siècle. 1910.
Charlier, G. Le Sentiment de la nature chez les romantiques français. 1912.
Claudin, G. Mes souvenirs: les boulevards de 1840–1870. 1884.
Clouzot, H. "L'Art décoratif du second Empire", in *Revue des Etudes Napoléoniennes*, 1915.
Dayot, A. Journées révolutionnaires, 1897.
Dayot, A. La Restauration, d'après l'image du temps. 1902.
Deberdt, R. La Caricature et l'humour français au xixe siècle. 1899.
Debidour, A. Histoire des rapports des églises et de l'état en France de 1789 à 1870. 1898.
Dechamps, J. Sainte-Beuve et le sillage de Napoléon. 1922.
Delzant, A. Les Goncourt. 1889.
Des Granges, C.-M. La Comédie et les mœurs (1815–1848). 1904.
Desnoiresterres, G. La Comédie satirique au xviiie siècle. 1885.
D'Estrée, P. Le Théâtre sous la Terreur. 1913.
Dickinson, G. L. Revolution and Reaction in Modern France. 1892.
Dimier, L. Histoire de la peinture française au xixe siècle, 1793–1903. 1914.
Dimnet, E. France herself again. 1914.
Dorbec, P. "La Peinture française de 1750 à 1820", in *Gazette des Beaux-Arts*, 1914.
Dorbec, P. "La Peinture française au temps du romantisme, jugée par le factum, la chanson et la caricature", in *Gazette des Beaux-Arts*, 1918.
Dorbec, P. "La Peinture française sous le second Empire", in *Gazette des Beaux-Arts*, 1918.
Droz, E. P.-J. Proudhon. 1909.
Du Camp, M. Souvenirs littéraires. 1882–1883.

BIBLIOGRAPHY 313

Duclaux, M. Twentieth-Century French Writers. 1919.
Eaton, D. C. Handbook of Modern French Painting. 1909.
Eggli, E. "Le Régionalisme", in *French Quarterly*, 1922.
Elton, G. The Revolutionary Idea in France, 1789–1871. 1923.
Espinas, A. La Philosophie sociale du xviiie siècle et la Révolution. 1898.
Estève, E. Byron et le romantisme français. 1907.
Estève, E. Etudes de littérature préromantique. 1923.
Fabre, J. Les Pères de la Révolution française. 1910.
Faguet, E. L'Anticléricalisme. 1906.
Ferrère, E.–L. Le Dictionnaire des "idées reçues" de Gustave Flaubert. 1913.
Fleury et Sonolet. La Société du second Empire. 1911 ff.
Florian-Parmentier. Histoire de la littérature française de 1885 à nos jours.
Fonsegrive, G. De Taine à Péguy, l'évolution des idées dans la France contemporaine. 1917.
Forster, Ch. de. Paris et les Parisiens. 1848–1849.
Français peints par eux-mêmes, Les, by various authors. 1840 ff.
Fusil, Louise. Souvenirs d'une actrice, 1774–1848. 1904.
Gaiffe, F. Le Drame en France au xviiie siècle. 1910.
Gaillard de Champris, H. Emile Augier et la comédie sociale. 1910.
Gaultier, P. Le Rire et la caricature. 1911.
Gautier, Th. Les Jeunes-France.
Geffroy, G. L'Enfermé. 1896.
George, W. L. France in the Twentieth Century. 1908.
Ginisty, Paul. Le Mélodrame.
Girardin, Mme de (Delphine Gay). Lettres parisiennes. 1843.
Giraud, V. Essai sur Taine. 1901.
Goncourt, E. et J. de. Histoire de la société française pendant la Révolution. 1854.
Goncourt, E. et J. de. Histoire de la société française pendant la Directoire. 1855.
Goncourt, E. et J. de. Journal des Goncourt. 1887–1892.
Gonnard, Philippe. Les Origines de la légende napoléonienne. 1906.
Grand-Carteret, J. Le Dix-neuvième Siècle en France. 1893.
Grand-Carteret, J. Les Mœurs et la caricature en France. 1888.
Grillet, C. "Le Satanisme littéraire", in *le Correspondant*, February, 1922.
Gros, J. Alexandre Dumas et Marie Duplessis. 1923.
Gros, J.–M. Le Mouvement littéraire socialiste depuis 1830. 1904.
Guérard, A. L. Five Masters of French Romance.
Guérard, A. L. French Prophets of Yesterday. 1913.
Guérard, A. L. Reflections on the Napoleonic Legend. 1924.
Guex, J. Le Théâtre et la société française de 1815 à 1848. 1920.
Gunn, J. A. Modern French Philosophy. 1922.
Guy-Grand, G. Le Conflit des idées dans la France d'aujourd'hui. 1921.
Guy-Grand, G. La Philosophie nationaliste. 1911.
Guy-Grand, G. La Philosophie syndicaliste. 1911.

Guy-Grand, G. Le Procès de la démocratie. 1911.
Hartog, W.-G. Guilbert de Pixerécourt. 1912.
Hourticq, L. Art in France. 1911.
Huard, Ch., et Billy, A. Paris vieux et neuf. 1909.
Isambert, G. Les Idées socialistes en France de 1815 à 1848. 1905.
Jaime, E. Musée de la caricature. 1838.
Janet, P. Philosophie de la Révolution française. 1892.
Jaurès, J. (editor). Histoire socialiste (1789-1900).
Jousset, P. La France, géographie illustrée.
Jouy, E. de. L'Ermite de la Chaussée d'Antin, 1812-1814; le Franc Parleur, 1814; l'Ermite en province, 1818-1824.
Jullien, B. Histoire de la poésie française à l'époque impériale. 1844.
Kahn, A. Le Théâtre social en France de 1870 à nos jours. 1907.
Killen, A. M. Le Roman "terrifiant" ou roman "noir". 1915.
Kropotkin, P. A. The Great French Revolution. 1909.
Lacour-Gayet, G. "La Princesse de Metternich", in *Revue de Paris*, 1924.
Lalou, R. Histoire de la littérature française contemporaine. 1922.
Lasserre, P. Le Romantisme français. 1907.
Lavisse, E. (editor). Histoire de France contemporaine. 1920 ff.
Leblond, M.-A. La Société française sous la troisième République. 1905.
Le Breton, A. Le Roman français au xixe siècle. 1901.
Le Brun, Henri. L'Ancienne France, étude géographique, historique et littéraire sur les anciennes provinces françaises. 1901.
Lenient, C. La Comédie en France au xixe siècle. 1898.
Leroy-Beaulieu, A. Les Catholiques libéraux, l'église et le libéralisme de 1830 à nos jours. 1885.
Lichtenberger, A. Le Socialisme et la Révolution française. 1899.
Locke, A. W. Music and the Romantic Movement in France. 1920.
Lote, G. "Zola historien du second Empire", in *Revue des Etudes Napoléoniennes*, 1918.
Madelin, L. La Révolution. 1914.
Maigron, L. Le Roman historique à l'époque romantique. 1912.
Maigron, L. Le Romantisme et la mode. 1911.
Maigron, L. Le Romantisme et les mœurs. 1910.
Marcel, H. La Peinture française au xixe siècle. 1905.
Martino, P. Le Naturalisme français, 1870-1895. 1923.
Martino, P. Le Roman réaliste sous le second Empire. 1913.
Mathews, Shailer. The French Revolution. 1923.
Matthey, H. Essai sur le merveilleux dans la littérature française depuis 1800. 1915.
Mauclair, C. L'Art indépendant français sous la troisième République. 1919.
Mauclair, C. Charles Baudelaire. 1917.
Mauclair, C. Paul Adam. 1921.
Mauclair, C. Servitude et grandeur littéraires. 1922.
Merlant, J. Le Roman personnel de Rousseau à Fromentin. 1905.

BIBLIOGRAPHY 315

MERLET, G. Tableau de la littérature française, 1800–1815. 1878.
MEYER, A. Ce que mes yeux ont vu. 1911.
MEYER, A. Ce que je peux dire. 1912.
MICHIELS, A. Histoire des idées littéraires au xixe siècle. 1863.
MONTFORT, EUGÈNE. Vingt-cinq ans de littérature française.
MORNAND, F. La Vie de Paris. 1855.
MURET, TH. L'Histoire par le théâtre. 1865.
NEBOUT, P. Le Drame romantique. 1895.
NETTEMENT, A. Histoire de la littérature française sous la Monarchie de Juillet. 1854.
NETTEMENT, A. Histoire de la littérature française sous la Restauration. 1858.
NOËL, C.–M. Les Idées sociales dans le théâtre de Dumas fils. 1912.
Paris, ou le livre des cent-et-un. 1831–1834.
PARODI, D. La Philosophie contemporaine en France. 1919.
PARODI, D. Traditionalisme et démocratie. 1909.
PEIXOTTO, JESSICA B. The French Revolution and Modern French Socialism. 1901.
PELLISSIER, G. Etudes de littérature contemporaine. 1898–1901.
PÉRICAUD, L. Le Théâtre des funambules. 1897.
POIZAT, A. Le Symbolisme. 1919.
POSTGATE, R. W. Out of the Past. 1922.
POTEZ, H. L'Elégie en France avant le romantisme. 1898.
PRUDHOMMEAUX, J. Icarie et son fondateur, Etienne Cabet. 1909.
RAMBAUD, A. Histoire de la civilisation contemporaine en France.
RAWLINSON, G. C. Recent French Tendencies. 1917.
RAYNAUD, E. La Mêlée symboliste. 1918 ff.
RECLUS, O. Le Plus Beau Royaume sous le ciel. 1899.
REICHARDT, J.–F. Un hiver à Paris sous le Consulat (French edition by A. Laquiante). 1896.
RENARD, G. Les Etapes de la société française au xixe siècle. 1913.
RETINGER, J.–H. Le Conte fantastique dans le romantisme française. 1909.
RETTÉ, A. Le Symbolisme. 1903.
REYNAUD, L. L'Influence allemande en France au xviiie et au xixe siècle. 1922.
RIOU, G. Aux écoutes de la France qui vient. 1913.
ROSENTHAL, L. "La Genèse du romantisme avant 1848", in *Gazette des Beaux-Arts*, 1913.
ROSENTHAL, L. La Peinture romantique. 1900.
ROSENTHAL, L. "La Peinture romantique sous la Monarchie de Juillet", in *Gazette des Beaux-Arts*, 1912.
ROSENTHAL, L. Du romantisme au réalisme; essai sur l'évolution de la peinture en France de 1830 à 1848. 1914.
ROUSTAN, M. La Littérature française par la dissertation, xixe siècle.
SABATIER, PAUL. L'Orientation religieuse de la France actuelle. 1911.
SABATIER, PIERRE. L'Esthétique des Goncourt. 1920.

SAINTE-BEUVE, C.-A. Proudhon. 1872.
SALGUES, J.-B.-S. De Paris, des mœurs, de la littérature et de la philosophie. 1813.
SALOMON, M. Charles Nodier et le groupe romantique. 1908.
SCHENCK, E. M. La Part de Charles Nodier dans la formation des idées romantiques de Victor Hugo. 1914.
SCHINZ, A. French Literature of the Great War. 1920.
SCHINZ, A. "Le Roman militaire en France de 1870 à 1914", in *Publications of the Modern Language Association of America*, 1919.
SCHNEIDER, R. "L'Art anacréontique et alexandrin sous l'Empire", in *Revue des Etudes Napoléoniennes*, 1916.
SÉCHÉ, A. Les Caractères de la poésie contemporaine. 1913.
SÉCHÉ, L. La Jeunesse dorée sous Louis-Philippe. 1910.
SEILLIÈRE, E. Edgar Quinet et le mysticisme démocratique. 1919.
SEILLIÈRE, E. Le Mal romantique. 1908.
SEIPPEL, P. Les Deux Frances et leurs origines historiques. 1905.
SENCIER, G. Le Babouvisme après Babeuf. 1912.
SIMOND, C. Paris de 1800 à 1900. 1901.
SIZERANNE, R. DE LA. "Ce que l'art doit à Napoléon", in *Revue des Deux Mondes*, December, 1921.
SLOANE, W. M. The French Revolution and Religious Reform. 1901.
STENGER, G. La Société française sous le Consulat. 1903-1908.
STEPHENS, H. MORSE. The French Revolution. 1886 ff.
STROWSKI, F. "Le Romantisme humanitaire et philosophique", in *Revue des Cours et Conférences*, 1913-1914.
TAINE, H.-A. Vie et opinions de M. Frédéric-Thomas Graindorge. 1867.
TEXTE, J.-J. Jean-Jacques Rousseau et les origines du cosmopolitisme littéraire. 1895.
THACKERAY, W. M. Paris Sketch-Book.
THOMAS, P.-FÉLIX. Pierre Leroux. 1904.
THUREAU-DANGIN, P. Histoire de la Monarchie de Juillet. 1884-1892.
TIERSOT, J. Les Fêtes et les chants de la France révolutionnaire. 1908.
TROLLOPE, MRS. T. A. Paris and the Parisians in 1835. 1836.
TURQUET-MILNES, G. Some Modern French Writers. 1921.
UZANNE, O. La Femme et la mode. 1892.
VAN TIEGHEM, P. "Les Idylles de Gessner et le rêve pastoral dans le préromantisme européen", in *Revue de Littérature comparée*, 1924.
VAN TIEGHEM, P. Ossian en France. 1917.
VÉRON, E. Eugène Delacroix. 1887.
VÉRON, L. Mémoires d'un bourgeois de Paris. 1856.
VIDAL DE LA BLACHE, P. Tableau de la géographie de la France. 1903.
VIEL CASTEL, H. DE. Mémoires sur le règne de Napoléon III. 1883-1884.
VILLEMESSANT, H. DE. Mémoires d'un journaliste. 1884.
WEBSTER, NESTA. The French Revolution. 1919.
WEILL, G. "L'Anticléricalisme sous le second Empire", in *Revue des Etudes Napoléoniennes*, 1915.

WEILL, G. Le Catholicisme libéral en France, 1828–1908. 1909.
WEILL, G. L'Ecole saint-simonienne. 1896.
WEILL, G. Histoire du mouvement social en France, 1852–1910. 1911.
WEILL, G. Histoire du parti républicain en France de 1814 à 1870. 1900.
WELSCHINGER, H. Le Théâtre de la Révolution. 1881.
YOUNG, ARTHUR. Travels in France.
ZÉVAÈS, A. Le Parti socialiste de 1904 à 1923. 1923.
ZYROMSKI, E. Maurice de Guérin. 1921.

INDEX OF NAMES

Names of fictitious characters are in quotation marks

About, Edmond, 187
Acker, Paul, 259
Adam, Adolphe, 149
Adam, Charles, 74
Adam, Mme, 301
Adam, Paul, 36, 250, 264
Adams, Henry, 9
Addison, 106
Agathon, 259
"Agnès", 228
Aicard, Jean, 17
Alacoque, Marie, 18
Alcibiades, 40
Allais, Alphonse, 7
Allard, L., 41
Alméras, d', 46
"Alphonse, Monsieur", 228
"Alvimar, Alfred d'", 124
"Amaëgui, marquesa d'", 115
"Ambrosio", 64
Ancey, Georges, 279
Andrieux, 50
"Ange, baronne d'", 225
"Angot, Mme", 44, 48
Angoulême, duchesse d', 73
Antier, 134
"Antonia", 153
"Antony", 137, 142, 149, 160, 161, 162, 163, 170, 173
Apollinaire, G., 299, 302
"Arabin, Mr.", 112
Arago, Etienne, 120
"Ardan, Michel", 278
Arène, Paul, 17
Aristides, 44
"Arlequin", 44, 48, 136
Arlincourt, vicomte d', 162
Arnaud, Etienne, 119
Arnault, 54
"Arthur", 108
"Astrée", 5
"Atala", 57, 63, 64, 162

Aubanel, 17
Auber, 112, 149
Aubernon, Mme, 301
"Aubry, Père", 57, 161
Aude, 48, 49
Augier, Emile, 106, 115, 120, 183, 185, 187, 188, 201, 204, 208, 214, 221, 223, 227, 250, 281
Aulard, 22, 27

Babeuf, 32, 34, 88
Badinguet, 177
Bakunin, 263, 264
Baldensperger, F., 287
Balzac, Guez de, 14
Balzac, Honoré de, 11, 36, 51, 58, 64, 74, 75, 76, 78, 82, 83, 100, 105, 106, 114, 115, 119, 120, 123, 124, 125, 128, 130, 134, 142, 143, 156, 161, 204, 206, 227, 264, 272
Banville, Théodore de, 109, 118, 121, 216
Baour-Lormian, 50, 63
Barateau, 119
Barbès, 88
Barbey d'Aurevilly, 9, 114, 156, 221
"Barbicane, President", 278
Barbier, 125, 196
Barras, 40
Barrès, Maurice, 18, 83, 234, 240, 245, 250, 254, 258, 259, 260, 261
Barrière, Théodore, 135, 227
Barry, Mme du, 39
Barthélemy, abbé, 41
Bashkirtseff, Marie, 283
Bastien-Lepage, 293
Bataille, Henry, 283, 284
Batteux, 138
Baudelaire, 7, 153, 156, 222, 233, 290, 291, 302
Baudin, 177
Baudry, 226

Bayard, 130
Bayle, Pierre, 22
Bazard, 89
Bazin, René, 13, 18, 259, 267
Beauclair, Henri, 292
Beaunier, André, 254
Beauvoir, Roger de, 121, 149, 159
Becque, 284
Bédier, Joseph, 16
Beffroy de Reigny, 48
"Bel-Ami", 124, 286
Bellamy, Edward, 265
Bellay, du, 11
Benoît, 69
"Benoîton, Mme", 229
Béranger, 52, 71, 75, 76, 91, 97, 98, 101, 116, 125, 132, 152, 172, 279
Bérat, Frédéric, 172
Berchoux, 51
"Bergeret, Monsieur", 272, 274
Bergson, 242, 243, 265
"Berlichingen, Goetz von", 160
Berlioz, 64, 142, 160, 163, 173
Bernardin de Saint-Pierre, 7, 42, 139, 156
Bernhardt, Sarah, 289
Berquin, 54, 55, 56
Berry, duc de, 73
Bertall, 219
Bertaut, 288
Berton, Germaine, 202
"Bertrand", 83, 134
Bertrand, Louis, 260
Bèze, Théodore de, 5
"Bézuquet", 272
"Bifteck, M.", 112
"Bilboquet", 135
Binet, 239
Biré, 27
"Birotteau, César", 124
Bismarck, 226
Blair, 57
Blanc, Louis, 22, 77, 92, 93, 175, 176, 177
Blanqui, 77, 88, 175, 191, 198, 199, 200, 201
"Blas, Gil", 10
"Blas, Ruy", 146, 160, 161, 238
Blocqueville, Mme de, 302
"Bluebeard", 13
Bocage, 163
Boieldieu, 149
Boileau, 51, 52, 62, 106
Bonald, 74, 80, 260

Bonaparte, Jerome, 185, 187, 230, 254
Bonaparte, Lucien, 213
"Bonhomet, Tribulat", 192, 276
Bonington, Robert, 172
Bonjour, Casimir, 125
Bonmariage, Sylvain, 302
"Bonnard, Sylvestre", 74
Bordeaux, Henry, 17, 234
Borel, Pétrus, 130, 142
Bornier, Henri de, 233
Boschot, 173
Bossuet, 8, 18, 80
Botticelli, 291
"Boubouroche", 274
Boucher, 65, 66
Bouffar, Zulma, 210
Bouguereau, 297
Bouilhet, Louis, 132
Bouilly, 46, 49, 50
Boulanger, General, 250
"Boum, General", 180
Bourgeois, Anicet, 130
Bourgeois, Léon, 241
Bourget, Paul, 234, 239, 242, 244, 245, 258, 266, 273, 284, 286, 288
Boutet de Monvel (eighteenth century), 45, 64
Boutet de Monvel (nineteenth century), 112, 114
Boutroux, 242
"Bouvard", 120, 190
Bouvier, 118
"Bovary, Mme", 158
Boylesve, René, 11
"Bramble, Colonel", 112
Brantôme, 15
Bréon, Commandant de, 252
Briand, Aristide, 201
"Bridau, Philippe", 75
Brieux, 274, 278, 288, 289
Brifaut, 47
Brillat-Savarin, 51
Brizeux, 10
"Brouhaha, Princess", 213
Bruant, A., 266
Brummell, Beau, 112
Brunetière, 238, 239, 243
Brutus, 40, 44
Bugeaud, Marshal, 101, 132
Bulwer, 112
Buonarroti, 34, 88
Bürger, 153
"Buteux, Cadet", 49
Byron, 143, 147, 153, 155, 156, 195

INDEX OF NAMES 321

Cabanel, 230, 297
Cabet, Etienne, 91, 93, 175, 196
Cæsar, 6, 40, 44, 212
Cahuet, Albéric, 283
Caigniez, 163
Caillaux, Mme, 236
Caillavet, 257
"Calicot", 103
"Calino", 135, 177
Calvin, 6, 8
"Camors, Monsieur de", 214, 228, 229
Camp, Maxime du, 132, 141, 145
Canova, 66
Capus, Alfred, 227, 254
"Carabas, marquis de", 71
"Cardinal, Madame", 276
Carlyle, 19, 21, 38
Carnot, President, 13, 263
Carpeaux, 203
"Cassandre", 136
Castiglione, Countess of, 213
Cavaignac, General, 176
Cavour, 213
Cayla, Mme du, 73
Caylus, comte de, 65
"Céladon", 5
Cézanne, 296, 297
"Chabert, Colonel", 75
Chambord, comte de, 10, 141, 218, 248
Champfleury, 118, 123, 132, 134, 142, 143, 222
Champlain, 7
Chancel, Ausone de, 145
Charcot, 239, 240
Chardin, 54
Charlemagne, 34, 130, 184
Charles II (of England), 213
Charles VII, 12
Charles X, 73, 124, 137, 141, 192
Charles the Bold, 162
Charles-Brun, 188
Charlet, 97, 98, 133
"Charlus, M. de", 302
Chastellux, chevalier de, 46
Chateaubriand, 10, 27, 42, 57, 59, 62, 64, 65, 74, 138, 144, 148, 154, 156, 158, 161, 192
Châteaubriant, A. de, 272
Châtel, abbé, 83
Chatterton, 126, 145, 160
Chauvin, 98
Chénier, André, 41, 50

Chénier, Marie-Joseph, 44, 45, 50
Chevalier, Michel, 89
Choiseul-Praslin, duc de, 174
Chopin, 173
"Chouette, la", 128
"Chourineur, le", 128
Cladel, Léon, 14
"Clarkson, Mistress", 278
Claudel, Paul, 245
"Claudine", 289
Clemenceau, 2, 201, 252, 254, 256
Clement VI, 12
"Cœlina", 64, 123
Colette, 276, 289
Collin d'Harleville, 49
"Colombine", 136
Combes, 256
Comte, Auguste, 89, 94, 95, 190, 191, 260
Condillac, 138
Confucius, 83
Considérant, Victor, 91, 175, 196
Constable, 172
Constant, Benjamin, 145
"Constantin, abbé", 279
"Consuelo", 81, 92
Cooper, J. F., 276
Coppée, François, 254, 271, 298
"Corinne", 57, 64, 81, 102, 148, 162
Corneille, 7, 47, 149
Corot, 172
"Corsair, The", 155
"Cosette", 128
"Cotonet", 120, 144, 153
Cottin, Mme, 59, 63, 102
Courbet, 172, 231, 294
Courier, Paul-Louis, 76
Courteline, 274, 279
Cousin, Victor, 77, 79, 81, 85, 188, 189, 190, 191
Couture, 227
Cowper, 152
Crabbe, 152
"Crac, M. de", 49
Crébillon *fils*, 208
Curel, François de, 243, 273

Dalayrac, 45
Dancourt, 125
Dante, 95, 168
Danzig, Duchess of, 40
Darc, Jeanne, 11, 18, 245, 261
Daudet, Alphonse, 2, 9, 17, 189, 260, 272, 274, 275, 288

Daudet, Léon, 260
Daumier, 79, 83, 132, 134, 181, 223
David, Félicien, 89
David, Louis, 23, 40, 65, 66, 68, 167, 169, 230, 297
David d'Angers, 172
Dayot, 53
Debraux, Emile, 75
Deburau, 136
Dechamps, 100
Degas, 285, 300
Delacroix, 140, 159, 168, 169, 196, 197
Delaroche, 166, 169
Delavigne, Casimir, 7
Delavigne, Germain, 64
Delille, 51, 58
"Delobelle", 275
Delord, Taxile, 229
Delorme, Marion, 145, 146, 195, 226
"Delphine", 64
Delvau, Alfred, 109
Demolins, Edmond, 234
Denis, Jean, 7
"Denis, M. et Mme", 52, 103
"Déodat", 183
Depaquit, Jules, 301
Déroulède, Paul, 250
Désaugiers, 49, 52, 58, 103
Descartes, 11, 22
Descaves, Lucien, 234, 266
Deschanel, Emile, 177
Deschanel, Paul, 177
"Desgenais", 207
Destouches, 49
Dickens, 36, 135, 229, 278
Diderot, 8, 38
"Didier", 135, 160, 195
Dimier, 260
Doche, 49
"Docre, chanoine", 279
"Dodolphe", 108
Dombrowski, 202
Domenichino, 102
Donizetti, 148
Donnay, Maurice, 266, 303
Donnersmarck, Count Henckel von, 226
Dorvigny, 48
Dostoevsky, 287
Dreyfus, 47, 251, 253, 254, 256
Droz, Gustave, 208
Dubois, 130
Ducange, 163, 164

Ducray-Duminil, 63, 64, 123, 158
"Dumanet", 101
Dumanoir, 135
Dumas fils, 192, 221, 223, 225, 226, 227, 228, 278, 281
Dumas père, 11, 100, 124, 137, 142, 143, 159, 161, 162, 163
Du Maurier, 298
Dumersan, 112, 135
"Dumollet, M.", 54
Dupanloup, 182, 187, 189, 240
Dupin, 103
Duplessis, Marie, 226
Dupont, Pierre, 126
Dupré, Jules, 171, 172
"Dupuis", 120, 144, 153
Duras, Mme de, 63, 165
"Duricrâne", 45
Durkheim, Emile, 241
Duruy, Victor, 189, 212
Duval, 226

Ecouchard-Lebrun, 51
Elizabeth, Queen, 166, 169
"Elodie", 162
Emerson, 91
Enfantin, 83, 89, 90
Erckmann-Chatrian, 18
Escousse, 147
"Esseintes, Des", 273
Estaunié, E., 279
Estissac, Geoffroy d', 13
Etienne, 50
Eugénie, Empress, 177, 184, 212, 215

Fabre, Ferdinand, 4, 190, 279
Fabre, Lucien, 233
Fabre d'Eglantine, 52
Faguet, Emile, 201, 234
Falloux, 85, 182
Fanchon, 49
"Fanfan-la-Tulipe", 75
"Fantine", 128
Fau, Fernand, 301
Fauchery, 135
Fauriel, 156
"Faust", 148, 155, 173
Favart, 45
Fayard, Jean, 287
Ferny, Jacques, 301
Ferry, Jules, 87, 203, 249, 250
Feuillet, Octave, 9, 212, 214, 218, 222, 227, 228, 229
Field, Cyrus W., 174

INDEX OF NAMES

Fiévée, 63
"Figaro", 44
"Flambeau", 98
Flaubert, 7, 105, 110, 120, 132, 158, 187, 190, 222, 272
Flaxman, 66
Flers, Robert de, 257
"Fleur-de-Marie", 119, 128
Floquet, Charles, 82, 87
Florian, 54, 165
"Floupin", 132
Fontaine, 69
Forain, 297
Fourier, 82, 90, 91, 93, 95, 149
"Fouyou", 130
Fragonard, 65
France, Anatole, 36, 74, 190, 204, 232, 240, 254, 259, 262, 265, 268, 272, 274, 275, 279
Francis I, 7, 14
Franklin, 276
Frénilly, baron de, 46
"Frétillon", 116
"Frollo, Claude", 161
Fulgence, 148
Furetière, 48
Fusil, Louise, 39
Fustel de Coulanges, 195

Galliffet, marquis de, 213
Gambetta, 14, 87, 187, 188, 191, 201, 226, 246, 248, 249, 256, 301
"Gamp, Mrs.", 135
"Gargantua", 11
Garibaldi, 17
"Gaudissart", 124
Gauguin, 95
Gautier, Théophile, 103, 105, 118, 141, 143, 156, 163, 169, 223
Gavarni, 108, 110, 117, 119, 128, 135, 177, 223
"Gavroche", 128, 130
Gay, Dephine. See Girardin, Mme de
Geffroy, Gustave, 199, 200, 266
Genlis, Mme de, 37, 62, 142
"Gennaro", 143
Géraud, Edmond, 58
Géricault, 157, 168
Gérôme, 230, 293, 297
Gessner, 54, 69
"Giaour, The", 155
"Gibou, Mme", 135
"Giboyer", 201, 210
Gide, André, 245

Gill, André, 181
"Gillenormand, M.", 74, 103
Girardin, Emile de, 207, 225
Girardin, Mme de, 81, 102, 109, 110, 112, 115, 121, 125, 142, 170, 208
Girodet, 68
"Goddam, M.", 112
Godin, 91
Goethe, 57, 148, 154, 160, 168, 195
"Gogo", 134
Goncourt, Edmond and Jules de, 108, 146, 202, 207, 208, 211, 213, 222, 224, 233, 281, 282, 283, 284, 286, 297
"Gondremarck, baron de", 206
Gounod, 64, 173
Gourmont, Remy de, 9, 298
Gracchi, 31, 40
Grand-Carteret, 72
"Grandet", 124
"Grandet, Eugénie", 11, 115
"Grandgousier", 11
Gras, Félix, 36
Grave, Jean, 263
Gray, 57
"Graziella", 154, 160
Greenough, 66
Greuze, 54, 65
Grévin, A., 297
Grévy, Jules, 177, 249
Grey, Lady Jane, 169
Grimm, 46, 49
Grisi, 148, 173
Gros, 68
Guesde, Jules, 262
Guex, 83
Guillaume, 277
Guillaumin, Emile, 11, 272
Guimond, Esther, 225
Guiraud, 17, 62
"Guitrel, abbé", 279
Guitry, Sacha, 136
Guizot, 78, 80, 206
Guttinguer, 147
Guyau, 241, 242
Guy-Grand, Georges, 255
Gyp, 270

Halévy, Ludovic, 206, 209, 210, 214, 276
Hamerton, P. G., 5, 18
"Hamlet", 155
"Han d'Islande", 143, 161
"Harold, Childe", 142, 144, 155
"Harris, Mrs.", 229

Harrison, Frederic, 94
Haussmann, 105, 202, 203
Hawthorne, 91
Hébert, 28, 37
Heine, 99, 168, 169
Helvétius, Mme, 37
"Henriette", 228
Henry, 263
Henry IV, 6, 15, 34
Herder, 86
Hermant, Abel, 190, 234, 270
"Hernani", 118, 130, 132, 137, 146, 147, 160, 162, 164, 210
Hervé, Gustave, 238
Hervey, 57
Hervieu, Paul, 274, 288, 289
"Hiroux, Jean", 135
Hoffmann, 153
"Homais", 132, 187, 272, 276, 278
Homer, 59, 150
Horace, 50
Hortense, Queen, 182
Houssaye, Arsène, 207
Hugo, Victor, 18, 36, 48, 58, 59, 81, 96, 98, 100, 103, 121, 126, 128, 130, 132, 137, 139, 140, 143, 144, 145, 149, 150, 151, 153, 154, 156, 158, 161, 162, 163, 164, 165, 169, 173, 177, 188, 204, 206, 220, 222, 290
"Hulot, Baron", 124
Huysmans, 9, 156, 234, 243, 273, 279, 297, 302

Ibsen, 286
Ingres, 140, 168, 169, 230, 297
"Iroux, Jean", 135

Jal, 50
"Jalin, Olivier de", 207
Jammes, 245
Janet, Pierre, 239
Janin, Jules, 116, 125
"Janot", 48
"Janotus de Bragmardo", 49
Jarry, Alfred, 276, 299
Jaurès, 22, 26, 32, 256, 263
"Javert", 161
"Jean, Père", 126
"Jeannot", 48, 49
Jefferson, 78
"Jenny l'ouvrière", 119
"Jobardière, M. de la", 72
"Jocrisse", 48
"Jones, Paul", 161

Josephine, 70
Jouaust, Colonel, 253
Jouffroy, 138
"Jourdain, M.", 134, 135
Jouvenel, R. de, 236
Jouvin, Benoît, 194
Jouy, Etienne de, 51, 52, 72, 106
Jouy, Jules, 301
"Jovard, Daniel", 142
"Juan, Don", 100, 155, 195, 228
"Julie", 63
"Julien", 268
"Juliet", 155
Jullien, 46

Karr, Alphonse, 109, 213
Klopstock, 154
Kock, Paul de, 63, 108, 116, 203
Kotzebue, 46
Kropotkin, 22, 26, 263

Labiche, 2, 120, 132
Lachelier, Jules, 242
Laclos, Choderlos de, 22
Lacordaire, 84, 240
Lacroix, Paul, 159
La Fayette, 5, 42, 58, 78
Laffitte, 83
La Fontaine, 8, 54, 135
Laforgue, Jules, 292
La Harpe, 36, 41, 138
Lallemand, General, 91
Lamartine, 18, 22, 59, 81, 82, 100, 102, 114, 121, 126, 144, 148, 151, 154, 156, 165, 174, 175, 176
Lambert, Mme de, 302
Lamennais, 10, 74, 83, 92, 125
"Lantaigne, abbé", 232
Lantier, 41, 68
"Lantier, Claude", 296
"Lara", 155
La Rochefoucauld, 14
Las Cases, 96
Lasserre, 147, 260, 261
Launay, vicomte de. *See* Girardin, Mme de
Lavedan, 243, 270, 273, 286, 289
Lavisse, 239
Laya, 44, 45
"Léandre", 136
Le Bossu, 65
Lebras, 147
Le Braz, Anatole, 10
"Lechat, Isidore", 274

INDEX OF NAMES

Leconte de Lisle, 188, 223
Ledru-Rollin, 175, 177
Le Goffic, Charles, 10
Legouvé, Gabriel, 57
Lemaître, Frédérick, 134
Lemaître, Jules, 240, 254, 274
Lemercier, Népomucène, 47
Lenin, 201
"Lenore", 153
Leo XIII, 257
Leonidas, 44
Leroux, Pierre, 82, 84, 89, 92, 95, 100, 175
Leroy, Charles, 234
Le Roy, Eugène, 105
Le Sage, 10
"Lessay, M. de", 74
"Leveau", 274
Lewes, G. H., 94
Lewis, Matthew, 64, 161
Lhéris, 135
"Lisette", 116, 172
Liszt, 173
Littré, 49, 94, 100, 191
Lockroy, 130
Loisy, abbé, 244
Longpré, 106
"Lothario", 153
Loti, 2, 9, 288
Louis IX, 184, 185
Louis XIV, 4, 34, 80, 213, 260
Louis XV, 39, 72
Louis XVI, 19, 22, 27, 54, 73
Louis XVIII, 71, 72, 77, 137
Louis-Philippe, 73, 78, 79, 82, 88, 95, 100, 105, 107, 108, 118, 120, 123, 124, 125, 129, 130, 136, 137, 170, 174, 178, 190, 206, 208, 221, 227, 230
"Louise", 268
Louvet de Couvray, 38
Louÿs, Pierre, 298
Lowell, James Russell, 9
Loynes, comtesse de, 254, 302
Loyola, 76
"Lucifer", 154
Lurine, Louis, 204
Luxemburg, Rosa, 202
Lycurgus, 44

"Macaire, Robert", 83, 132, 134, 135, 276
McKinley, President, 263
MacMahon, 248

Maeterlinck, 292
Magdalene, 195
"Magnus", 161
Magny, Olivier de, 14
Maigron, 130, 155
Maillot, 48
Maintenon, Mme de, 13
Maistre, Joseph de, 17, 74, 80, 183, 260
Maistre, Xavier de, 17
Malherbe, 9
Malibran, 173
"Malingear", 120
Mallarmé, Stéphane, 292
Malon, Benoît, 262
"Malvina", 59, 61, 162
Manet, 294, 296
"Manfred", 144, 155
Manlius, 40
Mantoux, Paul, 177
"Mapah, le", 83
Maran, René, 165
Marat, 28, 45, 77
Marcelin, 208, 217
"Maréchal", 187
Margaret of Navarre, 14
"Marguerite", 148
Marguerite de Bourgogne, 161
Margueritte, Brothers, 178
"Marianne", 196
Marie-Antoinette, 12
Mariéton, Paul, 17
Marius, 58
Marmontel, 54
"Marneffe, Mme", 112, 124, 225
Marot, Clément, 14
"Marsay, Henry de", 124
Marsollier, 45
Martin, Homer, 8
Martin du Gard, Roger, 254
"Martine", 48
Marx, Karl, 92, 191, 198, 200, 248, 264
Massa, marquis de, 213
Mathilde, Princess, 213
Mauclair, Camille, 264, 302, 303
Maupassant, 8, 124, 273, 274, 282, 284, 286, 298
Maurois, André, 112
Maurras, Charles, 245, 260, 261
"Mayeux", 99, 132, 135, 276
"Mazeppa", 153
Mazères, 105, 125
Meilhac, 206, 209, 210, 214

Mendès, Catulle, 223, 289
Menken, Adah Isaacs, 226
"Mephistopheles", 155
"Mercadet", 124
Mercier, Sébastien, 116
Mérimée, 17, 114, 188, 212
Merlet, Gustave, 208
Messager, André, 118
Méténier, O., 287
Metternich, Mme de, 204, 212, 213
Meyer, Arthur, 208
Meyerbeer, 173, 210
Michel, Louise, 202
Michelet, 21, 82, 84, 86, 87, 100, 188, 278
Michon, abbé, 188
Mickiewicz, 82
Mignet, 21
Mill, John Stuart, 94
Millerand, Alexandre, 201
Millet, 7, 172
Millevoye, 50, 62
Milton, 50, 154
"Mimi", 109, 116, 275
"Mimi Pinson", 116
"Minoret, Dr.", 74
Mirbeau, Octave, 266, 274, 288
"Mirliflor, Prince", 54
"Mirouët, Ursule", 74, 83
Mistral, 17
Mogador, Céleste, 109
Molière, 48, 54, 76, 95, 207, 228
Mollien, 135
Monet, 294
Monnier, Henry, 108, 123, 132, 134, 135
Montaigne, 14, 15
Montalembert, 84, 182, 183, 185
"Montbaillard", 208
"Monte-Cristo, Count of", 160
Montégut, Emile, 13
"Montéjanos", 206
Montesquieu, 14, 24, 26, 27
Montesquiou-Fezensac, Robert de, 114, 302
Montez, Lola, 226
"Moor, Karl", 160
Moore, Thomas, 154
Moreau, Hégésippe, 126
Morny, duc de, 207, 212
Moselly, Emile, 18
"Munchausen, Baron", 49
Murger, 105, 116, 118, 221
"Musette", 109, 116

Musset, 60, 76, 114, 115, 116, 120, 138, 143, 144, 146, 147, 148, 149, 150, 151, 153, 160, 163

Nadaud, Gustave, 16, 103, 109
Napoleon I, 5, 8, 17, 21, 30, 34, 35, 36, 40, 46, 47, 50, 59, 64, 68, 69, 70, 71, 75, 77, 80, 83, 96, 98, 99, 137, 142, 147, 150, 155, 170, 176, 178, 184, 206, 230, 257
Napoleon III, 6, 17, 19, 82, 87, 98, 105, 107, 108, 173, 176, 177, 178, 179, 182, 183, 184, 186, 187, 202, 204, 212, 213, 220, 229, 230
Necker, Mme, 37
"Népomucène", 130
Nerval, Gérard de, 143, 156
"Nicodème", 44, 48
"Nina", 45
"Ninette", 148
"Ninon", 148
Nodier, 139, 152, 153, 156, 160
"Nomophage", 45
Nordau, Max, 235
Norvins, 98
"Nucingen, baron de", 124

Offenbach, 164, 180, 209, 210
"Ophelia", 155
Orléans, Duke of (eighteenth century), 22, 24, 26
Orléans, Duke of (nineteenth century), 255
Orsay, Count d', 115
"Orsini", 143
"Oscar", 59
"Ossian", 59, 63, 114, 144, 150, 155, 156
"Oswald", 57, 102, 195
"Ourika", 63, 165
Owen, Robert, 91

Pailleron, 302
Pain, 49
Païva, marquise de, 226
"Pandore", 103
Parmentier, 83
Parny, 52, 62
Pascal, Blaise, 4
Pascal, Félicien, 100
Pasta, 148, 173
Patti, 180
"Paturot, Jérôme", 90, 136, 144
Paulmier de Gonneville, 7

INDEX OF NAMES

Paulus, 250
Paulyanthe, 134
Pearl, Cora, 226
Pecqueur, 92, 175
"Pécuchet", 120, 190
Péguy, 245, 262
"Pelham", 112
Percier, 69
Pérochon, E., 272
"Perrichon, M.", 120, 132
"Petrowlski, General", 202
Peyrat, Alphonse, 188
Philipon, 132, 134
Philippe, Charles-Louis, 287
Picard, 50, 105
"Pierrot", 136
Pigal, 123
Pigault-Lebrun, 63, 64
"Pigeon, M.", 122
"Pinson, M.", 54
"Pipelet, M. and Mme", 135
Piranesi, 57
Piron, 18, 109
Pius IX, 184, 185, 186
Pixerécourt, 64, 163, 165
Plutarch, 24, 38
"Pochet, Mme", 135
Poincaré, Henri, 242
"Poirier, M.", 106, 120
Pomaré, la Reine, 109
Ponsard, 115, 221, 227
Ponson du Terrail, 192
Pontius Pilate, 185
Pope, 50
Portsmouth, Duchess of, 213
Postgate, R. W., 201
Pottier, Eugène, 266
"Pourceaugnac, M. de", 54
Pourtalès, Mme de, 212, 213
Poussin, 170
Pouvillon, Emile, 14
Praslin, duchesse de, 174
"Presles, Gaston de", 106
Prévost, Marcel, 284, 286, 289
"Prig, Betsey", 135
Prince Imperial, 204, 249
"Priola, marquis de", 286
Proudhon, 92, 93, 94, 175, 197, 200, 201, 248, 262, 263, 264
Proust, Marcel, 114, 254, 302
"Prudhomme, Joseph", 101, 108, 121, 131, 132, 134, 135, 137, 276
Prud'hon, 68
Psichari, Ernest, 245, 259

"Puck", 153
Puvis de Chavannes, 295, 297
Pyat, Félix, 126

"Quasimodo", 161
Quatremère de Quincy, 66
Quinet, 84, 86, 87, 98, 100, 177, 188, 191

"Rabagas", 201, 274
Rabany, 46
Rabelais, 11, 12, 13, 49, 51
Racine, 47, 138
Radcliffe, Mrs., 63, 64
Raffet, 98
Raiz, Gilles de, 13
"Ramollot, Colonel", 234, 235, 279
Raspail, 77, 88, 175
"Rastignac", 124
"Ratapoil", 180, 181, 182
"Ratinois", 120
"Raton", 135
Rattazzi, Mme, 213
Ravachol, 263, 264
Ravaisson, 191, 242
Rawlinson, 240
Raynouard, 47
Reboux, Paul, 213
Récamier, Mme, 102
Reclus, Elisée, 263
Régnier, Henri de, 7
Reichenberg, Suzanne, 228
Renan, 2, 10, 77, 190, 192, 193, 194, 195, 233, 238, 239, 240, 259, 286, 302
"René", 64, 65, 144, 145, 152, 162, 173, 195
Renoir, 283
Renouvier, 191, 238
Restif de la Bretonne, 32
Revel, Jean, 7
Reybaud, 90, 136
Ribot, 239
Richelieu, 14
Richepin, Jean, 275, 276
Richter, Jean-Paul, 153
"Riflard", 50
Rivarol, 51
Robert, Hubert, 57
Robespierre, 19, 21, 28, 29, 30, 31, 32, 38, 45, 77, 93
Rochefort, Henri, 208, 249
Rod, Edouard, 287
"Rodin", 128

"Rodolphe", 118
Rohan, Cardinal de, 12
Roland, Mme, 37
"Rolla", 160
Rolland, Romain, 238, 245, 257, 279, 288, 289, 298
Rollinat, Maurice, 13, 291
Ronsard, 11, 12, 150
Roqueplan, Nestor, 109, 118, 119, 207, 208
Rosny, J.-H., 266
Rossini, 148, 161, 173
Rostand, 98, 234, 259, 302
Roucher, 51
Rouget de Lisle, 18
Roumanille, 17
"Roumestan, Numa", 2, 274
Rousseau, Henri, 299, 302
Rousseau, Jean-Jacques, 21, 24, 27, 28, 29, 30, 31, 32, 38, 42, 54, 62, 65, 93, 126, 139
Rousseau, Théodore, 172
"Roussel, Cadet", 49
Roussel, François, 155
Royer-Collard, 77, 79
"Rubempré, Lucien de", 114, 124
Rude, 172
Ruskin, 292
Rute, Mme de, 213

Saint-Armand, 134
Saint-Arnaud, maréchal de, 250
Saint-Evremond, 9
Saint-Lambert, 51
Saint-Pierre, abbé de, 24
Saint-Pierre, Bernardin de. *See* Bernardin de Saint-Pierre
Saint-Saëns, 210
Saint-Simon, 89, 90, 93, 149
Sainte-Beuve, 93, 100, 130, 152, 154, 187, 188, 190, 192
"Salluste, Don", 161
Sand, George, 5, 12, 13, 65, 81, 82, 83, 92, 95, 110, 115, 123, 128, 142, 145, 146, 147, 148, 149, 154, 161, 176, 188, 218
Sandeau, 71, 106
"Sapho", 288
Sarcey, Francisque, 189
Sardou, 40, 103, 132, 201, 218, 229, 274, 276, 289
"Satan", 154, 155, 159
"Sbogar, Jean", 153
Scaliger, Julius Cæsar, 14

Scarron, 54
"Schaunard", 118
"Schedoni", 64
Schiller, 160
Schneider, Eugène, 211
Schneider, Hortense, 180, 210, 211
Scholl, Aurélien, 208
Schwob, Marcel, 264
Scott, 158, 168
Scribe, 64, 103, 122, 123, 125, 135, 148, 173
Sébastiani, Marshal, 82
Ségur, vicomte de, 58
"Seiglière, marquis de la", 71
Seillière, 87, 100
Sewrin, 112
Seymour, Lord Henry, 115
Shakespeare, 95, 138, 155, 168
Sieyès, 35, 36
Silvestre, Armand, 298
Simpson, Sir Walter, 9
Socrates, 30, 44
"Sol, Doña", 160
Solms, Mme de, 213
Solon, 31, 44
Sorel, Agnes, 12
Sorel, Albert, 7, 22, 239
Sorel, Georges, 256, 264, 265
"Sorel, Julien", 96, 100
Soulié, Frédéric, 115, 142, 161
Soumet, 62
"Spiridion", 83, 92
Spuller, 256
Staël, Mme de, 35, 42, 46, 57, 59, 62, 64, 81, 138, 148, 195
Stendhal, 17, 96, 148, 278
Stevenson, R. L., 5, 9
Sue, Eugène, 91, 108, 119, 128, 135, 142, 161, 174
"Surville, Clotilde de", 59
Syveton, 260

"Taffetas, Mlle", 214
Tailhade, Laurent, 259, 264
Taine, 20, 21, 22, 59, 189, 190, 192, 193, 194, 195, 216, 226, 233, 238, 239, 240, 260, 286
Talleyrand, 5, 58
Tallien, Mme, 40
Talma, 47
Talma, Mme, 37
"Tartarin", 17, 49, 173
"Tartuffe", 44, 76
Tasso, 50

INDEX OF NAMES

Thackeray, 83, 110, 123, 134, 165, 210
"Thénardier", 128, 161
Theocritus, 54
Thérésa, 180, 211
Theresa, St., 289
Theuriet, André, 18
Thierry, Augustin, 89
Thiers, 6, 21, 98, 121, 124, 203, 246, 248
Thomas, Antoine-Léonard, 38
Thomas, W., 57
Thomson, 51
Thorwaldsen, 66
"Tigrane, abbé", 279
Tocqueville, 276
Tolstoy, 287
"Tortillard, le", 128
Tortoni, 108
Tourneux, 46, 49
"Trailles, Maxime de", 124
Traviès, 99, 127, 132, 135
"Trenmor", 146
Tressan, comte de, 43
"Triboulet", 161
"Trissotin", 52
Tristan, Flora, 95
Trollope, Anthony, 112
Trollope, Mrs., 141, 147, 150
"Troubert, abbé", 76
Troyon, 172

"Ubu roi", 276
Urfé, d', 5
Uzès, 235

Vadé, 48
"Valjean, Jean", 124, 128, 146
Vallès, Jules, 201
Vanderburch, 130
Vandérem, Fernand, 268
Van Tieghem, 59, 60
Varin, 135
Vaugeois, 260
"Vautour, M.", 52
"Vautrin", 124
Vaux, Clotilde de, 95
Vercingetorix, 6
Verlaine, 156, 292
Verne, Jules, 8, 278
Vernet, Horace, 75, 170

"Vernouillet", 209
Véron, Dr., 120, 121
Veuillot, 48, 183, 184, 185, 209
Vicaire, Gabriel, 292
Vico, 87
"Victor", 161
Victor-Emmanuel, 185, 213
Viel-Castel, 214
Vien, 66
Vigny, Alfred de, 12, 60, 61, 81, 98, 100, 114, 126, 132, 144, 145, 146, 150, 154, 160
Villard, Nina de, 223
Villemessant, H. de, 194, 208
Villiers de l'Isle-Adam, 192, 221
Vincent de Paul, St., 30
Vintras, 83
"Vireloque, Thomas", 135
Virgil, 50, 51, 54, 206
Vogüé, Melchior de, 242
Vollard, 297
Voltaire, 24, 42, 47, 49, 83, 85, 109, 138, 183, 187
Vulpius, 160

Wafflard, 148
Washington, 30, 66, 71, 98, 276
Webster, Mrs. Nesta, 22
Weill, 74, 77, 176
Weishaupt, Adam, 24
Welschinger, 42
"Werther", 63, 147, 152, 155, 160, 195
Whistler, 296
Willette, 136, 297
William I, 9
William III, 78
Willy, 289
Winckelmann, 66
Winterhalter, 212, 215
Wolff, Albert, 208
Wordsworth, 152
Worth, 212

Young, Arthur, 20, 25, 39
Young, Edward, 57

"Zampa", 161
Zola, 17, 47, 91, 178, 229, 233, 239, 252, 254, 257, 264, 265, 272, 281, 282, 284, 288, 296, 301

mid year. Wright p. 74
            Strowski 324
         Dumas   Henri III

       Choose 1 { Anthony
                 { Angèle
                 { Richard Darlington
                 { La Tour de Nesle

         Hugo   Préface de Cromwell
                Hernani

    Racine   Phèdre.